THE PRINCETON REVIEW

Job Smart

D1301937

THE PRINCETON REVIEW

Job Smart

BY MICHELLE TULLIER, PH.D.
TIMOTHY HAFT, M.A.
MARGARET HEENEHAN, M.ED.
MARCI TAUB, M.A.

Random House, Inc.
New York 1997
http://www.randomhouse.com

Princeton Review Publishing, L.L.C.
2315 Broadway
New York, NY 10024
E-mail: info@review.com

ISBN 0-679-77355-X

Editor: Amy Zavatto
Designer: Illeny Maaza

Manufactured in the United States of America on partially recycled paper.

9 8 7 6 5 4 3 2 1

First Edition

DEDICATION

This book is dedicated to the truly
smart ones in our lives.

J. Scott Tullier
Patricia and Ronald Gann
Michael James Gazelle

Arlene Karetnick
Adam Jesse Taub
the memory of Harold Karetnick

Bob and Vicky Haft

David and Ann Heenehan.

ACKNOWLEDGMENTS

A heartfelt thanks to our colleagues who shared their expertise and knowledge, especially: John Aigner, Lauren Buxbaum, Cheryl Goldstein, Erica Gray, John Johnson, Helen LaFave, Alexis Lucas, Nina Segal, and Manley Walker.

Our appreciation also goes to Ken Blye, Robin Edelstein, Jacqueline Einstein, Jonathan Golub, Martha Pierre, Suzannah Richmond, Jeff Rosen, and Randi Rosen for taking the time to discuss their job search and hiring experience with us. Thanks also to Michael for keeping us well-informed and well-fed as host to our many marathon meetings.

Letitia Chamberlain and Marion Flomenhaft have provided opportunity, guidance, and collegiality through our affiliation with the Center for Career, Education, and Life Planning at New York University's School of Continuing Education.

Special thanks to our editor Amy Zavatto and to our resourceful intern Sabera Saadullah.

Our deepest appreciation goes to the clients with whom we have had the privilege of working. They often teach us more than we teach them.

CONTENTS

Introduction

For more than a decade, we've been helping people find their dream jobs, or sometimes just plain old jobs to pay the bills. The philosophy behind our counseling, which we've carried over into this book, is that job search coaching is kind of like teaching. We don't just get our clients jobs or tell them what to do with their lives. We educate them about how to get a job and how to make career choices. In keeping with this mission, this book equips you with the skills you need to land a job now and to conduct successful job searches in the future.

WHO THIS BOOK IS FOR

The labels that might describe ideal readers of *Job Smart* tend to be either too narrow or too hokey—terms like entry-level, young adult, young professional, recent grad, student, twentysomething, or thirtysomething. Maybe you see yourself in one of those categories, but if not, don't worry. Much of the advice in this book is relevant to most any age or level of job seeker. There are probably even a few corporate CEOs who could learn a thing or two from these pages. We have, though, made a special point of gearing all the advice, resources, and real-people examples in this book to the unique needs of those in the early stages of the career journey.

HOW *JOB SMART* WILL LEAD YOU

The world of work has become a confusing and often intimidating place. Some of you are likely to have seen your parents laid off from jobs in the past several years and might have experienced such downturns yourself. Even if you haven't directly experienced the negative impact of these changes in the '90s, you've undoubtedly been bombarded with media reports of downsizing, reconfiguring, and general chaos in the labor market and wondered what it all means for you.

With job market changes happening at such a rapid pace, conventional wisdom about how to get a job may miss the mark. All too often, job search methods are based on hearsay and the advice of people who are out of touch or misinformed. In this book, we've taken an innovative but practical approach to job search that's fundamental enough for those of you new to the world of work but sophisticated enough for seasoned travelers on the road to a job.

We give you techniques for customizing a search that is tailored to the type of job, organization, or industry you're aiming for. In chapter 5 you'll find all the traditional and not so traditional resources for finding jobs. We present the pros and cons of all methods and guide you in creating a personalized job search strategy.

HOW TO USE *JOB SMART*

Your success in a job search will result from careful preparation, a well thought out strategy, and a structured framework for the process, so we suggest that you read this book from cover to cover. We realize, though, that you might have a job search crisis on your hands and need quick advice on some specific topic. To that end, we've made each chapter independent enough that you can turn to it and know what we're talking about. So, if you have an interview tomorrow morning and no clue how to handle it, or someone with an opening for the perfect job needs you to fax a resume today and you haven't even started on one, then you can turn straight to those chapters and get cut-to-the-chase advice. Once the crisis has passed, though, we hope you'll sit back in a comfortable chair and read the rest.

Think of *Job Smart* as a trusted companion to see you through those rough days of job hunting. Treat it as a workbook—mark it up, stick post-it notes on the most relevant parts for you, and just generally get to know it.

HITTING THE PAVEMENT

As you embark on your job search journey, we ask you to do one thing. Keep it all in perspective! A job hunt is not a race or a competition. Even though it does require assertive tactics and persistence, one of the best things you can do for a search is to enjoy yourself from time to time and have a life. Remember, employers hire people, not some alien creature called "Job Hunter." So, get to work, but take some time for YOU along the way. We wish you the best on the road to your ideal job.

L. Michelle Tullier
Timothy D. Haft
Margaret M. Heenehan
Marci I. Taub
March 1997

1

How You Get Hired

GETTING A CLUE:
THREE SECRETS TO JOB SEARCH SUCCESS

Before having to face nearly three hundred pages of job search realities, let us treat you to a few minutes of virtual reality. Come with us to a happy land where job seekers can wallow in the comfort of good intentions and New Year's resolutions and never really have to do anything about getting a job.

Here's the scene. It's Sunday morning and you're sitting in the most comfortable chair in the world with your feet propped up and the Sunday paper in your lap. You've turned straight to the help wanted ads because last night you decided once and for all to do something about your career. You were out with friends who were all complaining about their jobs (or about not having jobs) and you decided that at least you were going to do something about it. You would turn over a new leaf, get out of your rut, and get a great job.

So, it's the morning after, the leaf has turned, and the classifieds beckon. Armed with a bright red pen and a stockpile of determination, you meet the challenge by scanning the paper for the perfect job. Since this is a virtual reality, there are plenty of perfect jobs to circle, so by mid-afternoon you've painted the town crier red. "This job search stuff isn't so bad," you say to yourself, taking a break to have some waffles.

The rest of the afternoon is spent cutting out the ads you've circled and pasting each one onto an index card. It's kind of fun and you're feeling good. But wait. There seems to be a bit of real reality creeping into this imaginary world.

On closer inspection of the ads, you see that most of them are asking for skills and qualifications you don't have, and the ones that don't require much experience want you to type fifty words a minute. That could be a problem since you type about fifty words a week. Then the real momentum-buster strikes when your dad, or sister, or significant other, or roommate, or cat comes in and says, "When are you gonna get a job?" Welcome back to the dreaded Real World! We wouldn't blame you for crawling back under the covers and never coming out.

A METHOD TO THE MADNESS

Finding your place in the world of work is rarely easy, we admit, but it doesn't have to be as difficult as most people make it. There is a method to the madness of choosing careers and getting jobs that, unfortunately, is rarely taught in school, college, or at home. Chances are, lots of people have offered advice, claiming to know the secret to getting hired. Rarely, though, do these well-meaning friends, family, and advisors have the time or expertise to take you through every step of the job search process. That's why we've made *Job Smart* a comprehensive companion to take all the guess-work out of job hunting and maybe even make it a little bit fun.

Before we get into the nitty-gritty of all the steps in the job search process, this chapter is devoted to letting you in on three secrets to getting hired. Now before you say, "Yeah, I've heard that one before," hear us out. The three secrets are only "secrets" in that they are the most often overlooked things to do connected with your job search. They're actually quite simple steps to take that really aren't a big deal—unless you skip them. We've seen the positive results that come from thinking about the issues raised and taking the actions suggested for these three points:

1. Learn What "Job" and "Career" Really Mean

2. Know Yourself and What You Want

3. Know What You Have to Offer

To build a solid foundation for your search, start with the strategies described in this chapter, then you'll be ready to tackle the rest of the book.

JOB SEARCH SECRET #1—DEFINE WHAT "JOB" AND "CAREER" REALLY MEAN

Like anything in life, you have to know what you're looking for in order to find it. The first job search secret, therefore, is to know what we mean by the words "job" and "career"—not necessarily how your parents or friends define them or how you've always thought of them, but how they really are in the '90s and for the 21st century.

We're not talking about knowing if you're looking for a job as a cosmetics salesperson, a bond trader, or a salmon fisher. While it's important (if not downright essential) to know what occupation you're aiming for, it's even more important to think about bigger picture issues, like expectations, identity, and lifelong career paths. Pretty lofty subjects.

AND WHAT DO *YOU* DO?

It's hard to avoid being identified by the job you do or the occupational field you're a part of. Whether applying for a credit card, renewing a passport, or making small talk at a party, everybody wants to know what you do. We obviously do lots of things in life, but what most people care about is what we do for a living.

This cultural norm can be a real pain for people who get their intrinsic rewards from pursuits other than the activity that brings the paycheck. We all know the type—wannabe actors schlepping trays of food, cab drivers writing the next Great American Novel between fares, and secretaries who don't find their clerical duties all that fascinating, but get their kicks instead from the volunteer work they do after hours and from wind surfing on the weekends.

Add to this list those who do jobs that are just stepping stones to long-term career goal—recent grads in the mailroom on the slow road to CEO or aspiring attorneys proofreading for misplaced semicolons during summers off from law school. The jobs recent grads hold don't always hold their interest or attention, and rarely (yes, rarely) make use of that expensive college education. Education, especially a liberal arts one, usually pays off down the road, but initially you're likely to find yourself with a job title and job duties you'd rather not be identified with.

This frustrating irony can be particularly problematic for entry-level job seekers or twentysomething career changers who are often judged by the mark they're making in this world. You know those commencement speakers who implore you to take that hard earned sheepskin and make a difference? They get you all hyped up to go out and be wildly successful, while saving the world at the same time. Those speeches probably seem kind of remote now as you stand at the Xerox machine mastering the fine art of double-sided, collated copying. If you feel an identity crisis coming on at that moment, consider these words:

> *Your worth as a person and your professional success are not defined by the job you hold at any one point in time.*

Is a twenty-five year old earning $60,000 a year at a high-profile investment bank more successful than a twenty-five year old who's working as a waiter while doing two unpaid internships? Not necessarily. If the investment banker is happy with her job, then she is successful; but if she's miserable then she's no better off than the waiter who's earning a quarter of the banker's salary and not working in a "real" full-time job.

Answers to these questions of success and respectability depend upon how we define a "real job." Most people getting started tend to think of themselves as successfully ensconced in a career only when they have a steady, full-time job with an ample paycheck and a respectable title. But isn't a career more than the actual job you do?

> *A career is all the things you are doing at any given point in time to create a satisfying life while setting and working toward goals.*

You might work as a waiter for money but also intern and take classes to develop your career. Whether you're twenty-two or fifty-two, that combination is just as respectable as being on the fast-track in a traditional, full-time job. So, as a first strategy for getting a job, reflect on your own definition of what a "good" job is, and consequently, what success means to you.

EVOLUTIONARY MATTERS

Okay, so that first job, or even the second and third job, may not go down in history as the be-all and end-all, but where is it leading? As you've probably noticed, we're basically saying that careers evolve over time and that to understand whether any given job is worthwhile and right for you, you have to know what careers are all about. Most every career expert will agree that careers are developmental. You don't just choose to be a whatever at the age of 18 or 22 or 26 and do that for the rest of your life. You're likely to have several different occupations (i.e., the specific fields you work in) and many different jobs (i.e., the positions you hold) over a lifetime.

This fact has become an accepted part of working life as economic factors and technological advances have altered the status quo. What used to be called "job hopping" has become the more acceptable "career transitioning." And people who have part-time jobs in different fields or work as consultants and maybe go to school part-time are no longer called "scattered" or even "unemployed" (because they don't have one full-time job). They're now given the more impressive label "portfolio people" because they've creatively patched together a career out of a variety of skills and experiences. What these different occupations and jobs amount to is a "career."

You may already see themes and patterns in your life—a commitment to social service, a love of learning, an enterprising, entrepreneurial streak. All these traits interact with life circumstances and opportunities to create your career. Your objective now should be to start building on those themes. As you make your way in that process, you will find that the shortest distance between two points is usually not a straight line, despite what you learned in geometry class. So, while your career development is somewhat out of your hands and cannot be perfectly planned (and shouldn't be or you'd miss out on life's adventures), you can seek out opportunities that weave together the patterns in your interests, skills, values, and personality.

JOB SEARCH SECRET #2—KNOW YOURSELF AND WHAT YOU WANT

Job Search Secret #2 has to do with knowing who you are and where you want to be. This is a how-to-get-a-job book, not a how-to-choose-a-career book, but it just so happens that the same steps you take to identify your best career direction are the same steps you take to market yourself for jobs and get what you want. One of the easiest ways to sabotage your search is to come across as unfocused. True, in Job Search Secret #1 we did say that it's okay not to have a definite career direction because it's sometimes unrealistic to think that you can perfectly plan out a career path. However, you do have to be focused during a job search. You can be crystal clear that a job you are applying for is right on target for you at that point in time, even if you're a little fuzzy on your long-range goals.

Whether through letters, phone calls, or interviews, every moment of contact with prospective employers must convey that you have a focus and that you arrived at that focus in a careful, thoughtful way. The focus is simply that you know why any given job would be right for you and why you should be hired.

ME, MYSELF, AND I

Getting focused typically involves asking yourself three questions: What do I like? What do I do well? and What do I care about? The answers to these questions correspond to the categories "interests, skills, and values," which are often seen as the ABCs of career choice. By contemplating these questions, you're also addressing the question: "Who am I and which kinds of environments will I thrive in?"

Our interests are those things that we enjoy doing, discussing, or daydreaming about. They can include hobbies, sports, academic subjects, work activities, topics you read about, and anything else you like. They might be lifelong passions or just passing fancies. Your job is to decide which interests need to be a part of your work life. You can have an interest in the ocean, for example, without being a marine biologist. You can major in art history but work as a banker, reserving your art appreciation for museum visits on the weekends. Or, you might have an interest that is so strong it must be a part of your daily work life.

The category of skills is a broad one in that it encompasses three main areas: learned skills (tangible things we've learned how to do, like using a computer or writing a newspaper article); innate skills (aptitudes or talents, like mechanical or writing abilities); and personality skills (like being hard-working, detail-oriented, or creative). Deciding which skills you enjoy using is an important factor in defining a career focus, but is especially critical in obtaining a job. (Job Search Secret #3 talks much more about assessment of your skills and their role in marketing yourself for a job.)

The category of values can be a tough one. At times, making money might be a priority, while at other points in life doing good for the world might be more important to you. If you're in college or recently out, it's likely that you haven't had enough experience to know definitively where you stand on these things, but again, you can look for patterns you've already developed. Were you the kid in school who was always selling something, or the one off in the corner drawing pictures? Values like entrepreneurial spirit and creative expression are often formed at a young age. That doesn't mean you're destined to become a business owner or an artist, but you probably will want your work (or other aspects of your life) to satisfy those values in some way.

How Do I Know What Jobs Are Right for Me?

To zero in on specific job goals, it helps to assess yourself in terms of interests, strengths, values, and personality style. You can take formal, standardized tests (often referred to as "inventories" or "assessment instruments"), or you can complete informal paper-pencil exercises found in career guidebooks or available through career counselors. You can also simply observe and analyze your daily thoughts and habits to find clues to what floats your boat. Whichever method you use on your own or with the help of a professional career advisor, you'll be gathering data about yourself that gives you a personal evaluation and profile, and points you in the appropriate career directions.

Whether you see a career counselor in private practice or go to your college's career development office, you may want to inquire about career assessment (also called vocational testing) to help you figure out what to do and to help you identify the personal qualities that make you marketable in a job search. Try to avoid the stab-in-the-dark approach of taking only one test, such as an interest inventory, and assuming you've "done testing." If you're going to have testing at all, it's usually most effective to take a well-rounded battery of assessment tools that cover interests, skills, values, and personality style.

Beware of old-fashioned testing "labs," which offer only aptitude testing and little, if any, follow-up counseling. There are two problems with this type of service. First, aptitude testing is often the least helpful type of assessment. Rarely does it tell you anything new about your abilities. (Those Ds you got in math classes year after year were a good indication that your quantitative aptitude wasn't so great; you don't need to sit through two or three days of fancy testing to prove it.) Secondly, this type of service places too much emphasis on the role of tests in your career decision-making. NO TEST CAN TELL YOU WHAT TO DO! Career assessment is simply a springboard for discussions with a counselor to help you reach the answers you need. If a counselor or counseling firm offers testing, be sure there's ample follow-up counseling available.

Some skilled career counselors don't even use tests. They can get the same information by simply talking to you. Usually, though, the less work experience you have, the more helpful testing can be. Tests and informal exercises can help you articulate your personal profile and also do a little of the work for you by listing career fields that match your responses.

Regardless of the method, your basic goal is to decide what you want out of a job and a career in general. Once you've identified your interests, skills, and values, you need to define your priorities. You might have a strong interest in oil painting, for example, but you value job security and making a lot of money. The starving artist route is probably not for you then, so you'll need to aim for jobs that are more stable and lucrative—maybe something on the business side of an arts-related organization. Or, you may choose to keep your art interest "pure" by painting in your spare time and doing a non-arts job to make money. However you combine your interests, skills, and values, it all comes down to deciding what your priorities are, so you can focus on getting a job that meets your needs. Some typical ways entry-level job seekers state their priorities are:

- a foot-in-the-door of a career field in which I have a definite focus.

- just any old job that I have the ability to do and at least a basic interest in that will let me get experience and establish myself in a work routine.

- a job that will reasonably fit my interests, skills, and values but that most importantly gives me the amount of money I need to gain financial independence.

- a job that bridges the gap to a new career field.

TAKING THE SCENIC ROUTE

Consider the example of Jennifer, a twenty-four year old who went through an assessment of her interests, skills, and values but decided that her priority was to get any old job that would let her gain some independence from her parents. After college, Jennifer spent a summer in Wyoming enjoying the outdoors and working as a telemarketer. She then worked for a year in Mexico with a social service organization teaching English to the locals and improving her proficiency in Spanish. She loved languages and music and enjoyed helping people. She also liked the job as a telemarketer and found the fields of marketing and advertising interesting.

When she returned home and was eager to settle into a regular full-time job and get her own apartment, she couldn't decide which route to take. She considered teaching music, counseling Spanish-speaking people, teaching ESL (English as a Second Language), or training to be a music therapist. She also thought of working for an ad agency or marketing firm. Her test results and discussions in counseling sessions confirmed that she seemed equally suited for all those options.

While worrying about the decision she faced, a job offer fell unexpectedly into her lap. It came from a friend of her parents who needed an assistant in his area of a major finance services company. Her parents were urging her to take it because they felt her priorities should be to get any job just to establish herself in a routine, gain some independence, and take on responsibility. As Jennifer's career counselors, we had a difficult time going along with that plan because it was clear that this job didn't fit into any of her possible long-range goals (except maybe marketing or advertising of financial products in the future). We realized, though, that her parents were right. Jennifer was in no position to make a decision at that point. She needed time to learn more about herself, especially her values, and to explore the world of work. There was also a recession on at the time, so in the tight job market there was no telling how long it would take her to find a position in one of her areas of interest.

Her father's friend assured her that the position would equip her with valuable computer and general office skills, and would expose her to many aspects of the business world. She would also be working around a lot of other young people, giving her the chance to have some fun and reestablish a social network in the hometown she had left several years before. We endorsed Jennifer's decision to take the job, with the promise that she would continue to explore her other options. Sure enough, she contacted us six months into the job when she felt settled in and ready to start exploring future options. She then spent several months going on informational interviews to evaluate her options, taking a couple of evening classes, and doing some volunteer work, all the while receiving a nice paycheck and benefits from her "day job" at the prestigious finance company. She eventually decided to apply to graduate school for a counseling degree and felt comfortable with her decision, knowing that if she had rushed the decision a year earlier, she wouldn't have felt as certain about her goals.

Like Jennifer, you just might not have done the things you need to do and taken the time you need to take in order to set appropriate and realistic career goals. If you're not comfortable saying, for example, "I'd rather be in public relations than advertising," because you just don't feel ready to make that decision, then why not aim for any job in communications to get your feet wet and take it from there? If you do, on the other hand, know exactly what you want to be doing five or ten years from now and have known it since you were born, then by all means make a commitment to that goal and have the job you seek now be a stepping stone to it.

JOB SEARCH SECRET #3—KNOW WHAT YOU HAVE TO OFFER

When people in your life are dispensing wisdom about how to get a job, they probably say things like:

> *"Networking's the only way to get a job."*
> *"Forget the classified ads."*
> *"Make your cover letters short and powerful."*

There's nothing wrong with that advice, but all the job leads in the world are useless unless you can present yourself as qualified for the job and capable of adding value to the prospective employer. It sounds obvious, but you have to focus on what you have to offer before you can expect to get a job.

Ask Not What They Can Do for You, Ask What You Can Do for Them

Prospective employers want to know one simple thing from you. What can you do for us? BE PREPARED TO TELL THEM! Getting a job requires looking at yourself as a product that must be marketed, packaged, advertised, and sold. Whether writing a cover letter or resume, being persuasive in an interview, or closing the deal to get a job offer, you have to be fluent in the language of "you." The reality of job hunting is that to get a job, you have to sell a prospective employer on your talents, skills, and potential, and, like selling a product, you're not going to be convincing unless you can articulate your best features.

Doing the self-assessment we advocated in Secret #2 is one way to do that. The profile of your interests, skills, and values forms the basis of the self-marketing campaign. It shows how you'll add value to an organization. While interests and values are important in the self-marketing campaign (a prospective employer on Wall Street, for example, wants to know that you find reading the *Wall Street Journal* interesting and that you value making money), strengths and skills are hands down the most important facet of your campaign.

But I Don't Have Any Skills

So many college students, recent grads and entry-level workers believe they have no skills, so if you fit into those categories you're probably not thrilled to hear about this emphasis on skills. Don't worry, the fact is that employers are hiring you as much for your potential as for your concrete, job-related skills. They can teach you how to work their computer program or process their papers or sell their products, but they can't teach you how to think. It's the age-old argument for a liberal arts education. Even if you did major in something practical like engineering, computer science, or journalism you might still feel you are unskilled when comparing yourself to experienced professionals in your chosen field, so remember that you, too, are being hired for your aptitude and potential, not just for what you already know.

If you happen to have physical or learning disabilities and have spent your school years having to focus on your difficulties and strategies for overcoming them, then you're likely to feel lacking in job-related skills. Well, take heart, because you'll find that some of the most successful people in a variety of fields are disabled. The skills that have enabled you to cope and adapt are usually more useful in the job world than the skills that have enabled your classmates to ace academia or sports.

Now that we've established that everyone has skills and potential, let's look at how you're going to put together a profile of those strengths. This "Skills Package" will be the foundation for so many things you'll have to do throughout your job search, so don't skip this part. When we take you through writing letters and resumes, interviewing, and negotiating job offers, you'll need to refer back to your Skills Package. It will serve as the basis for your self-marketing campaign.

I YAM WHAT I YAM

One way to demystify the confusing process of declaring your strengths is to think of them as falling into three categories:

I am   I can   I know

The I am skills are the broadest ones in that they reflect your capabilities, talents, and general areas of strength. They even border on being personality characteristics. For example, you might say "I am artistic, I am mechanically inclined, I am easygoing, I am detail-oriented." The skills in this category are highly versatile and can be valued in any number of career fields.

The I can skills are next broadest but a little more specifically linked to activities. They are such things as "I can speak French fluently, I can do word processing, I can balance a budget." The I can skills are also transferable among many different fields.

The I know skills are the most narrowly defined and most closely connected to a particular activity or content area. They might be, for example, "I know French business vocabulary, I know Microsoft Word and WordPerfect, I know how to monitor accounts payable and receivable in a retail business."

Look through the checklists of skills in each of these categories on the following pages and pick out those that best describe you. You will probably be pleasantly surprised at how many skills you have. If you think you're being too hard on yourself and not checking enough skills, do this exercise with a friend, family member, or counselor who can help you think of real-life examples of ways you've demonstrated some of these abilities.

When you've gone through the lists, follow the instructions for transferring some of the skills to the "Skills Package" page that follows the checklists. You might want to put a marker on that page, because you're going to be referring to it throughout your job search process. Your Skills Package is the backbone of successful letter and resume writing, interviewing, and negotiating. You'll also want to keep your skills in mind as you read chapter 2 on the job market. The Skills Package can help you see where you might find a place for yourself in the world of work described in that chapter.

The I Am Skills
Read the following list of skills and check off the ones that sound like you. Consider also showing this list to someone who knows you well so you can get a truly objective reading on your personality strengths.

I am.....

adaptable
analytical
artistic
assertive
athletic
calm
cheerful
confident
congenial
conscientious
cooperative

creative
curious
dependable
detail-oriented
disciplined
diplomatic
discreet
efficient
energetic
enterprising
enthusiastic
expressive

flexible
funny
good with languages
honest
idealistic
independent
industrious
inventive
loyal
mathematically/
   quantitatively-inclined
mechanically-inclined
musically-inclined
observant
open-minded
outgoing
organized
patient
perceptive

persevering
persuasive
poised
practical
punctual
quiet
realistic
reserved
resourceful
responsible
scholarly
sensitive
serious
sincere
tactful
team-oriented
technically-inclined
thoughtful
visionary

After checking off the characteristics that describe you, go back and circle the six words that BEST describe you. If you aren't sure, ask people who know you well to tell you which traits best fit you.

When you've done that, turn to the Skills Package form on pages 15–16 and write those six words in the I am section.

The I Can Skills

Check off the ones that you can do or that you think you have the potential to develop. Don't worry about your level of proficiency. Remember you're being hired as much for your capabilities as for your acquired skills.

advise or counsel others
analyze quantitative data
analyze situations or
   problems
appraise value
assess needs
brainstorm
budget

calculate/compute numbers
   with ease
care for animals
care for children
carry out plans/follow-
   through
coach
collect payments/money
compete

concentrate for long periods of time

conduct meetings

converse with others comfortably

cook well

coordinate events

create works of art

debate issues

delegate duties or responsibilities

design programs or procedures

edit written works

entertain

estimate costs

evaluate quality or performance

explain things

follow instructions or orders

handle details

hire people

host others/make people feel welcome

influence people

instruct

integrate ideas and information

interview others

investigate

keep in touch with people

keep records or logs

learn languages

listen attentively

make, build, or fix things

make decisions

make friends easily

make plans

manage people

manage projects

mediate conflicts

motivate others

negotiate/bargain

nurse or treat others

observe

organize projects or spaces

perform for an audience

play sports

proofread

raise funds for a cause

read well

research

sell

serve as a liaison

serve others

speak to groups

summarize information

supervise others

teach or train

translate languages

troubleshoot

use computers

use mechanical abilities

visualize physical spaces or designs

work with my hands

write creatively

write essays or reports

Others:

After you've checked off the skills you possess, go back and circle the ones that you think will be the real selling points for getting a job. (These should also be the skills you'd like to use on a job.) Now record these in the "I Can" section of the following Skills Package.

The I Know Skills

Since the I Know skills are connected to specific activities and knowledge areas, it would take thousands of pages to list all the possible skills in this category. Your I Know skills are the ones that are likely to be the most unique to you and your experience.

To identify your I Know skills, reflect on your experiences and accomplishments in the following categories, then complete the phrase "I know how to..." by filling in the blanks. Then, fill in the I Know section of the following Skills Package form.

> Academic subjects
>
> Jobs
>
> Internships
>
> Hobbies/Interests
>
> Activities/Affiliations/Clubs
>
> Home/Family Life

THE SKILLS PACKAGE

I Am

_____   _____

_____   _____

_____   _____

I Can

_____   _____

_____   _____

_____   _____

_____   _____

I Know

_____

_____

_____

_____

_____

_____

_____

_____

Refer to these pages throughout your job search process as you present yourself to prospective employers in writing, on the phone, and in person.

2

Real Facts About the Real World

DEBUNKING JOB MARKET MYTHS

If you're even thinking of looking for a job, you need to know that today's job market is very different from the one you witnessed when you began college and selected a major. And tomorrow's job market? Who knows. But one thing you can probably bet on is it will continue to transform at as rapid a pace. These ongoing changes can leave you feeling overwhelmed and disillusioned, wondering how to keep on top of current and future job market trends and how to use this information to your advantage during your job search.

From our years of experience working with college grads, we'll walk you through some of the biggest myths about today's job market. Not only will this make you feel a little less jittery, but it will help challenge your misconceptions about getting a job and build upon your knowledge from chapter 1 about job search success.

Myth #1

All you read and hear about is downsizing. If you notice that a company has just laid off a bunch of employees, don't even bother to consider looking for a job there. Applying to those kinds of places is a waste of time.

Reality #1

There are lots of companies in many different industries that are going through what is sometimes called "downsizing," "reengineering," or "restructuring." Whatever they call it, it means layoffs and changes in the way the organization does its business. Often, layoffs cause big problems for the employees who still have their jobs. These workers sometimes feel afraid of losing their jobs, guilty about having their jobs when their colleagues lose theirs, and frustrated by heavier workloads and constant changes in their workplace.

Just because you hear that a company has recently laid off workers, though, doesn't mean that you can't or won't want to work there. When organizations cut back the number of employees in certain areas, they usually expand other parts of the business that they think will have more growth and earnings potential. So the likelihood of finding a job with a downsizing company depends on whether or not your skills and interests fit with the new jobs they may be creating as a result of the reorganization.

With change also comes the opportunity to join an organization that is moving forward and really taking a look at how they do things. That can be an exciting and rewarding (though sometimes intense and unstable) experience. For example, you may end up getting a job in a place with newly flexible work hours or locations, increased rewards for being a good performer, and a chance to help make day-to-day decisions.

Myth #2

You deserve a good job because you're a college grad who made good grades and paid your dues in school. But, instead, you're doomed to take a dead-end job for which you're overqualified and didn't even need to go to college to get anyway.

Reality #2

It's true that lots of grads initially take jobs they are overqualified for and end up being essentially "underemployed" because of a tight job market. But the situation is not as bad as it seems. First of all, the sense of entitlement that many grads seem to have is a leftover attitude from their parents' generation. It's just not realistic anymore to assume that a college degree by itself will enable to you find a good job right out of school.

As we talked about in chapter 1, working as a waiter while interning and taking classes to develop your career may not be your idea of the good life. But it may be the best alternative you have to a traditional full-time job that puts you on the fast track. Besides, you can position yourself to get on the fast track of your choice depending on your initiative and attitude. It just won't happen as fast as you might like. The good news is that many graduates are only underemployed for a brief time.

Myth #3

Liberal arts majors don't have a lot of hard skills to offer an employer. Their job searches are tough, since everybody wants you to have specialized, technical knowledge these days.

Reality #3

In most cases, technical, specialized knowledge is important. The "I know" skills we mentioned in chapter 1, which are the most narrowly defined and most closely connected to a particular activity or content area, correspond to this knowledge.

But to launch a successful job search, you also need to develop and present a wide range of the "I can" skills we talked about in chapter 1. Again, these skills are a little broader than the "I know" skills, but are still linked to activities. Sometimes, the "I can" skills are referred to as competencies in the work world.

Myth #4

You can't do what you love and still make a decent living without juggling several other part-time jobs on the side. And then you won't have the time or energy to really make your dreams happen.

Reality #4

It is possible to do what you love and survive without feeling overextended. Many people have dream jobs that meet their basic needs without needing to survive on four hours of sleep and working seven days a week at jobs they don't like.

Myth #5

You need to find a job at a large organization in order to make a living. That's really the only way to look at the job market in terms of opportunities that make sense for college grads. Check out your fields of interest and go after large organizations that hire people in these fields.

Reality #5

Ironically, this generation of college-educated job seekers is in the right place at the right time. No, we're not kidding. With all of the economic and technological reconfiguring of the world of work that we discussed in chapter 1, there are actually more, unusual job opportunities than ever before available for grads. And since people at all stages of their careers are loosening up about the "right" way to do things, you don't have to worry that by deciding to try out a job that the choice is irreversible or will damage your professional credibility. So the fun, and sometimes hard part, is discovering the best job opportunities for you.

Myth #6
Every area in the U.S. is experiencing an equally tough job market for college grads. Even if I'm living in a place with a lot of job competition in my field and a really high cost of living that makes it tough to get by, there's no point in relocating to try out another place and get a better quality of living.

Reality #6
Relocation can be an effective job search tactic. As organizations in both the public and private sectors go through a period of great change, opportunities for you to relocate may come up. Sometimes relocating to another geographic area will improve your chances of getting a job and can be a fun, valuable way to start a new phase of your career.

Now that we've demystified what's going on in today's ever-changing job market, we're going to give you some key strategies for how to navigate your way to job search success.

Strategy #1
When you learn that a company you might be interested in is downsizing certain areas, check up on what's going on in terms of staffing other parts of the business. Ask people you know and read newspaper and magazine articles, to determine for yourself whether there might be jobs that you have the background for and interest in. Don't assume that it's a lost cause or let other people talk you into believing it either, especially those who might potentially compete with you for the same jobs. The only way to know for sure is to check it out for yourself.

Strategy #2
To beat the underemployment game, take advantage of a no-brainer job to pursue an internship, apprenticeship, volunteer position, or take classes on the side. Remember, though, to set a time limit on postponing your job search. For example, decide that in six months you'll complete your internship and resume your job search, using your new experience as leverage. This way, you'll stay motivated and on track, rather than getting stuck in your no-brainer job indefinitely. (In chapter 7 we'll tell you more about ways to bridge the gap and continue your education.) Also, actively use the job search places and techniques we recommend in chapter 5 to get what you want. It's a hard situation to be in but there are practical ways to make the most of it and search for a job successfully.

Strategy #3

Distinguish yourself from other job candidates by showing what competencies, or "I can" skills, you have to offer an employer. Some key competencies, which apply to many fields, are analytical skills, computer skills, flexibility, foreign language fluency, interpersonal skills, leadership skills, oral and written communications skills, and teamwork skills. Marketing yourself as having a strong combination of technical "I know" skills and competencies will enable you to stand out from other applicants.

FYI

Presenting these examples of competencies to a prospective employer will cause you to blow it, big time!

analytical skills: your accuracy at determining how long it will take before your manager will go off on you for coming to work late every day for a week

computer skills: your on-the-job mastery of the latest games (unless, of course, you work for a game designer)

flexibility: your uncanny knack for taking a lunch break at 11:30 A.M., 12:30 P.M., and 2:30 P.M.—all on the same day

foreign language fluency: your prowess at pig latin, which you spoke with your brother growing up so your parents wouldn't understand what you were talking about

interpersonal skills: the time you got sued for sexual harassment because you repeatedly complimented your coworker on his body instead of his work

leadership skills: your ability to run a meeting into the ground in 60 seconds flat by making all of the important decisions yourself and not letting anybody get a word in edgewise

oral and written communications skills: your inability to listen to anyone without daydreaming about what you're having for lunch and how you can write the longest memo using more SAT vocabulary words than anyone else in your office

teamwork skills: how you play well but don't work well with others, since you like to let them do all the work

---

Strategy #4

Open your eyes to the possibility of combining your passions with growth fields. Let's take the healthcare industry as an example. If you really want to work in healthcare, there are many fields in which you might be interested that have a need for qualified workers. Gerontology is one of them. Caring for the growing number of elderly people in the U.S. is big business now and will continue to boom for many years.

How can you connect your areas of expertise and interest to gerontology? You can do what Alexandra did. She loved social work and had spent many summers and school breaks working at a residential living facility for the elderly. After graduating with a bachelor's degree in social work she had a lot of student loans to pay and couldn't afford to go to grad school right away. So she wasn't qualified to get a higher paying job in social work. Moving back to her parents' home, she wondered how she was ever going to do what she wanted and still get out on her own.

After listening to her parents discuss their frustration with figuring out how to arrange care for her grandparents, she realized that there might be a way to combine her love of social work with the hot field of gerontology. She approached one of her mentors, a social worker in the community with an M.S.W., about starting an eldercare referral service, which would help adults find affordable, quality services for their aging parents. The service took off and gave her a way to do what she loved, go back to school part-time, and fill an immediate need in her community.

Brandon took another approach to gerontology. He decided to combine his passion for architecture, a very competitive profession, with this growth field. As a young architect for a medium-sized, struggling firm, he approached his manager about bidding on contracts to develop living communities for elderly people who needed only partial support. His manager recognized the value of Brandon's idea, and they researched the feasibility of the project. When they discovered that it was indeed a relatively untapped market, they embarked on a campaign to design model units with communal dining rooms, special apartments with support rails and easily accessible buzzers in every room in case of emergency, and other amenities. Brandon's firm become well-known as one of the premier designers of facilities that enabled the elderly to live with dignity, and Brandon ultimately was promoted to manage the division that handled related projects.

So you can see from these two examples that whether your passion is to be a human services worker, a businessperson, or any other position you want to pursue, there are a myriad of ways in which you could combine your talents with a growing field. Some of these jobs you come up with by using this approach will be traditional ones with a special twist, like the social worker who does eldercare referrals or the architect who designs living communities for the elderly.

Other jobs will require your ability to work with professionals in other fields. The multimedia industry, for instance, is creating many of these jobs. Imagine working as part of a professional team, designing educational CD-ROMs. You could be the graphic artist who develops the visuals. You could be the marketer who determines how to pitch the product to the public. You could be the computer programmer who writes the code that makes the CD-ROM run. Fun and sometimes funky jobs like these exist in many up and coming industries where you can apply your background to a new, dynamic job and transform your career.

FYI

The 10 industries with fastest projected job growth, 1994–2005, moderate alternative projection

Industry	Percent change
Health services	84.1
Residential care	82.7
Computer and data processing services	69.5
Individual and miscellaneous social services	68.8
Miscellaneous business services	68.4
Child day care services	59.4
Personnel supply services	58.1
Services to buildings	58.0
Miscellaneous equipment rental and leasing	50.8
Management and public relations	46.5

[Source: Bureau of Labor Statistics, U.S. Department of Labor, December 1, 1995, p. 6]

Note: This data assumes that the economy will grow at a moderate rate, rather than at an accelerated or depressed one. This projected growth pattern is the one typically used by job seekers and career development specialists to evaluate trends. But it is subject to change, given the uncertainties in the economy.

When you take the time to brainstorm job ideas related to the hot industries, you'll realize that so much is out there for you. The answer to the question, "What do you want to be when you grow up?" is taking on a whole new world of possibilities. By getting involved in areas you care about and that have lots of growth potential, you can leverage your experience immediately after college and keep in synch with the job market.

Strategy #5

An innovative job search strategy is to look at the job market not just in terms of specific industries or jobs. Instead, you can take advantage of the growing employment opportunities that have emerged as a response to economic and technological changes in the job market. There are three main types of such opportunities: small businesses, contingency work, and self-employment; and a fourth secondary type, telecommuting.

It's no longer just the big companies that can offer you jobs with growth and the opportunity to build a career. The benefits of hands-on learning and often a more casual, team environment also make small companies an appealing place to work.

Jim joined a small, graphic design firm two years after graduating from college with a fine arts degree. The large firm he had worked for immediately after college went bankrupt and there was a hiring freeze at all of the other large firms in his city. He ended up finding an opportunity at a small design company through his college roommate's mother, who had a contact there.

Within a few months, he realized that he had been lucky to land a job in a small, busy place. It was exactly what he needed to learn the ins and outs of the business. And what made it even better was that thirty employees all knew each other by name and often enjoyed socializing together after work to unwind. Jim's hard work and cooperative nature quickly earned him the respect of the firm's owners as well as his coworkers. He was able to hold increasingly responsible positions and his input into new projects was actively sought by others.

"In the past decade, small employers have provided the greatest growth in employment. This trend is likely to continue, and there's a good chance that [as a college graduate] you'll work for a small employer."

("Small Employers: How, When, & Who They Hire,",
Planning Job Choices: 1996, Constance J. Pritchard NACE, p. 67)

Contingency work—temporary, part-time, or contract employment—is another place you can direct your job search. This type of work has steadily increased due to organizations' changing needs, such as reducing the costs of hiring full-time employees, gaining the expertise of individuals with specialized knowledge, handling projects with highly confidential natures, addressing temporary staffing gaps, meeting cyclical or seasonal work needs, and buying time while sorting out their needs after a reorganization.

You can pursue a managerial role in an agency that hires out contingency workers or become a contingency worker yourself. You can use this work either as a stepping stone to a job in the same field or as a stabilizer while you are seeking full-time employment in another field.

Chelsea took as job as a project manager for a vice president of a major insurance company on the East Coast after graduating from college in California. With a degree in business administration, she was recruited by a company representative who did on-site interviews at her college career center. She was happy for the first year, since she was told by everyone how lucky she was to get a job with such a reputable company and didn't have to graduate jobless and then settle for some less desirable position at a second rate organization just to get going.

As she approached her one-year anniversary, however, she started questioning whether this was a job she really wanted to stay in for much longer. Her manager was a fair, responsive person who took a keen interest in her career development. Her colleagues were pleasant enough and her hours weren't bad. The pay was pretty decent, too. On the whole, she had a stable, good thing going.

She couldn't quite understand what was bothering her at first and then she realized that she missed being able to pursue the outdoor sports she loved as often as she had during college. She was an avid rock climber and cyclist, and there just wasn't time or easy access to these activities where she lived. Besides, at that point in her life, she felt that spending a lot of time outdoors being physically active was something she didn't want to miss out on. The weather in the east was cold and rainy or snowy much of the time, and sitting behind a desk much of the day, wearing formal business clothes, and the routine nature of the job turned her off.

So she checked out her options and decided to leave her position shortly after her one-year anniversary to move back to California and live the lifestyle she craved. Her former adviser at school hooked her up with her brother, who ran a temporary agency, and she arranged to work temp jobs to pay her living expenses while she rock climbed and cycled after hours.

Even with 5.5% unemployment and a recovering labor market, many companies depend heavily on temporary help. Temp outfits have added more than 1 million workers over the past three years, and their employment is rising at 17% annually.

(The Temp Boom Is Here To Stay: Low Joblessness Doesn't Faze It , Edited by Michael Mandel, Business Week, May 8, 1995)

You may also want to consider turning to self-employment. This is a challenging, high risk option. But it can be a good one if you have a lot of drive and desire. This option can also help you develop a more flexible and autonomous, though labor-intensive, lifestyle.

Gabriella found that becoming self-employed was a natural step for her. After working in the marketing department of a magazine for a few years and making jewelry on the side as a hobby, she was ready to make her move. She had built up a strong clientele of friends, family, and their referrals. In addition, a local newspaper article showcasing her work generated orders from three major department stores and several small, exclusive boutiques in her city. When she realized that she could finally make the transition from hobby to full-time job, she went for it and took a chance. Knowing that she could always get another job in marketing or temp if necessary for a while to make ends meet, she got to work filling her orders. It wasn't easy, and she worked longer and harder than ever before. During a dry spell several months later, she did have to take on a temp job and move to a smaller apartment to pay her rent. But after two years, she was able to support herself entirely through her jewelry business.

A fourth, less available, option to seeking a regular job in a large company is telecommuting. Increasingly, organizations are offering employees the chance to work at home at least part of the week. This arrangement, called telecommuting, makes many organizations and employees equally happy. Organizations get to reduce their overhead costs and employees can better balance work/family responsibilities and their overall lifestyle needs. To telecommute, you generally need a computer, fax, separate telephone line, and work space. The equipment may or may not be provided by your employer.

Dan and his wife Sharon had two children right after college. After a few years, they agreed that he would take on more of the child care responsibilities so Sharon would be able to go back to school part-time to earn a graduate degree. In order to be home when his kids came home from school, Dan arranged to telecommute two days a week. His job as a computer programmer made it easy for him to work at home and at different hours when necessary. He scheduled conference calls on those days during the hours the kids were in school and began working from home at 7:00 A.M. This arrangement worked for everyone and set a precedent in his department.

Strategy #6

Relocation can be a successful tactic when you do your homework before you move. Checking out places first will help you maximize your opportunities and minimize your costs and stress.

There are three steps to take when you're thinking of relocating: determine job growth areas, evaluate your options, and calculate the cost of living.

In order to pick a winner, it's advisable to research job growth areas by region, state, and city or town. Books on relocation such as *The Moving and Relocation Sourcebook* by Diane Barlow (Omnigraphics, 1992) can help you get started.

After you've come up with some places where you think you may want to live, consider whether or not each one is a realistic option for you. There are many factors to consider when you screen a potential living place. What are the job opportunities in my fields of interest? Are they on the rise or at least stable for now? Are there interesting, varied places to hang out, like coffee houses, art galleries or museums, and movie theaters? Are there places I could take classes, such as colleges or universities, learning centers, or public libraries? Do there seem to be people who I can relate to on an intellectual, artistic, spiritual, recreational, or other level that is important to me? What's the housing like? Is it plentiful, affordable, and desirable? How about the public transportation systems? Do I need a car? Can I park a car if I want or need one? Remember to consider these and any other issues relevant to your situation. And, of course, ask yourself the big question: What is the relative cost of living?

As a final step, you need to figure out how much money you would need to live in your new place as compared to where you are now. Contact the local Chamber of Commerce in your prospective new location for accurate cost of living information. Chambers of Commerce also offer relocation packets, usually for a nominal fee. Also, most cities now have websites that include their major types of employers, housing, and other relevant information for relocaters.

Another, high-tech option for getting cost of living information is to check out The Center for Mobility Resources' website on the Internet. The Center currently maintains a Salary Calculator on the Internet at:

http://www.homefair.com/homefair/cmr/salcalc.html.

This website lists cost-of-living indexes updated quarterly for over 450 U.S. cities based on data collected from local real estate boards, Chambers of Commerce, and other sources. The calculator enables you to estimate the income you would need in a new city in order to maintain your current standard of living.

You simply enter your current annual income in one box, your current city code in a second box, your destination city code in a third box, and click on a fourth, "calculate" box. A list of cities and codes is provided. The salary calculator then provides you with the annual income you would need in your new city. You can repeat this process as many times as you wish.

There are two limits to the calculator: (1) neither taxes nor government services are included, but the Center for Mobility Resources provides their e-mail address where they will respond to city tax rate questions; and (2) there is no one standard index of cost-of-living measures; each index weights items differently; this index more heavily weights housing more than other indexes. The Center claims on their website, however, that "Our weighting generally follows the guidelines provided by the U.S. Bureau of Labor Statistics."

You can use these six strategies to help you kick off and keep your job search on track. They give you a sense of how to manage the many factors that affect a successful job search. In the end, you want to keep two things in mind: What are the myths and realities of today's job market? What strategies can I use to make my job search work given these realities and their advantages as well as restrictions? The answers to the second question will become the basis for your personalized job search strategy.

3

Preparing for Your Journey

BUILDING AND MAINTAINING A SUPPORT TEAM

Now that you have an idea of how to get hired and where the jobs are, it's time to dive right into the search. Or is it? Just as you wouldn't dive into a pool without first making sure there's water in it, you also have to look before you leap into a job search. As with most pursuits in life, a little foresight goes a long way for a successful job hunt. There are three main steps to take now in preparation for your search:

1. Assemble a support team and learn how to manage it.

2. Get organized and learn how to make time for the search.

3. Compile your hit list of target employers.

STRENGTH IN NUMBERS

Life's most challenging tasks are rarely solo efforts. The real movers and shakers of this world usually owe much of their success to an inner circle of supporters. Can you imagine presidents without their advisors? Olympic athletes without coaches? Hollywood stars without agents?

Whether you like it or not, as a job seeker, you are dependent on the people around you, either for emotional support, strategic input, or actual contacts and job leads. A job search is not—and should not be—conducted in a vacuum. Besides interacting with prospective employers, you will have to deal with people in your daily life such as family, friends, and classmates if you're in school. The people in this inner circle can be incredibly helpful, doing things like staying up half the night to type your resume or putting you in touch with all sorts of people to interview with. Or, they can be incredibly annoying—nagging parents who keep asking when you're going to get a job or alleged friends who suddenly turn competitive, gloating about every interview they line up as if they're The World's All-Time Greatest Job Seekers. We'll show you how to manage these people so that they help more than they hurt.

Then there are the outside experts you should bring into this inner circle of family and friends. These may include career counselors, job search coaches, resume writers, professors or deans, and anyone else who can guide you through the intricacies of job search. We'll tell you how to find the people who can help.

A support team is important not only because multiple heads are better than one when it comes to brainstorming job search strategies, but also because you're undergoing a major transition. Psychologists who study career development have found that the success of a transition is highly dependent on the strength of one's support system. Whether you're making a transition from college to a first postgraduate job or changing careers after working for several years, you will undoubtedly encounter many hurdles in the process. One way to get over those hurdles is to have a supportive network of people close to you.

School-to-work transitions, moving from job to job, and changing career fields are all significant life changes, often made even more complex by the fact that people involved in one transition are usually undergoing other changes as well. Think about what else is going on in your life as you look for a job. Are you moving back home and reestablishing your role as your parents' child under their roof? Are you leaving college as well as the friends and student identity you'd grown comfortable with? Are you changing careers and getting married? Are you relocating to another part of the country? Our life roles are so intertwined, that a job search is likely to affect, and be affected by, many other areas of our lives and many other people.

With all this in mind, it's wise to put together a team of people who can help with the day-to-day management of your search. It's also a good idea at this point to learn techniques for coping with the people around you who may inadvertently—or even deliberately— hinder your efforts. This team, for better or worse, will include parents (and other family), friends, and outside experts.

IT'S A FAMILY AFFAIR

No matter what your age, your parents are likely to be involved in your search on at least some level. The relationship between parents and adult children is difficult enough without the added stress of a job search. If you have stepparents, grandparents, or aunts and uncles involved in your life, then the situation is even more complex. Their various agendas and expectations can be mind boggling. It might seem like you can never please them. They ask such annoying questions as "Do you have a job yet?" "Shouldn't you be out looking for a job now instead of watching TV?" "How did the interview go with my dear friend Bob over at The Boring Corporation?" It's inevitable that conflicts will arise as you try to please yourself and your family.

Let's look at a couple of the realities of family-job search dynamics, as well as strategies for making family members (especially parents) valuable members of your support team.

The Mixed Message Reality

As you attempt to get a career going, the degree to which you are dependent on your parents is likely to fluctuate. You may need their help in a number of ways—from basic food and shelter to job search advice and contacts. With more and more adults these days moving back home with their parents throughout their twenties and thirties, the issues of dependency are becoming increasingly significant.

While you and your parents struggle with these changes, you're likely to get mixed messages from them. They might say that they want you to be independent and act like an adult, yet sometimes they treat you like a child. You might not even know what you want yourself. You want to be left alone to do your own thing, but you also expect them to help you find a job and may want them to support you until then. If you recently graduated college and spent four or more years away from home, then the situation is likely to be even more tense. You suddenly find yourself back at home at their mercy, following their rules. You might even be relying on their contacts to help you find a job.

- *Remember that this is a difficult time for them too. They might have expected that once you left the nest for college, you were gone for good. They'd already dealt with the painful cutting of the ties that bind, only to find you back in the nest. As wrapped up as you are in finding a job, try to keep their perspective in mind. They may see it as a mixed blessing that you're back under their wings. Parents grapple with separation issues as much as children do, so be patient and respect their point of view.*
- *To ease the strain of being totally or partially supported by them, see what you can do to act more like an adult. Sit down together and go over any ways that you can help out, whether it's with household chores or working in their business—whatever makes sense. Even if your contributions don't equal theirs in monetary value, at least they'll be more inclined to see you as a mature adult.*

THE "WHEN I WAS YOUR AGE" REALITY

At some point in your search, you might find that your parents expect your job search and your career in general to proceed as theirs did. They live by such rules as "Never stay at a job less than a year or you'll look like a job hopper," "Never leave a job without having another one," "Working in one full-time job for a respectable company is the only way to go." These and other alleged truths about career management fill the minds of parents but aren't always accurate.

That was the case with Eileen, a twenty-four year old who had held two jobs since college, the latest one for about nine months. She was working in cable television in an area that required she work an overnight shift every other week. She'd come to loathe her job and really wanted to leave it. Not only had she decided that TV was not a field she wanted to pursue long term, but the crazy schedule of her job was making her prone to illness. She wanted to leave the job since she found it hard to look for a new one with that schedule. During the weeks when she did have daytime hours free, she was unable to get anything done because she felt so out of it.

Her plan was to quit her job and do temporary office work while conducting informational interviews in other fields that interested her. Her mother, though, would hear nothing of it. In her mind, Eileen was breaking all those rules of career management.

They ended up reaching a compromise in which Eileen agreed to stay at the job until a year was up, but then she could leave to pursue other options. Instead of just taking the easy way out by quitting, Eileen listened to her mother and also worked to make her job more tolerable by discussing some concerns with her boss. She managed to get a more regular schedule and took on a new project that made her job more interesting.

She also wrote out a plan of action for how she would spend her time if she did quit her job. This showed her mother that she wouldn't just be wasting time but would be actively defining a new career direction and working toward a new job.

Strategies:

- Sometimes, parents need to be educated about the current job market and the job search process. Look for objective sources of advice about how to handle job situations so that it's not your word against your parents'. Turn to career counselors, professional associations, or do a search of articles about the job market in popular magazines or newspapers.

- Reassure your parents that the path you want to take is a productive one. In Eileen's case, for example, doing temp work sounded to her mother like "being unemployed." If you have top-notch office skills, as Eileen did, then temporary work is a viable option. Whatever you might be doing that concerns your parents, sit down with them and go over how you are going to spend your time. It's easy to have a lot of idle hours in a job search, so do yourself and your parents a favor by putting yourself on a schedule.

No matter what problems you encounter with your parents as you go through your job search, remember to be patient and respectful and try to keep their perspective in mind.

"Happiness is having a large, loving, caring, close-knit family in another city."

George Burns

FRIENDLY FIRE

Like family, friends can be a much-needed source of support during the job search, or they can be the bane of your existence. There's so much going on in the job search process that can affect your relationships. For instance, are you and your friends conducting job searches simultaneously? Are you looking for jobs in the same field? Is a friend relying too heavily on you for job leads, or vice versa? To college seniors, recent graduates and career changers who find themselves in these situations, we say beware! We've watched many a close friendship become strained during the stressful months of on-campus recruitment programs and during off-campus searches for employment as well.

Why Can't We Be Friends?
Rosemary and Chuck had been good friends all through school. Not only did they hang out a lot together, but they had been in some of the same classes because they were both majoring in political science. Many a late night they could be found studying together over a pizza or quizzing each other for the next day's test. They were both interested in getting a job as a paralegal, with the ultimate goal of going to law school. All year long their professors, parents, and friends had been telling them "You'd better start looking for a job!" or "I just read an article that says there are no jobs out there!" or "They say by the year 2005 there will be too many lawyers and too few jobs, are you still thinking about going to law school?" Over the course of senior year, a sort of mass hysteria seemed to break out about their job prospects, leaving Rosemary and Chuck more than a little stressed out and suddenly feeling like they were in direct competition for the few jobs that were out there. Unfortunately, the panic caused by all of these misconceptions affected their friendship.

What can you do to keep the pressure from coming between you and your friends? While there can be a great deal of pressure to secure that perfect job in today's challenging job market, cooperative efforts between friends and classmates are often the keys to a successful search. Rather than viewing the job search as a competition, why not focus your energy on making yourself the best and most informed candidate for the job market. Instead of putting energy into getting one-up on a friend, why not spend time organizing your job search, honing your interviewing skills, or researching prospective employers?

With Friends Like These, Who Needs Enemies?
Roommates Susan and Christine were conducting their job searches through the senior recruitment program at their college, both looking for jobs in finance. While they had always been close friends, they found their interactions becoming more and more strained. Susan, upon hearing through the college career center that a spe-

cific firm had suddenly decided to come to campus for interviews, "forgot" to tell Christine about it. Similarly, while conducting industry research, Christine found some information that would be extremely helpful for an upcoming interview. Even though Susan had an interview with the same firm, Christine chose not to share the information with her, feeling it would give her an edge in the interview process. Susan and Christine's relations became so tense that they were not even speaking to each other by the end of the semester.

Instead of competing with each other, consider forming a job search support group among your friends or classmates. These don't have to be led by a career counseling professional, but instead can simply be a chance for you to get together with friends and do everything from venting about the hassles of job seeking to critiquing each others' resumes or sharing contacts and ideas. Many working adults in a variety of professions have these kinds of groups for ongoing networking. All around the country, there are informal "breakfast clubs" or "happy hour groups," which meet maybe once a month for people to talk about their jobs and share tips on how to be more successful at work. Establishing a job search group early on in your career can be a great way to make lasting friendships and valuable contacts that can help you professionally later on.

Don't Put All Your Eggs in One Basket

Bill, twenty-seven, had worked as a high school English teacher since graduating from college. He was starting to get bored with his job and was considering a career change. He had always enjoyed newspaper journalism, having been a teaching assistant in one of his college journalism courses, so he decided to pursue that field. It just so happened that his good friend Jim was an assistant editor at the local newspaper. Rather than conducting research on all the newspapers he might apply to and using Jim as one of his resources, Bill focused his search solely on the paper for which Jim worked. After months of constant phone calls from Bill asking him to use his pull, Jim began avoiding Bill's phone calls. "I felt like I was solely responsible for getting Bill a job," replied Jim when asked why the friendship had cooled.

As the job seeker, try to remember that although friends can be used as possible resources for job information, they are only one resource to be used in conjunction with your own strategies. Cover your bases, in other words. In Bill's case he should have tried to make contacts with people who worked at a number of newspapers in his geographic area. Or he might have asked Jim for some contact names so he could try to get interviews on his own. Remember, you are ultimately responsible for your job search.

Calling All Experts

To get expert advice on job search strategies, it helps to include a career development professional in your support team. These experts can't get you a job per se, but they can guide you through the search with fewer headaches and pitfalls than if you were to go it alone.

If you're still in college, take advantage of any career counseling available on campus, whether in the form of individual sessions or group workshops. Some college career development offices also provide services for alumni, either free or for a reasonable fee. We talk more about these offices in the Campus Resources section of chapter 5. Some professors can also be a good source of advice. Depending on their field of study, many academics work as consultants or have businesses in addition to being scholars. That real-world knowledge can make them useful members of your job search team.

If your alma mater is not an option, check around for community-based career counseling centers that provide free or low-cost advice to the general public. Some major universities also have career offices open to the community rather than to students through their Adult Education or Continuing Education divisions.

If you've been in the work world a while, contact your industry's professional association to find out about any job search coaching or seminars available to members. Also, counseling is often offered through groups that cross over various industries but represent a specific population such as women or ethnic groups. We've listed some resources for finding these associations at the end of this chapter.

You Get What You Pay For

If those aren't options, or if you want more personalized attention, then a career counselor in private practice may be the answer. Be aware that the career counseling profession is not regulated by any licenses or credentials, so you have to be careful about who you're getting. You might see the initials "N.B.C.C." after some career counselors' names. This is an optional credential, which does ensure that you're getting a counselor who has met certain basic criteria for education and experience, but be aware that many experienced, skilled, and well-educated career counselors have chosen not to obtain this credential.

If you want help choosing a career direction, then look for a counselor with a master's or doctoral degree in counseling, psychology, or social work. Experience is just as important as the degree, however, so be sure to ask how long they've been doing career counseling and what type of clients they typically work with. If they've been using their Ph.D. to do pet therapy, then that fancy degree doesn't do you much good. Assuming they have been working with humans, ask about their areas of expertise. Career counselors accustomed to dealing primarily with senior executives, for example, may not know what to do with a twenty year old, or even a thirty year old entering the job market.

If you want help with job search issues or mid-career transition strategies, you may also consider career counselors with M.B.A.s or maybe no advanced degree at all but with solid business backgrounds who can help you with the less psychological aspects of career planning. These professionals often call themselves consultants, advisors, or coaches since they aren't really counselors.

Beware of any career development professionals or firms that promise you placement in a job or who ask for fees that seem excessive. Some firms charge several thousand dollars and actually have salespeople doing the intake counseling who earn a commission on the package you sign up for. Most reputable counselors, on the other hand, charge on an hourly basis with fees typically ranging from about $50 to $150 per hour. Outside major cities, fees may be lower. Some good counselors may also offer package rates of multiple sessions or sessions with testing in addition to their hourly rates. These typically cost anywhere from a couple hundred to several hundred dollars and can be a more cost-effective option than paying by the hour.

Whether you work with a private career counselor on a regular basis throughout your search, or whether you simply stop in to chat with an advisor in your college career center, remember that these experts can have valuable knowledge about the job search process. Making them a part of your support team is a smart move.

GETTING ORGANIZED: LIFE IN THE FAST LANE

Let's face it, whether you're a college student, recent graduate, or mid-level professional your life is probably moving at a frenetic pace. It's likely you feel you don't even have time to organize your closet let alone your job search. "I'll manage," you say. "Post-it notes on the fridge have always kept my life together in the past." But a job search is an entirely different animal.

With a job search, the amount of research that needs to be conducted and the quantity of information that needs to be managed (e.g., facts, figures, names, phone numbers, dates, addresses, and so on) is staggering. We're talking big with a capital B.

Not to scare you, but the biggest difference between trying to succeed as a student and trying to succeed as a job hunter is that as a student you can often make a mistake or two with relative impunity, whereas as a job hunter even a small mistake can ruin your chances of obtaining employment. Consider the following examples. John, a senior at the University of Virginia, mistakenly thought his history paper was due on Friday, when in fact it was due on Wednesday. When his professor asked everyone to turn in their papers at the conclusion of Wednesday's class John was in a state of shock. He begged and pleaded with his professor for an extension, which the latter finally granted with the proviso that for each day John's paper was late, a half grade would be deducted. That night John worked into the wee hours, managed to complete his assignment and turned it in the following day. As a result, his grade was slashed from a B to a B-, a penalty John could live with, especially since it had virtually no effect on his overall GPA.

To help my clients manage their time, I suggest they develop a detailed daily schedule for job search related activities. A person should have something planned for each day of the week, even if it's just recreational. Doing nothing can lead to a loss of motivation, and in some cases paralysis.
Erica Gray, Career Counselor, New York University

Burt's mistake, on the other hand, was a bit more costly. He had just completed his B.A. in sociology at Northeastern and was aggressively looking for work with an organization that specialized in consumer opinion research. After sending out over one hundred letters and receiving over one hundred rejections, Burt was finally offered an interview by the National Opinion Research Center in Chicago. Overwhelmed by the good news, Burt hastily jotted down the date and time of the interview in his planner. Unfortunately, he marked it down for 2 P.M. on March 23rd when in fact it was scheduled to take place on March 22nd at 3 P.M. So when Burt trotted in to the National Opinion Research Center on the 23rd, a day late for his interview, he was more than a bit surprised by the icy reaction he received from the Director of Human Resources who told him in no uncertain terms that such an oversight could not be tolerated by the organization and that Burt's status as a viable candidate was "kaput." Burt pleaded to reschedule, citing dyslexia, being bitten by a rabid dog, visiting a deathly ill grandma, and searching for a stolen car—all to no avail. The National Opinion Research Center wouldn't budge. Two years later, Burt approached them again for an interview, hoping that the previous incident was water under the bridge, but alas the black mark on Burt's personnel folder was as indelible as the marinara stain on his best tie.

THE BASICS OF GETTING ORGANIZED

In light of Burt's horror story, let's talk about the basics of good job search organization. Ultimately, being well organized comes down to following four simple principles:

- manage your time effectively
- take thorough notes
- unclutter your workspace, and
- create an organizational system that works.

No Pain, No Gain

As you embark on your job search, it is likely that the issue of time will cause you some anxiety—both in terms of how much time you devote to your search, as well as how much time it will take before the fruits of your labor finally pay off. Obviously, all things being equal, the more time you can spend looking for a job each week, the better the chance that you will find what you want faster. How much time should you allocate to your search on a daily or weekly basis? Well, that really depends on your priorities. If you can go about your job hunt as though it were your full-time job that's great, but for many of you that's not realistic—especially if you're already working full-time, and are taking care of your two kids plus grandma. Let's put it this way: To get good results, you should probably try to spend at least 2 hours a day, 6 days a week on your job hunt. Always give yourself one day off per week to recuperate and recharge your batteries. Job hunting is a high-stress activity. Every now and then you need to kick your feet up, pour a hot bath, burn some incense, and relax.

How Long Has This Been Going On?

As far as how long it will take you before you find the right position, that depends on a number of factors including how much time you devote to your search, the supply of and demand for workers in the field you're pursuing, your level of skill and experience, and plain old luck. Job search experts throw out wildly divergent figures regarding how long a search should take. Typically, these range from three months to a year. The reality is that no one can really predict how long it will take you to find a job. It depends on so many different factors that it's impossible to put a concrete number on it., but we can guarantee that once you're offered and have accepted a position you'll have the answer to your question.

The bottom line is that you've got your work cut out for you and you're going to have to manage your time carefully so that you a) don't get overwhelmed and, more importantly, b) don't make the same kind of costly error that Burt made. How to do this? First off, be realistic about how much time is required to accomplish your job search goals. For example, if it takes you roughly an hour to write a targeted cover letter, and your goal is to send out ten tailor-made letters each week, then your job hunting meter is already at ten hours. Factor in the time you need to research each organization, follow up on previous inquiries, develop new contacts, and you can quickly see that the hours are starting to pile up. Whatever figure you arrive at, pad that by at least 15 percent to account for the dreaded x factor (e.g., your hard drive crashes, your printer runs out of toner, you succumb to writer's block, etc.).

Now that you have a rough estimate of how much time you'd like to spend each week on your search, step back and look at the big picture. What are your other time commitments at the moment? Is there any place where you can cut back temporarily so that you can borrow time for your job hunt? Perhaps you've allocated too much time to your search and you need to cut back to avoid burning out. Whatever you decide, keep it in perspective and go with what feels right to you.

When In Doubt, Write It Out

During the course of your job search you will come across many useful bits and pieces of information from a variety of sources—newspapers, magazines, books, friends, professors, and so on. Some of these bits and pieces could eventually turn into job leads that might actually result in your getting hired, unless of course you lose the little bits of paper on which you jotted down all those wonderful tips. To prevent such a disaster from happening, get in the habit of keeping a notebook with you at all times and take extremely thorough notes. You never know when they may come in handy. Even if you're making a follow-up call to an employer, keep your notebook by your side. This will allow you, for example, to jot down the name of the friendly receptionist who fielded your phone call. Then the next time you call you can win some brownie points by addressing him by name.

It's these little intangibles that can make the difference between getting hired or not, or at least getting an interview. The point is that you can't keep all this minutiae in your head—you've got to write it down and have it accessible at all times.

ORGANIZATIONAL TOOLS FOR THE JOB SEARCH

As we've already mentioned, managing a job search requires you to efficiently and accurately keep track of voluminous amounts of information and communications. For the non-detail-oriented person this can be a tremendous challenge. We're going to try to make this process as easy as possible by carefully walking you through it. Granted, there is no one correct way to organize a job search, but our method has proven to be effective with a wide range of job seekers, and at the very least will serve as a jumping-off point, which you can later modify to suit your own needs, taste, and style. First let's look at the tools and supplies that you're going to need. We've tried whenever possible to recommend items that will put the smallest possible dent in your checkbook. With more expensive items, such as a computer, begging, borrowing, or sharing will help keep your costs down.

File Box

You should have one of these for letter-size hanging pendaflex folders. We like the Flip-top Storage/file Crate by FREM—it's not a thing of beauty, but it's inexpensive, portable, and holds roughly 30-40 folders, depending on how stuffed they are. You will probably need at least two of these.

Letter-Size Pendaflex Folders with Tabs

Get the cheap ugly green ones that allow you to insert five tabs across the top (they're called 1/5th cut). They usually come in boxes of 25. Start with two or three boxes. You might also want to pick up a package of colored inserts to slide into the plastic tabs. These will enable you to color code your files and dazzle all your friends.

Letter-Size Manilla Folders

A box of 100 should do.

Notebook

Pick up the kind with perforated 3-hole punched paper in the event that you want to transfer your notes to a loose-leaf binder.

Rolodex

Choose one large enough for filing business cards (2" x 3 1/2"). We like the rotary model, which you can flip incessantly when you're bored.

Planner

Get either the daily or weekly variety with preprinted 15 minute time slots. Either should cost less than $15 as long as you don't object to vinyl. Another option is the Uncalendar (of which there are numerous varieties) by People Systems, Inc. (1-800-844-6586), which allows you to customize your planner according to your needs. Although the Uncalendar affords you the greatest flexibility, be warned that the dates of the month and times of the day are blank — you have to fill them in yourself.

Computer

Now this is obviously a huge topic that we don't have room to get into here in any depth, but suffice it to say that in this day and age owning, or at least having access to, a computer borders on necessity. A computer allows you to efficiently manage large quantities of information, such as a database of prospective employers, or 99 versions of your resume. If you're going to buy one, go for what you're most comfortable with. If you're still a student or somehow affiliated with a university, Apple has a very cool student loan program, which will help you finance your purchase. For more information, contact Apple at 1-800-277-5356. For the ultimate in convenience and practicality, get a laptop, which will virtually eliminate the need to keep notes on paper. Also, the simple addition of a modem and some faxing software will enable you to use your computer to send and receive faxes, and to surf the net. It can also save you the time, not to mention the huge expense, of running to the local copy shop to send or receive faxes. If you buy a computer, try to get the fastest machine (measured in megahertz) with the most memory (at least 8 megabytes of RAM), the highest quality monitor (15" or larger), and the largest amount of hard disk storage (at least 500 megabytes) that you can afford.

Software

At the very least you'll need a good word processing package (WordPerfect, Microsoft, and ClarisWorks are all quite robust) for composing and designing letters and resumes, but we also recommend you purchase database management software that will enable you to keep track of all your contacts and prospective employers.

Portfolio

This is where you will store all the masterpieces that you're going to bring with you on your interview. Our favorite is the Itoya Profolio, which comes in a variety of colors and has polypropylene sleeves in which you can insert any letter-sized document you'd like to display. The smallest version of the Profolio, which holds 12 pages, is less than $4.00.

Envelopes, Paper, and Thank You Notes

You're going to need matching paper and envelopes for your resumes and cover letters. If you're printing them yourself, get at least 100 of each. When it comes to paper, there are countless excellent options, although it is generally best to go for a conservative color and a heavier weight such as 24 pound. For envelopes you have two options—the standard business size (#10), or the larger, 9" x 12" size. The latter are more expensive and will cost you more in postage (a minimum of .11 as of this writing), but they do make a nicer presentation, and practically guarantee that your resume will arrive flat—a big bonus if your resume is going to be scanned into a computer (more on that in chapter 4, pp. 106–107). And while you're at it, pick up a box of thank you notes. Something plain and simple will do.

Answering Machine

This is an absolute must. It really doesn't matter whether it's digital or tape as long as it works. Make sure you get one that allows you to retrieve messages from a remote location.

KEEPING ON TRACK

Okay, so now that you know all the fancy tools you'll need to store, sort, track, retrieve, and display all kinds of stuff, what's next? Not to worry, we're going to walk you through each phase of the job hunt and explain how you'll be using your new toys.

IN THE BEGINNING, THERE WAS PENDAFLEX

At the beginning of your search most of the information you accumulate will result from the research you do on your field. You'll have notes and photocopies of articles about the field and where it's going, descriptions of various jobs, lists of resources you've used, as well as names of people you might want to speak with. To keep yourself from getting overwhelmed right out of the starting gate, set up a pendaflex folder in your filing box for each field that you're investigating.

Now it's time to shift gears to manilla folders. Are we having fun yet? The manilla folders will allow you to categorize the information that you're keeping in your pendaflex so that it is easier to retrieve. We suggest you create manilla folders to keep track of books, CD's, magazines, articles, etc. that have proven helpful in your search, and contacts (names, addresses, and phone numbers of people who can provide helpful information).

Organizing Employer Information

Once you decide on the type of work you're going to pursue, your next task will be to figure out who you want to do it for. You'll be compiling a large list of prospective employers, which you will gradually winnow down by matching up the criteria you have deemed most important (e.g., size of organization, geographical location, growth potential, etc.) against what each employer has to offer (later in this chapter, you'll learn how to compile a hit list). Those employers that make the grade get their very own pendaflex folder and accompanying "Employer Information Form" aka, E.I.F., which you'll use to record all the data you've tracked down about the organization being researched. In this same folder, you should also keep annual reports, articles, catalogs, statistics, and any other printed materials you've been able to collect about the prospective employer. As you progress through your search you will constantly be referring to your employer folders, so it's a good idea to keep them in alphabetical order.

Employer Information Form

Name of Organization _____

Contact 1 _____

Title _____

Phone _____

Address _____

Comments _____

_____

Contact 2 _____

Title _____

Phone _____

Address _____

Comments _____

Contact 3 _____

Title _____

Phone _____

Address _____

Comments _____

_____

Information Sources (e.g., *Infotrac*, *Good Works*, *Community Jobs*)

Organization Data

Number of employees _____

Products/Services _____

Structure _____

Reputation _____

Financials _____

New Development _____

Position Data

Job Title 1 _____

Responsibilities _____

Qualifications _____

Salary _____

Benefits _____

Job Title 2 _____

Responsibilities _____

Qualifications _____

Salary _____

Benefits _____

BABY IT'S YOU

In addition to retrieving materials about different organizations, you will also be generating some stuff of your own. Just about everything you create should be stored on disk so that it can be easily revised or re-sent should there be a problem with mail, fax machine, or modem. Make a copy of everything you send out—cover letters, resumes, thank-you letters, and rejection letters, and place it in the appropriate employer folder. In this way you will always know what you've sent to whom.

Have Portfolio, Will Interview

At this stage you should also be putting the finishing touches on your portfolio, which will mostly come into play during the interview process. Your portfolio should include copies of your resume, references, and letters of recommendation as well as any samples of your work you feel would be appropriate to show an employer (essays, research papers, published articles, poems, or artwork, brochures of programs or events you developed or managed, computer programs you designed, and/or copies of your transcript). The possibilities are limitless.

THE HUNT BEGINS

Your biggest challenge at this point will be keeping track of times and dates of important activities. This is where your planner moves to center stage. Make sure that you write down and regularly check the time and date of all your job hunting activities such as interviews, career fairs, career planning workshops, and networking events. Also note when you need to follow up with employers who you've approached but haven't heard from yet.

This Log Ain't for Lumberjacks

A typical week in your planner might look like this:

While you're trying to keep a handle on your hectic schedule, we suggest that for each company you approach, you maintain a detailed communications log. The log will be a place for you to keep notes about your impressions of your target employer and the people you meet and speak with there. It will serve as a comprehensive history of your interaction with a given company, and will help you in preparing for interviews, handling follow-up phone calls, and considering offers. Think of your communications log as a diary where you can store all your deep, dark insights. It serves as a complement to your planner, which is really just a tickler, reminding you when and where you have to be, and when you need to take certain action.

Job Hunt Communications Log

Company Name: Downsize, Inc.

Date	Action	Notes
6/8	Spoke to Dan at my Career Fair	Nice guy—Seemed interested in internship.
6/9	Faxed resume	Need to follow up on 6/20.

6/20	Follow-up call	Left message.
6/23	Dan called back	Apologized for delay—he was out sick Scheduled 1st interview for 6/30.
6/30	Interview with HR	Went okay—basically a screener. Indicated they would like to pass me on to the head of the Dept.
6/30	Mailed thank-you note	
7/5	Received call from HR	2nd interview scheduled for 7/8.
7/8	Interviewed with VP, Asst. VP, Product Manager	Really liked VP, Prod Mgr was Asst VP, and kind of a jerk. Not sure if I could work for him
7/8	Sent thank-yous	
7/9	VP extended offer	20K base + bonus - under VP jerko
7/10	Declined offer	

KEEPING IT IN PERSPECTIVE

Well, that's all folks. Purchase the basic tools we've recommended and follow the simple guidelines discussed above, and we're confident you'll be able to stay on top of your job hunt. There's no magic to it. Just hard work, persistence, and maintaining consciousness. If you slip up, never fear. There's no need to be neurotic or excessively anal about being organized—just do it. And obviously, if you devise a system that works better for you than the one we've outlined, then more power to you (just make sure you drop us a line and tell us all about it).

COMPILING YOUR HIT LIST

In this section, we're going to show you how to formulate a list of target employers for whom you might actually want to work—what we often refer to as a hit list. This list will serve as a road map for your job search, enabling you to devote the majority of your time and energy to researching and contacting organizations that seem to offer the best employment prospects given your goals and desires. Going through this process is crucial because it will provide your search with a focus and direction. Without a hit list, the job hunt can often be overwhelming since there are simply too many choices to consider. Why bother researching thousands of employers when you can zero in on the 100 or so that you most care about?. In the end, preparing a hit list will save you time, money, and increase your chances of finding a good employment match. But keep in mind that a hit list of employers is not set in digital stone. It's an evolving document. You will add to and subtract from it regularly. Even if your initial list is quite large, resist the temptation to stop digging, because as an archaeologist will tell you the buried treasure may lie just below the next shovel of dirt.

Making Up (Your Mind) Is Hard to Do

To compile a hit list you really have to know what you're looking for. Thus, we are assuming you've already self-assessed, reassessed, decompressed, and figured out more or less what you want to do for a living. If you're not at that point, then back up a bit and revisit some of the earlier steps of the career planning process or consider making an appointment to see a career counselor.

For those of you who say you know what you want and are just chomping at the bit to get there, hold on. Are you sure you really know what you want? Lisa, a marketing major at Arizona State told us in no uncertain terms she knew exactly what she wanted. "I'm so excited that I've figured this career thing out, I just want to run to my window, fling it open and yell to the world—I want to be in advertising!" Fortunately, Lisa's window was nailed shut. You see, saying you want to work in advertising is kind of like telling someone at a party who asks where you're from that you "reside in the Northern hemisphere." Could you be just a little more vague?

Every career field, as is the case with advertising, is highly complex, and encompasses a variety of subfields and job titles. Each of these, in turn, often requires different skills, credentials, and personality traits. For example, in advertising there is a world of difference between the work an account executive does and the work a copywriter does. They are two different animals who happen to inhabit the same zoo. If you're still at the stage our friend Lisa is at, then you've got a lot of work ahead of you to more precisely define what you want. Why is that necessary, you ask? Consider the following snippet from an on-campus interview between a recruiter from Shades of Grey, an advertising agency, and Jim, a college senior at a small liberal arts college. What you're about to read plays itself out many times every single day on college campuses around the country.

Interviewer: So, Jim, you're about to graduate this May and you're thinking about a career in advertising. What draws you to that field?

Jim: It's just such a fascinating business. It's creative, it's fast paced, it's everything I want in a career.

Interviewer: As you know, Jim, there are numerous opportunities within our agency. Which department do you think fits you the best—media planning, account management, or creative?

Jim: I can't say for sure, but I'm sure I'd be able to contribute in any of those areas. I really just want to be in advertising.

Interviewer: Well Jim, before you can get into advertising you have to know how to advertise yourself, and that means understanding your target audience. I suggest you go to the library and do a little reading on our industry, then perhaps we can talk at a later date.

Jim: (jaw drops open and stays there for many days)

"Stand in the place where you live. Now face north. Think about direction, wonder why you haven't . . ."
R.E.M., "Stand" from the album Green (1988, Warner Bros. Records, Inc.)

Jim was dismissed and rightly so because he wasted the interviewer's time. When you're not at all sure of where you are heading, as was the case with Jim and Lisa, and you forge ahead with your job hunt anyway, three things are likely to occur:

1. You will lose credibility with employers because it will be apparent that you haven't made the time, or effort to figure out what you want in a career.

2. Your search will take considerably longer than it would have had you carefully researched the occupational options available within the field you've identified.

3. Your odds of ending up in the wrong job will be vastly increased since you will be interviewing for a wide range of positions of which you have minimal knowledge, rather than just interviewing for the ones that you are confident will fit you best.

Help Is on the Way

Now if you're saying to yourself, "Gee, I shelled out $12.00 for this book, and I can't use it because all I know right now is that I want to be in advertising," don't despair—we'll help you out.

Your next step is to more narrowly define and investigate the occupational options that you think would be best for you. In a sense, you'll be compiling a hit list of job titles as opposed to a hit list of employers. As long as you have an idea of which of your interests really turn you on, the skills you want to use on the job, the values you hold dear, and the kind of environment that appeals to you, researching your field should be a snap. Right now try making two lists—one of what is most important to you in a job, and one of what you hope to avoid. Don't censor yourself. Just let it flow from the heart. Here's an example of a wish list from Max Grody, a recent graduate from Ohio State, who's hoping to pursue a career in publishing but is trying to narrow down his options within that field.

What I Really, Really Want

1. To do editorial work on science fiction novels or scholarly works

2. Laid back work environment where I don't have to worry about wearing a suit and tie

3. An opportunity to learn desktop publishing

4. A salary of at least $22K per year

5. Friendly coworkers

6. A chance to work on many projects simultaneously

7. To have personal or phone contact with authors

8. To work for a publisher that really believes in what they produce

What I Definitely Don't Want, Even if I'm Unemployed and Starving

1. A corporate environment

2. A boss who's a micro-manager

3. A job where all I get to do is proofread or do secretarial work

4. To deal with how-to or self-help books

Hold on to your lists, as you'll need them when you begin to research your field. A little later in this chapter we'll walk you through how to do just that, but first let's go over a few basic research tips.

LET THE SOURCE BE WITH YOU

During the research process, whether you're investigating careers, job titles, companies, or personnel, you will undoubtedly plow through tons of material, talk to many people, and maybe even dabble on-line. Some of the resources you encounter will be good as gold and others you can probably live without. In your haste to get "the answers" don't forget to make a list of all the sources you found to be helpful as well as where you found them. Write down names and phone numbers, titles of books and directories (note author and publisher information), the dates and page numbers of magazine and newspaper articles, addresses of web and internet sites, etc. You never know when you may have to refer to them again, and we're sure you don't want to spend another entire Saturday buried in the library trying to re-find stuff that you spent countless hours tracking down a week earlier.

DON'T BELIEVE WHAT YOU READ

Try to identify and access as many reliable sources of job and career information as possible, since as objective as each one may appear to be on the surface, they will nevertheless all be biased to some degree. Those organizations that have the greatest vested interest in your career decision, such as professional associations and the companies themselves, tend to publish the most biased materials. Many of their publications are slickly written PR pieces, which may give you the icing on the cake but not the whole enchilada. You also have to be wary about what you read in newspapers and magazines and the slant taken by the publication in question. In general, be aware that anyone who puts anything in print may have an agenda that doesn't necessarily coincide with yours.

By looking at numerous dependable sources and speaking with a variety of seasoned professionals, it's more likely you'll gain an accurate impression of the subject you're investigating. Failure to do so could leave you with a grossly distorted picture of what a particular field or company is like.

HERE TODAY, GONE TOMORROW

Today's world is hardly a stable place. Borders are crumbling, currencies are merging, and entire categories of workers are becoming redundant and centuries old disputes seem to be burning as hotly as ever. New technology is changing the way we work, live, eat, and play. Change has become the norm rather than the exception. So what does this have to do with job hunting? A lot. More than ever before the job seeker needs to be extremely careful to gather information that is timely and valid. Using old data substantially increases the chances that you will make costly errors in your job search. Do you really want to send letters to organizations that are no longer in business, pursue a field that was once hot and now is not, target a burgeoning metropolis that is now facing an economic crisis, or send a letter to a producer at NBC who now works for Fox? We didn't think so. Using obsolete data is a waste of your time and money, and can also damage your credibility with employers. Make sure that your information is current and pay attention to the date of your source. A book on manufacturing management careers written in 1964 may have amusing pictures of people with crew cuts on the cover, but is not likely to provide you with a bevy of useful information .

SMELLS LIKE BAD INFORMATION

Just as with food, the spoilage rate of information varies according to type. Generally, information about a field or industry is the most stable over time. However, even in this case, "stable" may mean no more than a few years or in some cases even months. A few years ago, many job search experts touted nursing as one of the "hottest" and most lucrative fields in the country for new grads. Today, many registered nurses are struggling to find employment, let alone high salaries. Perhaps next most stable is information pertaining to a specific company, but as we know from the recent slew of mergers and acquisitions in the banking world, companies come and go with alarming regularity. Finally, people data (i.e., information pertaining to employees) is the least stable of all. Be forewarned that if you're using a directory that was published two years ago to identify key individuals at Company X, there's a very good chance that some of those people will no longer be around. Even if you're using a brand new directory, much of the information concerning personnel may be obsolete before the publication actually hits the library shelves. And a final warning: As nifty as CD-ROM's appear to be on the surface, the information they provide is usually several months old by the time you sit down to spin the disc. That's because all those truckloads of information have to be indexed before the disc is usable and that process takes a lot of time.

The Librarian Is Your Friend

Librarians may be one of the most underrated and underutilized resources of all time, especially for job hunters. These professionals have an incredible amount of knowledge at their fingertips, and when it's not at their fingertips they know exactly where and how to get it. They can save you countless hours by pointing you to the right sources from the outset of your search. No matter what else you do, make nice with all the librarians you encounter — in your university library, public library, and campus career center. Whatever it takes to get them on your side (usually good manners and a smile will suffice), do it. You will not be disappointed.

Researching Your Field

By now you're probably thinking you'll never compile a hit list. Don't fret, we're getting there. Although you may be tempted to start snooping around for places where you can actually work and get a paycheck, researching your field should always precede researching prospective employers, especially for those of you who are still considering a broad range of career options. By investigating your field, you will gain a sense of the range of jobs available, the language spoken among your future coworkers, and where your profession is heading. Most importantly, you will be arming yourself with valuable knowledge that will make you a savvier job hunter and a more competent interviewee. While researching your field, try to answer the following questions:

- Which jobs within the field provide the best match with my credentials, skills, interests, values, personality, and experience?

- What are the typical responsibilities of workers in these jobs?

- What are the biggest challenges faced by workers in these jobs?

- What are the major rewards and frustrations related to this type of work?

- Does this job frequently require travel, relocation, or long hours?

- What is the work environment like? (e.g., dress code, physical conditions)

- How much supervision is typically received by people in these jobs? To what extent do they supervise others?

- How is job performance in this field evaluated?

- What are the opportunities for advancement like?

- Is more education or another degree a prerequisite for career advancement? Would it be wisest to go directly to graduate school or to first gain some work experience?

- What are the opportunities for on-the-job training and development?

- What is the range for starting salaries? What can I expect to earn within five years? Ten years?

- Which regions of the country offer the best opportunities for this field?

- What are the short- and long-term outlooks for this field? In which direction is it moving?

- What are the most effective ways to look for a job in this field?

- Which professional associations are linked to the field and what types of activities do they sponsor? Are there any with which I can become involved right away?

- What other sources can I look at to find more information?

PEOPLE VS. BOOKS AND OTHER INFORMATION SOURCES

When researching a field, or, for that matter, conducting any type of career research, the most helpful and reliable information will generally not come from books, but from people working in the field. They know from experience what it's really like to design widgets or whatever it is they do, and can paint you a more complete and accurate picture of life on the job than you would be able to find in any book or magazine article. In spite of this, people are usually the last source you should tap into for information, unless of course you have an Uncle Ernie who likes you a lot and has the patience of a saint. Because people working in your field of interest are so crucial to the success of your research mission, you must be very careful to approach them only after you have milked dry every other resource you can possibly track down. Doing so will guarantee that by the time you meet with these folks (or speak to them on the phone) you will already be well-informed about your subject, and will be able to ask more intelligent, insightful questions than had you approached them from the outset. And whatever you do, never, ever ask them for a job! If they mention the "j" word of their own free will, that's another story, but let them bring it up first. Please be extremely sensitive to these people because while today they may be simply providing you with information about their job and industry, it is very possible that tomorrow they will be a source of job leads, and one day might even be your employer. As far as learning the nitty gritty of identifying contacts, and properly setting up, preparing for, conducting, and following up on information interviews, you'll need to turn to chapter 10 where we cover the entire process in great detail.

chapter 10

FYI

Getting the most from computer searches

A great deal of the research you'll be conducting about your field and for compiling your hit list will require extensive use of a variety of CD-ROMs. Since database searches can be both time-consuming and expensive, you need to approach them in a logical and thoughtful manner. First, determine the scope of your topic. Are you investigating "marketing," "direct marketing," or only "direct marketing in the Far East"? Once you've defined your topic select the appropriate database(s) for conducting your search. Next, carefully pick the keywords for use in your search. These are crucial since a computer can only look for what you tell it to. Some databases have a built-in thesaurus to assist with this process, otherwise you can consult the Library of Congress Subject Headings or a reference librarian. Try to use keywords that are as few in number and as specific as possible. For more effective data retrieval consider connecting the keywords you've selected with boolean logic and truncation. Boolean logic requires the use of the connectors "or" or "and" in your search. "Or" will retrieve all the terms you've specified (e.g., graphic design "or" desktop publishing), whereas "and" only retrieves items that satisfy both (or all) the conditions you've specified (e.g., graphic design "and" desktop publishing). Truncation, on the other hand, involves using a special symbol to ensure that you not only retrieve the exact terms you specified, but also others that are similar (e.g., "graphic design" and "graphic designers"). Check the guidelines of the system you are using to find out the correct symbols for Boolean logic and truncation. Before you download or print out your results, make sure that your search successfully retrieved the items you were seeking. If the results are not satisfactory, modify your search terms accordingly.

RESOURCES FOR RESEARCHING FIELDS AND OCCUPATIONS

ABI/Inform. CD-ROM database that indexes and abstracts articles from more than 800 business and trade journals over the past five years.

Career Guide to Industries. Bureau of Labor Statistics. Analyzes 40 industries and their prospects.

Dictionary of Occupational Titles. U.S. Department of Labor. Most recently updated in 1991, this resource is a bit cumbersome, but it provides some useful information regarding the specific tasks performed on each of the 12,741 jobs listed.

Encyclopedia of Associations. Gale Research, Inc.: Detroit, MI, 1996. Lists over 25,000 associations, clubs and other nonprofit groups. These organizations and their members are often excellent sources of information about a given field. Some may have local chapters in your region, and many offer reduced membership rates for students and recent graduates.

Infotrac (General Business File). CD-ROM database that indexes and abstracts articles from more than 800 business, economic management and trade journals, and newspapers from the past two years.

Job Hunter's Sourcebook. Michelle LeCompte, editor. Gale Research, Inc.: Detroit, MI, 1996. Provides a comprehensive listing of information sources for 155 popular occupations.

Jobs '96. Kathryn Petras and Ross Petras. Fireside: New York. 1995. Offers numerous descriptions of jobs in various industries. Includes average salaries and hiring qualifications. Describes current job and industry trends as well as national and regional employment trends. Highlights careers that have the best long-term potential.

National Trade and Professional Associations of the United States. Columbia Books, Inc.: Washington, DC. Annual. Provides a broad range of information on over 7,000 associations, including their history and purpose, when and where they meet, what they publish, and the names of key contacts.

Newsletters in Print. Gale Research, Inc.: Detroit, MI. Lists over 10,000 newsletters on a variety of subjects.

Newspaper Abstracts. (CD-ROM) Indexes articles from major U.S. newspapers as the *New York Times*, *Wall Street Journal*, *Washington Post*, and *Los Angeles Times*.

The Occupational Outlook Handbook. U.S. Department of Labor. Updated every two years. Offers a broad overview of over 250 occupations which account for nearly 85 percent of the labor force.

Periodical Abstracts. This CD-ROM indexes and abstracts over 2,000 popular and scholarly periodicals.

Predicasts F&S Index U.S. CD-ROM includes citations, abstracts, and complete text of articles from over 1,000 business and trade publications.

Professional Careers Sourcebook. Gale Research, Inc.: Detroit, MI. 1995 Information on 118 high profile occupations. Includes job descriptions, lists of career guides, professional associations, trade journals, and industry conventions.

Regional, State, and Local Organizations. Gale Research, Inc.: Detroit, MI. 1995. Similar to the Encyclopedia of Associations except that the more than 50,000 organizations listed are at the local, state, or regional level.

Standard and Poors Industry Surveys. Issued annually with quarterly updates. Provides general information and financial forecasts for 25 industrial groups.

U.S. Industrial Outlook. U.S. Department of Commerce. Analyzes current trends and future outlook for over 300 industries.

A Good Employer Is Hard to Find

Remember back in high school when you tried to figure out which college would suit you the best? Well, just as you weeded out the colleges that didn't meet your standards, you'll need to weed out employers that don't satisfy the criteria you've deemed most important. Also, in the same way that applying to a college did not guarantee you acceptance, approaching an employer for a job in no way guarantees you employment. Remember, the organizations on your hit list will not necessarily have openings at the present time, but as we have stressed repeatedly, opportunity can knock at any time. Do not make the mistake of only investigating companies that advertise jobs—they're a tiny subset of your actual employment possibilities.

THE MAGIC NUMBER IS . . . ?

Before going any further, take some time to revisit what you've decided is most important in an employer. Are you looking for a job in Atlanta because that's where your fiancee will be, or are you free to roam the country? Is a large corporation more appealing to you than a mom and pop operation? Would you be more at home in a formal or casual environment? Are you seeking a company that is sensitive to gay and lesbian issues? Is an innovative, risk-taking organization your cup of tea, or do you relish companies that are stable as a rock?

The nature and length of your hit list will be determined by the way you answer these and other questions. If you are not selective enough, your list might include the entire universe of employers in your field, which could number in the tens of thousands. Managing a job search with so many potential employers would be literally impossible, not to mention that calling and sending out resumes to all those employers would cost you a small fortune. On the other hand, if your selection criteria are too rigorous, only a few employers will end up making the final cut and you'll be setting your search up for almost certain failure. Although there is no magic number of potential employers to shoot for, the number should be small enough that you can adequately research each employer you identify, and large enough that there is a reasonable chance that one of the employers on your list will have an opportunity for you. Go through this decision-making process slowly and carefully, because it is your hit list that will serve as a road map for your job search. And don't forget to note contact information for each employer that you add to your list. Also keep a written log of all the sources you used to track down employers, as you may have to consult them again later.

RESOURCES FOR TRACKING DOWN NON-PROFIT EMPLOYERS

Community Jobs. Published by ACCESS: Networking in the Public Interest in New York City (212-475-1001). Community Jobs is a monthly newspaper devoted to the world of nonprofit employment. It features articles, resource lists, organization profiles, and job listings. For $25, ACCESS will compile a list of nonprofit organizations for you that meet the criteria you've set regarding field of interest and preferred geographic location. ACCESS also publishes the National Service Guide, which lists some of the best resources for finding a job in the nonprofit sector.

Directories in Print. Gale Research: Detroit, MI. 1995. Lists over 15,000 directories. Index includes over 3,500 subject headings.

Good Works: A Guide to Careers in Social Change (5th edition). Edited by Donna Colvin. Barricade Books, Inc.: New York, 1994. Describes over 1,000 non-profits across the U.S. Includes information on where job openings are advertised, how many jobs are typically available each year, and how much starting employees can expect to earn. Indexed by field and region.

How to Get a Job in... (available for several major cities/ regions). Surrey Books: Chicago, IL. Lists contact information of numerous employers across a wide range of fields. Includes very helpful sections on researching the local job market and networking.

The Job Bank Series (available for numerous major cities/ regions). Bob Adams: Holbrook, MA. Describes major employers of the region across a variety of industries.

Jobs and Careers with Non-Profits. Dr. Ronald Krannich. Provides contact information for hundreds of domestic and international nonprofit organizations.

National Trade and Professional Associations of the United States. Columbia Books, Inc.: Washington, DC. Annual. Provides a range of information on over 7,000 associations. Many of these associations publish directories of their membership.

Non-Profits' Job Finder. Daniel Lauber. Planning/Communications: River Forest, IL. 1994. Lists over 1,400 sources for finding employment in the nonprofit sector.

Professional Careers Sourcebook. Gale Research, Inc.: Detroit, MI. Date. Information on 118 high profile occupations. Includes job descriptions, lists of career guides, professional associations, trade journals, and industry conventions.

Regional, State, and Local Organizations. Gale Research, Inc.: Detroit, MI, 1995. Lists over 50,000 organizations, many of which publish directories of their membership. These directories can be extremely useful for identifying potential employers and contacts.

White and Yellow Pages. So obvious that we almost skipped it, yet it is a virtual gold mine of information. Check the yellow pages under categories that closely resemble your field of interest (e.g., child care centers). Many phone books also include non-profits in a special community service section of the white pages.

World Chamber of Commerce Directory—Loveland, CO. Annual. To identify employers in a particular town, city, or region, the local Chamber of Commerce is the place to go. Many publish directories of their membership and a fair number sell "welcome packages" to assist the job hunter who is relocating from another part of the country.

RESOURCES FOR TRACKING DOWN GOVERNMENT EMPLOYERS

Directories in Print. Gale Research: Detroit, MI. 1995. Lists over 15,000 directories. Index includes over 3,500 subject headings.

The Directory of Federal Jobs and Employers. Krannich and Krannich. Lists job hotlines and contact information for key personnel in all three branches.

Blue Pages. Many phone books have a special section where government agencies are listed. Sometimes these are called the blue pages.

Government Job Finder. Daniel Lauber. Planning/Communications: River Forest, IL. 1994. Details on over 1,700 sources of local, state, and federal government job vacancies in the U.S. and abroad.

RESOURCES FOR TRACKING DOWN FOR-PROFIT EMPLOYERS

American Business Disc. This CD-ROM lists over 10 million businesses in the U.S. You can search for organizations by yellow page category, SIC code (standard industrial classifications used by the U.S. Department of Labor), city or state, and number of employees.

Directories in Print. Gale Research: Detroit, MI. 1995. Lists over 15,000 directories. Index includes over 3,500 subject headings.

Directory of Corporate Affiliations. Lists almost 5,000 parent companies along with their subsidiaries, divisions, or affiliates. Can identify companies by line of business or SIC code.

Dun & Bradstreet's Million Dollar Directory. Provides basic information for major companies. Indexed by SIC code and geographic region. Also available on CD-ROM.

Hoover's Masterlist of America's Top 2,500 Employers. The Reference Press: Austin, TX. Includes company profiles and contact information for each entry. Comes with a free disk that can be used to search for companies and create mailing lists. Hoover's also publishes a number of other excellent directories of up and coming companies.

The Job Seeker's Guide to Socially Responsible Companies. Katherine Jankowski. 1994. Describes nearly 1,000 companies that have distinguished themselves as being socially conscious. Includes information on job application procedures.

How to Get a Job in... (available for several major cities/ regions). Surrey Books: Chicago, IL. Lists contact information of numerous employers across a wide range of fields. Includes very helpful sections on researching the local job market and networking.

The Job Bank Series (available for numerous major cities/ regions). Bob Adams: Holbrook, MA. Describes major employers of the region across a variety of industries.

National Trade and Professional Associations of the United States. Columbia Books, Inc.: Washington, DC. Annual. Provides a broad range of information on over 7,000 associations. Many of these associations publish directories of their membership.

Newspaper Abstracts. (CD-ROM) Indexes articles from major U.S. newspapers as the *New York Times*, *Wall Street Journal*, *Washington Post*, and *Los Angeles Times*.

Periodical Abstracts. This CD-ROM indexes and abstracts over 2,000 popular and scholarly periodicals.

Professional Careers Sourcebook. Gale Research, Inc.: Detroit, MI. Information on 118 high profile occupations. Includes job descriptions, lists of career guides, professional associations, trade journals, and industry conventions.

Professional's Private Sector Job Finder. Daniel Lauber. Planning/Communications: River Forest, Il. 1994. Describes over 2,500 sources of jobs in a wide variety of fields.

Regional, State, and Local Organizations. Gale Research, Inc.: Detroit, MI, 1995. Lists over 50,000 organizations, many of which publish directories of their membership. These directories can be extremely useful for identifying potential employers and contacts.

Standard & Poor's Register of Corporations, Directors, and Executives. Lists over 45,000 publicly held companies indexed by SIC code and geographic location.

Ward's Business Directory of U.S. Private and Public Companies. Provides data on more than 130,000 public and private companies. Includes SIC codes.

World Chamber of Commerce Directory. Loveland, CO, Annual. To identify employers in a particular town, city, or region, the local Chamber of Commerce is the place to go. Many publish directories of their membership and a fair number sell "welcome packages" to assist the job hunter who is relocating from another part of the country.

REFINING YOUR LIST

If you used some of the resources we suggested above, you've already identified a fairly healthy list of potential employers. Some of these may be ideal matches, while others may be duds. Unfortunately it's impossible to tell which is which without researching each employer further. Your next step is take a closer look at the employers that made the first cut and decide whether in fact they are worth approaching for a job. In theory this may sound easy, but in practice it can be excruciatingly frustrating. Finding basic contact information and financial data for an organization may be a breeze, but getting the inside scoop on the company's culture, management philosophy, and goals for the next five years can be extremely difficult. As with researching a field, the best information will most likely come from people rather than books; however, the resources listed below, especially some of the CD-ROMs, should also prove to be helpful with your detective work.

Resources for Researching Organizations

ABI/Inform. CD-ROM database which indexes and abstracts articles from more than 800 business and trade journals over the past five years.

Annual Reports. available at many libraries, campus career centers or by calling the organization directly. Includes information on the company's financial performance and other aspects of operation.

Better Business Bureaus. If you're researching a local company the BBB may be able to tell you how many complaints have been lodged against the firm. Ironically, some BBB's charge fees to provide this information.

Business Periodicals Index. This CD-ROM indexes roughly 350 periodicals covering all business fields.

Cracking the Corporate Closet: The 200 Best (and worst) Companies to Work for, Buy from, and Invest in If You're Gay or Lesbian—and Even if You Aren't. Daniel B. Baker, Sean O'Brien Strub, and Bill Henning. Harper Collins: New York. 1995.

Disclosure/Worldscope. This CD-ROM provides information abstracted from reports filed with the SEC on over 12,000 public companies.

Infotrac (General Business File). CD-ROM database which indexes and abstracts articles from more than 800 business, economic management and trade journals, and newspapers from the past two years.

Local Newspapers. Particularly helpful for learning about smaller regionally based organizations. Many local papers are indexed and can be found on microfilm at the public library.

Moody's Manuals. For companies listed on U.S. stock exchanges provides information on company history, products, and financials.

Newspaper Abstracts. (CD-ROM) Indexes articles from major U.S. newspapers as the *New York Times*, *Wall Street Journal*, *Washington Post*, and *Los Angeles Times*.

The 100 Best Companies for Gay Men and Lesbians. Ed Mickens. Pocket Books: New York. 1994.

Periodical Abstracts. This CD-ROM indexes and abstracts over 2,000 popular and scholarly periodicals.

Predicasts F&S Index U.S. CD-ROM includes citations, abstracts, and complete text of articles from over 1,000 business and trade publications. Indexed by SIC codes.

Public Libraries. A number of libraries maintain their own files concerning local businesses and news. They may also know of more obscure sources of information not listed here.

Shopping for a Better World. Council on Economic Priorities. If your preference is to work for a politically correct company, this handy guide rates approximately 200 employers in a variety of categories including charitable giving, advancement of women and minorities, family benefits, and environmental policies.

Standard and Poors Industry Surveys. Issued annually with quarterly updates. Provides general information and financial forecasts for 25 industrial groups.

10K Reports—Public companies must submit these to the Securities and Exchange Commission. One section of the report will let you know if any legal proceedings have been brought against the company.

4

The Tools of the Search

WHY DO YOU NEED A RESUME?

Because you need a job. To get a job you need an interview, and to get an interview you almost always need a resume unless you have connections in high places, in which case you probably don't need to be reading this book. Employers have decided that reviewing your qualifications on a piece of paper or a disk is the most efficient way to screen the hundreds and thousands of applicants who want to be hired. No employer has the time to read your autobiography, nor does she have the time to meet or speak individually with every person who applies for a job.

THE SKY'S NOT THE LIMIT FOR YOUR RESUME

A well-written targeted resume can help you obtain job interviews. During the interview it can guide the interviewer to your strengths, particularly those that relate most closely to the position for which you are applying. After the interview, your resume can function as a memory jogger, reminding employers of your key qualifications.

But the buck stops there. No resume, no matter how brilliant, can ever land you a job. Looking great on paper is important, but it only serves to set the tone for the employment interview.

SELLING YOURSELF

During the job hunt you may find it helpful to conceptualize yourself as a product, whereas the resume is your advertisement, and the employer is the consumer. Your goal is to convince the employer that you are the right candidate for the job. Your resume is one of the means by which you can do this. It must entice and intrigue the reader, and prove that you have the ability to get the job done. Because the job market is an employer's market, you must write your resume with their needs in mind. Think of yourself as a problem-solver. Your prospective employer's problem may be selling soda to octogenarians, providing a shuttle service to the moon, building a database of spas, or developing a new cure for rabies — whatever. Your resume must convince them that you can solve the problem.

And by the way, this is no time for modesty. If you don't tell the employer about yourself, who will? Just make sure that whatever you include on your resume is honest and accurate.

WHAT EMPLOYERS WANT AND DON'T WANT

Since your resume is being written strictly for an employer's eyes, why not give them what they want? Who cares if your friends think your resume looks cool. The bottom line is that if your resume isn't convincing a prospective employer to grant you an interview, then it isn't doing its job.

Recently, we surveyed and interviewed nearly 50 hiring professionals at some of the most prestigious organizations in the nation across a variety of fields. We asked them questions about what they look for in a resume. The consensus was that the ideal resume is easy to read (i.e., well-organized), professionally presented, concise, results-oriented, and tailored to the requirements of the job being applied for. Hiring managers already have enough headaches to deal with, so basically they want you to put together a resume that requires a minimal amount of effort to digest.

On the flip side, they cited sloppiness (e.g., typos, poor grammar, and misspellings) and wordiness as the major resume killers. They reason that if you can't take the time to carefully proof your own work, why would you be any more conscientious on the job? Fortunately, all the mistakes cited above can be easily avoided. To ensure that you don't fall prey to misspellings and poor grammar, always keep a dictionary and a good grammar guide (The Princeton

Review's *Grammar Smart* is great) by your side. In addition, have at least two trusted friends or relatives with a good grasp of the English language proofread your resume.

As far as being verbose goes, ask yourself the following question about each word on your resume: Does it add to the clarity of my statement or enhance my marketability? If the answer is "no," then the word should be history. After all, your resume is just a summary—the gory details can be supplied during the interview. Also keep in mind that you can only squeeze approximately 250 words onto the typical one page resume. Therefore, every word should be chosen with great care and consideration.

Consider the following example:

> *I compiled information and wrote the first draft for a launch book introducing the first sinus relief product with daytime and nighttime formulations in a single package.*

We revised this to read:

> *Completed draft of launch book introducing a unique sinus relief product.*

Note that in the revision the personal pronoun "I" and some of the articles have been omitted as they added nothing to the original statement. Editing has reduced the new version to one line, which is quite significant considering that the typical one page resume consists of only 33 lines. Each line, therefore, is equivalent to approximately 3 percent of your life. Waste three lines and you've just flushed nearly 10 percent of your life down the drain.

Show your resume to at least two other people for proofreading before you give it out—and don't depend on a computer's spell checking; you may have spelled the wrong word correctly. Another common mistake is the use of jargon abbreviations and acronyms. You may know that TSAA stands for the Tree Saving Association of America, but it's unlikely that anyone else will.

PLAYING DETECTIVE

The tricky part for you is figuring out what the employer's needs are. If you are applying for a position advertised in the classifieds, then it's fairly simple—the employer's needs are stated in the ad. However, since many jobs are never advertised, you will not always have this luxury, and it will be up to you to play detective and figure out what qualifications the employer is seeking. The information you need can be gathered from many of the sources reviewed in chapter 3 (Compiling Your Hit List, p. 49, as well as from the following):

The Employer
Why beat around the bush? Call the employer's Public Affairs, Public Relations, or Human Resources Department and ask them to send any information they may have on hand about the organization—annual reports, brochures, newsletters, etc. Let the person on the phone know that you are investigating employment opportunities with their firm. Offer to pick up the materials in person if they are reluctant to mail them.

Your Campus Career Planning Center
Ask if they have any information on file regarding your target employer. Organizations that recruit on campus often send an information package prior to their recruitment visit.

If you are an alum and no longer live near your alma mater, find out if your college's career planning office has a reciprocity agreement with a college in your area. If so, you'll probably be able to use some of the resources at that school.

The Library
Librarians can be a wealth of information. Tell them you're in the midst of a job search and are trying desperately to find more information about Company X. They are likely to have many suggestions.

The Insiders
Professionals who either work at your target organization or for a competitor are often the best sources of information since they have the "inside scoop" and can provide you with "classified" knowledge that would be impossible to obtain anywhere else. Check with your alumni relations office to see if they can provide you with a list of alumni working in your field of interest. Some of them may work at your target company and may be willing to sit down with you and give you inside info.

PRIORITIZE

After you've researched your target employer, prioritize the qualifications you list on your resume so they mesh with your prospective employer's needs. Start with your most relevant and impressive credentials. By going with your relevant strengths early, there is a good chance you will make a strong, positive impression on the reader right off the bat. That's important because many employers skim resumes very quickly (one employer we interviewed claimed to spend no more than eight seconds with each resume) and if nothing piques their curiosity at the beginning of your resume, they may not bother reading the rest.

DO WHAT YOU LOVE

If using a skill makes you miserable, then there is no sense stressing it on your resume, no matter how good you are at it and no matter how much it may increase your marketability.

Imagine that your dream is to write for *Rolling Stone* magazine. Also imagine that you are the fastest, most accurate typist in the West, but that you enjoy typing about as much as you enjoy listening to chalk screeching on a blackboard. Now it's true that by stressing your exceptional typing speed on your resume you could probably land a job at one magazine or another as a typist. "That's OK," you say to yourself, "as a typist I'll have my foot in the door, and eventually will prove myself to be the great feature writer I know I am." The question is how long can you stand pounding the keyboard all day before you pick it up and start pounding your boss' head? What toll will all the dreaded typing take on your mind, body, and spirit? Do typists at *Rolling Stone* have even the slimmest chance of being promoted? Only you can answer these questions, but in general if you want to be a writer then look for a job which will allow you to write.

CUSTOMIZING YOUR RESUME

If you are job hunting in more than one field, or considering different types of positions within the same field, you will need to have more than one version of your resume. For example, let's assume you are applying for two jobs as both an account representative at an advertising agency and as an editorial assistant at a publishing house. For each position you need to stress different skills. For the account rep job you need to emphasize your interpersonal, communication, sales, and marketing skills. For the editorial assistant slot you need to stress your detail orientation, ability to work under deadline pressure, and skills as a proofreader. Naturally, there will be some overlap on both resumes, but the thrust of each should be very different. You should also have a more generic version of your resume readily available, which you can use for networking purposes. This will come in handy when you meet a contact who wants to know more about your background, but isn't necessarily offering you any kind of employment opportunity.

RESUMEPHOBIA

Most people not only hate writing resumes, but are also afraid of the process. They either opt for total avoidance or hire people to write them. This is a big problem, since avoidance leaves you without a resume and puts a quick end to your job search, while hiring someone to write a resume for you is not only costly, but often results in the creation of a document that misrepresents you. We will now take a look at the three most common resume writing fears and try to put you at ease.

You The Man—Not

"How can I put my whole life story on one page?" you exclaim. "I have done so many amazing things that I need at least five pages to do my accomplishments justice." Wrong. A resume is not your autobiography. It is merely a summary of your qualifications—a highlight reel, if you will. Employers do not need or want all the gory details. On a resume, as is true with much in life, less is more.

My Life Is Zippo

"I haven't done anything in my life. I'll never be able to fill up one page," you whimper. Wrong again. If you think you haven't accomplished anything, odds are that you don't know yourself very well. Ask your friends and other supportive folks to give their opinions of your skills and strengths. Everyone, including you, has a unique combination of skills, accomplishments, and experiences that make him or her special, as well as valuable to an employer.

I Can't Write

"I'm not the next Shakespeare." Not a problem. Skilled writers often have the most difficulty writing good resumes, because, after all, resumes are concise, factual documents, not showpieces for elegant, stylish prose. Simple, direct language will do you just fine. If you can write a clear, intelligible sentence, you can write a great resume.

PUTTING YOURSELF ON PAPER

Like a sculpture in progress, your resume is an emerging work of art that must be prodded and molded to obtain the desired result. Instead of clay, stone, or steel, the medium of your resume is words—words that you will carefully piece together to create your final masterpiece. But before you can find the right words you will first need information. The information required can be found by taking inventory of your accomplishments, experiences, and skills drawn from work, school, and leisure. You may find it most helpful to record this information in a notebook using the lists that follow as a guide. (At this point, you should review your skills package on pages 15-16.)

You may also want to enlist the help of past and present employers, co-workers, professors, friends, acquaintances, and anyone else who may recall some of your more memorable and noteworthy exploits. Certain documents such as school transcripts, old job descriptions, and letters of recommendation may also come in handy.

In compiling your personal history inventory, be as thorough and descriptive as possible. Although some of the information in your inventory may not end up on the final draft of your resume, you may still find it handy for filling out a job application. For this reason, always bring a copy of your completed inventory with you on interviews and whenever you suspect that you might be asked to submit an employment application.

YOUR PERSONAL HISTORY INVENTORY

Graduate School Education

1. Name of the institution
2. Location of the institution (city and state)
3. Dates of attendance
4. Degree
5. Thesis topic and description
6. Course of study
7. Research interests
8. Overall GPA
9. Courses completed and grades received
10. Significant projects/papers
11. Merit-based scholarships
12. Academic honors
13. Other school-based honors or awards

College

1. Name of the institution
2. Location of the institution (city and state)

3. Dates of attendance

4. Degree

5. Major(s)

6. Minor

7. Overall GPA

8. Major GPA

9. Class rank (if known)

10. Courses completed and grades received

11. Significant projects/papers

12. Merit-based scholarships

13. Academic honors such as Dean's List, Phi Beta Kappa, Magna Cum Laude, etc.

14. Other school-based honors or awards

High School Education

1. Name of the institution

2. Location of the institution (city and state)

3. Dates of attendance

4. Diploma

5. Curriculum

6. Overall GPA

7. Class rank (if known)

8. Courses completed and grades received

9. Merit-based scholarships

10. Academic honors

11. Other school-based honors or awards

Non-Formal Education

List classes, seminars, and workshops you have attended in addition to your formal curriculum. For example, perhaps you attended several lectures and workshops at the American Marketing Association's national convention. Make sure to indicate the name of the class, the name and location of the organization that offered it, and the year you attended.

Standardized Test Scores

Feel free to skip over this section if your scores were less than stellar. It's rare that an employer will factor standardized test performance into her hiring decision.

SAT

GRE

MCAT

LSAT

GMAT

Work Experience

Include paid and volunteer positions, as well as internships.

Experience (repeat this section for each job you've held)

1. Name of employer

2. Employer's address

3. Type of business, industry, or field

4. Job title

5. Dates of employment (month and year)

6. Reason for leaving

7. Name and phone number of direct supervisor (will this person be a reference?)

8. What were your major accomplishments on the job? (e.g., Were you promoted? What did you initiate, create, design, revamp, etc.?)

9. What were your major job responsibilities? In what types of tasks or activities were you typically engaged? Try to recall and write down what seem like even the most mundane and obvious responsibilities.

10. What knowledge or insights did you gain? This question is especially relevant for those of you who have served as interns or volunteers. While working in a non-paid capacity, it's common that the responsibilities are menial and that the real value of the position is exposure to a field from the inside.

11. What skills did you acquire or improve upon (e.g., became adept at public speaking)?

Activities

List your participation in both school and extracurricular activities (e.g., student government, clubs and organizations, fraternities and sororities, sports, publications, and hobbies), and repeat this section for each activity.

1. Name of club, organization, or hobby

2. Your position or title (e.g., member, Treasurer). Were you elected to the position?

3. Dates of involvement

4. Principal activities of the club/organization

5. What did you accomplish while involved with this activity?

6. What were your major responsibilities as a member of this group?

7. What skills did you acquire or improve upon?

Skills

This list should be comprised mainly of what are commonly referred to as "hard" skills, meaning they can be measured in some way. "Soft" skills such as communicating, organizing, and managing should be omitted from this section. For each skill you list, indicate your level of competency (e.g., beginning, intermediate, advanced). The categories below are by no means exhaustive, but they're a good place to start.

1. Computers—software packages, hardware, and programming languages

2. Foreign Languages—specify whether and with what degree of proficiency you have the ability to write, read, speak, interpret, or translate

3. Math and Science—statistics, research methodology, lab procedures

4. Business—cost accounting, financial analysis, economic forecasting

5. Arts—film editing, camera operation, set design, sewing, graphic design

References

It is often best to pick former employers who can testify as to your competency in the career area that you are pursuing. Most prospective employers will ask for three references. You'll need to provide the name, title, address, and phone numbers of each.

LOOKING GOOD

The resume format you select will dictate the organization of your qualifications on the printed page, and thus has major implications for how the reader will perceive your credentials. Two resume formats have dominated in recent history: the "reverse-chronological" and the "skills-based." The reverse-chronological approach has been the more popular of the two for many years and for good reason—most employers find it easier to read, and most job seekers find it easier to prepare. Nevertheless, the skills-based approach also has its own loyal following, and in certain situations is very appropriate. Let's take a closer look at these two styles so you can determine which would be best for you.

REVERSE-CHRONOLOGICAL FORMAT

The logic behind the reverse-chronological format is that professional and academic progress occurs in a linear fashion—in other words, "you're not getting older, you're getting better." In the reverse-chronological format above, the applicant's work experience and education are listed and described sequentially. This approach, provides the reader with a clear sense of the applicant's career and academic progression through time. It also enables the employer to determine from just a quick glance where and when the applicant worked, as well as what was accomplished at each job.

The reverse-chronological format is a good choice for job hunters whose most recent work and educational experience is closely related to their current job objective. It also favors those who have demonstrated a stable work history with few or no employment gaps. Finally, it works well for those whose careers have progressed logically toward their current objective.

However, the reverse-chronological format is not for everybody. It is not for those who have an inconsistent work record, or history of job jumping. On a reverse-chronological resume, this kind of checkered past becomes blatantly obvious. Gaps literally jump off the page. The reverse-chronological approach is also not particularly effective for those whose most relevant experiences came earlier in their career. For example, imagine that you are applying for a job as an accountant. Five years ago you worked as a bookkeeper, but since then you have been employed as a beekeeper. On a reverse-chronological resume your experience as a beekeeper is the first thing the employer would see. Not very promising.

ANNE SEIN

203 Fifth Avenue • New York, NY 10028 • (212) 333-3333

Objective

Position as a staff nurse.

Education

Phillips School of Nursing, New York, NY
Associate in Applied Science Degree, Nursing, June 1996
Grade Point Average: 3.93

Honors:
- Dean's Honor List—all semesters
- Class Senator, 1993 - 1996
- Selected by faculty to participate in a conference sponsored by the Jacobs Perlow Hospice
- Representative for student body on the Faculty Curriculum Coordinating Committee

Experience

1993 - Present   **Beth Israel Medical Center**, New York, NY
Student Nurse Extern, Emergency Department
- Assist RNs and physicians with providing emergency care to patients in a 32 bed Emergency Department.
- Perform EKGs, insert foley catheters, administer glucose tests, and perform other procedures as requested under the supervision of a Registered Nurse.

1989 - 1992   **Bud M. Weiser, M.D.**, New York, NY
Office Manager
- Liaison between doctor and patient.
- Coordinated hospital admissions and arranged for various outpatient tests.
- Handled insurance, billing, and correspondence.

Community Service

- Burden Center for the Aging, Participant in the Friendly Visitor Program.

The reverse-chronological approach is also not the best choice for career changers, or for those who have limited direct experience in their chosen field. Let's say you want to get into publishing, but have no actual publishing experience. Preparing your resume in a reverse-chronological manner will only emphasize your lack of experience and give employers little cause to consider you as a serious candidate. If you find yourself in this predicament you will need to opt for the skills-based format to which we will turn next.

Reverse-Chronological Format Checklist
Use this format if:

1. Your most recent work and/or educational experience is related to your career goal.

2. You have a stable work history with few or no gaps.

3. Your work history shows a logical progression toward your current objective.

SKILLS-BASED FORMAT

The skills-based format above enables you to showcase what you can do, as opposed to where and when you did it. Your qualifications are grouped into skill-based categories (marketing, counseling, and research) that relate directly to the position for which you are applying. The abilities you present on a skills-based resume can be extracted from a wide range of experiences, not just the workplace. For the skills-based resume to be effective, the categories you choose must closely mirror what the employer is seeking.

The skills-based format affords tremendous flexibility and enables you to tailor your qualifications precisely to the needs of the employer. If you know they are looking for someone to write, edit, and conduct research, you simply group your qualifications into those headings (assuming you have abilities in all three areas). The skills-based approach is a particularly good choice for those who have limited, irrelevant, or spotty work histories, because it de-emphasizes gaps, career shifts, and lack of direct experience. It can also be advantageous for those who have acquired the bulk of their credentials from nonprofessional experiences such as volunteering, interning, continuing education, and traveling. Finally, it is a good choice for the job seeker who has held several similar positions over the course of their career in which he or she performed the same tasks repeatedly. A skills-based approach would enable such a job seeker to avoid the redundancy inherent in describing several identical jobs.

The major down side of the skills-based format is that many employers don't really care for it. In fact, in the recent survey we conducted of major employers, an overwhelming 78 percent said they preferred the reverse-chronological format. They find skills-based resumes more difficult and time-consuming to read, especially when the employer information is separated from the skills section. They are also fearful that people who use the skills-based format are actually trying to hide some glaring weakness or gap.

Evan Rogers

55 West Street, Apt. A • Iowa City, IA 30024 • (319) 777-7777

Education	**Bachelor of Arts, History**, May 1996 University of Iowa, Iowa City, IA • Financed 50% of college expenses through various part-time and full-time positions.
Activities	• Rugby Club, President • Judicial Review Board, Member • Academic Search Committee, Member
Organizational Skills	• Procured and managed annual Rugby Club budget of $50,000. • Coordinated fundraisers, special events, and other activities, including the annual food drive to benefit St. John's Center.
Leadership Skills	• Provided general guidance and counseling to educationally and economically disadvantaged 14-17 year-olds. • Elected Rugby Club President for two consecutive years.
Research Skills	• Conducted a comprehensive review of the ideologies underlying Iowa's educational policies regarding minorities since 1954. Submitted report to the Iowa Education Department's Office of Equity and Access.

Employment History

1993 - Present	Youth Aide, Iowa Division for Youth
1993	Intern, Iowa Education Department
1990 - 1992	Ski Instructor, Mountain House

Skills-Based Format Checklist

Use the skills-based format if:

1. You have limited direct experience in your chosen field.
2. Your skills have been acquired primarily through study, travel, volunteering, and interning.
3. Your work history is inconsistent.
4. You are changing careers.
5. Your work experience is highly repetitive or redundant

ALTERNATIVE FORMATS

These are basically variations on the reverse-chronological and skills-based themes that have been created by borrowing elements from one approach and integrating them into the other. If you want to try something a little different, then consider one of the following formats.

THE TARGETED REVERSE-CHRONOLOGICAL FORMAT

This format is ideal for the person who has past experience relevant to their objective, but whose most recent experience is not within their targeted field. By creating targeted experience headings, this approach will enable you to emphasize your most relevant experience and avoid an unfavorable chronology. The only drawback is that the employer will have to fish around a bit to figure out where you're currently employed.

Ray Copper

25 Union Square • New York, NY 10003 • (212) 999-9999

Education   **New York University**, New York, NY
               B.S., Accounting / Actuarial Science, May 1997

Honors   Stern Scholarship
               Nassau Community College, Garden City, NY
               A.A.S., Accounting, December 1993
               Overall GPA: 3.88
               Honors: Phi Theta Kappa
                         National Honor Society

Business Experience

1992 - 1994   **H&R Block/VITA**, Valley Stream, NY
               Tax Preparer

               • Prepared individual tax returns for a diverse clientele.
               • Acquired substantial knowledge of tax laws.

1989 - 1991   **Custodial Trust Company**, Princeton, NJ
               Assistant Accountant

               • Analyzed financial statements, and reconciled bank and
                 general ledger accounts.
               • Collaborated on designing a new billing system.
               • Accurately maintained clients' accounts.
               • Computed net equity reports and trading funds.

1989   **Whitehorse Savings and Loan**, Mercerville, NJ
               Bank Teller

               • Courteously satisfied customers' banking needs in a
                 heavy volume, high pressure environment.

Additional Work Experience

1994 - Present **New York University**, New York, NY
               Administrative Assistant

               • Maintain various databases and oversee alumni billing.

Computer Skills

               Excel, Lotus 1-2-3, Q & A, Filemaker Pro 2.0, Paradox, DOS, BMDP,
               Statistix, WordPerfect, Microsoft Word

The Reverse-Chronological Format with a Skills-Based Twist

This approach is especially effective if you want to draw the reader's attention to broad categories of your strengths while staying within the safe confines of the reverse-chronological format. To do this, simply insert skills-based sidebars or subheadings into each job description. This will clue the employer in on what you believe to be your most marketable strengths.

Bruce Rit

Maple Street • Burlington, VT 00011 • (666) 666-6666

Summary

- Extensive experience in a variety of non-profit organizations with proven ability in fundraising, marketing, public relations, program development, and counseling.
- Strong writing, communication, and interpersonal skills.

Education

University of Vermont, Burlington, VT
Masters of Social Work and Masters of Science in Non-Profit Management, May 1, 1996

University of Maryland, College Park, MD
Bachelor of Science, Business and Marketing, Cum Laude, December 1986

Non-profit Experience

FOUNDER, B.A.G.A.L., Brattleboro, VT   1992 - 1993
Marketing/Fundraising
Initiated and implemented various development activities including special events, direct mmail, advertising sales, and community solicitation. Increased membership by 200%.

Public Relations
Established, developed, and maintained positive working relationships with various community organizations resulting in increased public awareness of and support for the organization. Designed promotional materials. Published a statewide newsletter.

CONSULTANT, Brattleboro AIDS Project, Brattleboro, VT   1991 - 1992
Public Relations/Fundraising
Enhanced public relations through expanded community outreach, increased media contact, and the redesign of promotional materials. Planned special events; raised funds through community solicitation, and the initiation of fee-based services.

Program Development
Gathered and analyzed data on trends regarding the transmission of HIV/AIDS. Developed and implemented community AIDS educational campaigns.

CASEWORKER, The Brattleboro Retreat, Brattleboro, VT   1990 - 1991
Counseling
Developed and coordinated treatment plans as part of a multi-disciplinary team. Direct clinical experience with a diverse caseload of patients in recovery from substance abuse.

Program Development
Designed and implemented Stress Reduction and Journal Writing programs for patients.

Additional Experience

Marketing Assistant, Patriot Bank   1988 - 1990

SKILLS-BASED RESUME WITH EMPLOYER INFORMATION

Another option is to use the skills-based approach, but to indicate the name of the employer next to each accomplishment. For the reader, this technique takes the guesswork out of what happened where. The down side is that by adding employer headings you will undoubtedly be left with less space, and thus may be forced to do some creative editing.

CLANCY RUIZ

8th Street • San Diego, CA 11111 • (888) 888-8888

Education

University of California at San Diego, *B.A., English*, May 1995
Financed 100% of college education through full-time employment.

Writing/Editing Experience

Clearwater Revival
Wrote artist bios for annual environmental festival; interviewed sloop club directors.

Women's Action Coalition
Wrote press releases concerning the definition of women in the '90s.

Ultracomputer Research Laboratory
Assisted Director with editing academic papers prior to journal publication.

Community Service

Grace Opportunity Project
Tutored fourth grade Latino students in reading, math, and writing.

UCSD AHANA Mentor
Mentored incoming NYU minority underclassmen.

UCSD Higher Education Opportunities Program
Promoted higher education opportunities for their students.

Administration

Ultracomputer Research Laboratory
Maintained on-line resource library on Unix system. Managed office operations.

Department of Human Services and Education/Resource Access Project
Played major role in assembling 600+ person conferences.

Computerland
Assisted Director of Finance in all phases of transition to on-line payroll system.

Professional Experience

Ultracomputer Research Laboratory, 1994 - Present

Department of Human Services and Education, Resource Access Project, 1992 - 1993

Computerland, 1991

Skills

IBM: DBase IV, Lotus 1-2-3, WordPerfect, LAN • Macintosh: Microsoft Word

---

SIMPLE WORDS FOR SIMPLE MINDS

Your goal is to make the reader's job as easy as possible. Write in the active voice in a straightforward, style. Keep your sentences short and to the point. Personal pronouns are unnecessary. Helping verbs are passive so you can omit them as well. If you're short on space, you can get rid of most articles. Avoid cryptic abbreviations and obscure acronyms. Spell everything out so the reader knows what you're talking about. Finally, try to vary your language to keep the reader's attention.

Use language that is readily comprehensible to the layperson, but demonstrates your familiarity with the buzzwords and terms commonly used in your prospective field. This is particularly important for technical fields, such as computer science or engineering.

THE ENDS JUSTIFY THE VERBS

Employers are primarily concerned with the results you've achieved in the past. The most effective way to convey results on a resume is to begin your sentences with a power verb. Power verbs catch the reader's attention and help to draw her into your description. Depending on the accomplishment you're trying to describe, you can string together two or more power verbs to add some extra punch to your description. Examples of power strings are, "designed, developed, and implemented," or "established, cultivated, and maintained."

Also, employers aren't just interested in what you did, they want to know how well you did it and how much you achieved. In some instances it is difficult, if not impossible, to describe your work in qualitative or quantitative terms. When this is the case, simply state what you did and leave it at that. Refrain from adding fluff or embellishment. Nothing will turn off an employer faster.

Quantification

Provided customer service to over 200,000 callers annually.
instead of
Provided customer service to callers.

Qualification

Resolved staff-management conflicts in a diplomatic and sensitive manner.
instead of
Resolved staff-management conflicts.

Power Verbs That Demonstrate Leadership Skills

Advocated for the rights of the mentally ill.

Directed a team of five oceanographers seeking the lost city of Atlantis.

Enlisted the support of 20 volunteers to restore a community garden.

Formed a student committee to investigate alcohol on campus.

Founded a volunteer organization dedicated to serving the needs of the homeless.

Governed the University Senate, adhering to the highest standards of honesty and integrity.

Hired a staff of 15 phone interviewers for the alumni phoneathon.

Initiated the unionization of domestic workers, including housewives.

Inspired obese individuals to adopt a low fat vegetarian diet.

Instituted a more relaxed dress code to boost staff morale.

Led the soccer team to three consecutive national championships.

Managed an exclusive hair salon catering to entertainment personalities.

Moderated a panel discussion on the impact of nuclear proliferation.

Motivated volunteers to work extra shifts prior to the mayoral election.

Pioneered the national anti-fraternity movement.

Presided over monthly student council meetings.

Recruited, hired, and trained ten new staff members.

Represented the student body on the Faculty Recruitment Coordinating Committee.

Selected performers for the Senior Week Celebration.

Spearheaded efforts to ban the use of animals in lab experiments.

Sponsored a bill to make all tuition benefits tax-exempt.

Staged a benefit concert for victims of Hurricane Bill.

Started a campus-based travel agency.

Supervised twelve peer counselors.

Power Verbs That Demonstrate Organizational Skills

Arranged transportation to and from conference site for visiting scholars.

Assembled press kits and promotional packages for national rock 'n roll tours.

Centralized alumni credential files resulting in more efficient file maintenance.

Coordinated seating arrangements at fashion shows for media and retailers.

Catalogued the private art collection of David Byrne.

Distributed a weekly newsletter to 4,000 subscribers.

Disseminated pamphlets on HIV to Residence Life staff members.

Executed stock and option orders issued by retail brokers.

Formalized application procedures for the Alumni Mentor Program.

Implemented a computerized registration system.

Installed system software on over 250 computer stations.

Maintained a comprehensive log of acceptable sound takes.

Organized a ski trip to Utah during Winter break.

Planned a twelve part lecture series concerning international politics.

Prepared a list of low cost treatment centers throughout the city.

Processed over 100 financial aid applications daily.

Routed over 500 calls daily to a staff of 25.

Recorded minutes at weekly staff meetings.

Reorganized the Career Resource Center collection based on the Holland codes.

Scheduled weekly social outings for dorm residents.

Updated alumni mailing list for annual fundraising drive.

Power Verbs That Demonstrate Communication Skills

Apprised management of shifts in consumer buying patterns.

Answered callers' questions during an alternative music radio talk show.

Briefed reporters on recent developments in U.S. foreign policy.

Conducted campus tours for prospective students and their parents.

Contacted subscribers by phone to offer a special renewal rate.

Demonstrated CPR techniques to EMS trainees.

Drafted business correspondence for senior management.

Educated parents of the physically challenged about the Americans with Disabilities Act.

Explained academic requirements to incoming freshmen.

Familiarized Croatian refugees with American customs and practices.

Informed committee members of the various factors affecting student retention.

Instructed a group of inner-city junior high students in the basics of photography.

Interviewed varsity basketball players for a feature article in The Targum.

Lectured American physicians about the benefits of Eastern healing practices.

Listened to employee grievances.

Presented major selling points of the new swimwear collection to sales force.

Reported findings about campus safety at a public forum.

Spoke at the AMA Conference about the relationship between diet and overall health.

Taught basic English to children of Mexican migrant workers.

Trained bartenders on how to mix a drink properly.

Translated romance novels from English to Spanish.

Wrote a daily summary of New York Stock Exchange activity.

Power Verbs That Demonstrate Analytical Skills

Analyzed blood samples to determine cholesterol levels.

Assessed clients' readiness to return to the workplace.

Audited financial records of the Board of Education.

Consulted on the design of a virtual reality installation.

Discovered a new species of reptile in the Amazon.

Evaluated job readiness of newly arrived immigrants.

Examined supermarket poultry to determine salmonella bacteria levels.

Identified students in need of remedial help.

Interpreted entertainment contracts and prepared contract amendments.

Investigated the cause of heart failure in albino goldfish.

Researched the relationship between income level and political affiliation.

Surveyed over 2,000 Alabama residents to determine their opinions on TV violence.

Tested the effects of marijuana on short-term memory.

Power Verbs That Demonstrate the Ability to Create

Conceived the international blockbuster film, Transvestites in Turkey.

Conceptualized a twelve-step program for chocolate addicts.

Created in-store displays using glow in the dark mannequins.

Composed a film score for a documentary on the Russian Revolution.

Designed a five-week intensive Spanish conversation course for hospital personnel.

Devised a direct marketing campaign for a nondairy frozen dessert.

Established long-term objectives for a national community service initiative.

Invented a solar powered light bulb capable of illuminating a 300 square foot room.

Originated the "Fashion Compassion Ball," an annual fundraiser for battered women.

Produced the first ever on-campus comedy show for charity.

Revolutionized the use of Styrofoam models in print advertising.

Power Verbs That Demonstrate Helping Skills

Aided the homeless with all aspects of their job search.

Arbitrated a settlement between team owners and players.

Assisted students with the career decision making process.

Attended to the day to day needs of nursing home residents.

Collaborated on the design of a new billing system.

Comforted children suffering from various serious illnesses.

Contributed to the development of the restaurant's new outdoor seating area.

Counseled college seniors regarding making the transition from school to work.

Facilitated the installation of a multimedia exhibit honoring female athletes.

Fostered the reconciliation between African-American and Jewish residents in Crown Heights.

Guided high school students through the college application process.

Helped victims of child abuse regain their self-esteem.

Mediated conflicts between quarreling roommates.

Mentored high school students considering careers in physical therapy.

Resolved disputes between management and staff concerning salary increases.

Settled disagreements between landlords and tenants.

Supported sales efforts of brokers by maintaining up to date client records.

Treated patients with multiple psychological disorders.

Tutored elementary school students in basic math.

Power Verbs that Demonstrate the Ability to Convince or Sell

Convinced owner to introduce daily drink specials resulting in a 20% increase in profits.

Dissuaded union members from voting in favor of a walkout.

Encouraged dormitory residents to participate in weekly "town hall" meetings.

Marketed carpentry services via phone and direct mail.

Negotiated contracts on behalf of 1,200 union members.

Persuaded shoppers to sample perfumes and cologne.

Promoted long-distance services to businesses in the New York metropolitan area.

Publicized film screenings via flyers, posters, and ads in the local paper.

Sold advertising space to clothing retailers throughout California.

Secured new accounts by making in-person sales presentations.

Solicited alumni for contributions to restore the damaged cathedral.

More Useful Power Verbs

Attained the level of black belt after only three months of intensive karate lessons.

Augmented sales by 25 percent through extensive phone follow-up.

Awarded the Anderson Medal for superior sportsmanship.

Boosted net retail sales by 50 percent over the last quarter.

Built temporary housing for the homeless.

Calculated daily shifts in foreign exchange rates.

Decreased the average wait for registration by 25 percent.

Developed expertise on the subject of vintage French wines.

Ensured customer accounts complied with Federal Reserve regulations.

Eliminated dangerous admission rites for newly accepted fraternity brothers.

Exceeded monthly sales quotas for a record 15 consecutive times.

Excelled at providing professional, courteous, and efficient service.

Expanded retail operations to 50 sites nationwide.

Expedited the processing of transcript requests.

Financed 75 percent of college education through full-time work.

Gained experience with a variety of desktop publishing programs.

Generated significant student interest in CIEE's work abroad programs.

Improved relations between staff and management through monthly gripe sessions.

Increased paid membership by 200 percent within two years.

Launched a campus-wide public relations campaign for the Schick Tracer.

Mastered spoken Greek while traveling throughout Crete.

Modernized the recreation center by introducing the latest line of Nautilus machines.

Published a monthly newsletter listing internship opportunities nationwide.

Raised the ability and confidence level of beginning racquetball players.

Reduced campus waste by introducing a dorm-based recycling plan.

Revamped the school library, making it accessible to those with impaired mobility.

Revitalized cheerleading squad through modernizing costumes and dance routines.

Saved employer $20,000 by revamping vendor system.

Strengthened business relationships by providing superior customer service.

Supplemented lectures with role plays and interactive group exercises.
Tended bar at exclusive Soho drinking establishment.
Utilized spreadsheet software to aid with line planning.

THE COMPLETE RESUME

We're about to walk you through the process of writing a resume from start to finish. Grab a pencil and some paper because it wouldn't be a bad idea to take some thorough notes. Also, pull out your notes personal history inventory notebook (remember pages 75–80?). As we discuss each resume category, you'll need to refer to your notes to decide how you would like to present the information you've amassed on paper. Finally, take a moment to reacquaint yourself with the various resume formats presented earlier, and pick the one that lends itself best to your situation.

What's In a Name?

Your name should always go at the top of your resume. It should make a strong first impression—not flashy, but powerful. Your name generally looks best when centered or pulled out to the left hand margin. Make it larger than anything else on your resume. If you're using 12 point type, then see how your name looks at 16 or 18 points. Put it in bold to boot.

Address and Phone Number

List your complete address and phone number (actors applying for performance jobs being the exception—they can get away with just a phone number) as well as your fax number and e-mail address, if you have one. Keep in mind, however, that most employers will contact you by phone unless they have bad news in which case they will mail you the infamous rejection letter.

If you're living at a temporary address, it's a good idea to indicate on the resume for how long the address will be valid. And don't forget to list a second address where you can receive mail after you've moved.

You can list either your home or office phone number, or both. Of course, only list your office number if your boss knows that you're looking for another job and has given you the green light to receive calls from prospective employers at work. Otherwise, you might get tossed out the door before you even have a chance to quit.

The Profile—Your Opening Statement

To make a strong, positive impression from the start, lead off with a profile or summary statement. This strategy works particularly well for the more experienced job hunter, although recent graduates can use it effectively as well. The profile serves as a teaser to whet the appetite of the reader and hopefully intrigue him to read on. It is a carefully crafted sound bite that in just a few lines proves to the employer that you are tuned in to his needs, and that you have the qualifications he is seeking.

To create your summary you must know what the prospective employer is really looking for in a candidate. More importantly, you must have the qualifications being sought. The rest is easy. Try to come up with two to four sentences or bulleted statements that communicate your most relevant credentials. Keep in mind, however, that you will need to modify your summary depending on the requirements of each position for which you are applying.

Summary

Five years of experience in advertising and public relations, with a strong track record in account management, direct mail, print production, and traffic. Effective communicator with excellent organizational skills. Perform best under deadline pressure.

Profile

- Four years experience in the food and beverage industry.
- Excel at providing professional, courteous, and efficient service.
- Substantial knowledge of haute cuisine and fine wines.

THE OBJECTIVE

Over 60 percent of the recruiters we surveyed favor the inclusion of an objective on the resume of a recent college grad. If you choose to include an objective it should be focused, concise, and employer-oriented. This is an opportunity for you to demonstrate to your prospective employer that you not only know what you want in a job, but also what they want in a candidate. Although your objective should be focused, be careful not to make it too narrow, or else you run the risk of limiting your range of employment options. Also, it is conceivable that your resume may end up in the hands of an employer who doesn't have a suitable opening, but knows of a colleague who does. If the objective on your resume isn't too constraining, the employer may pass your resume on to his or her colleague for consideration.

Objective

Position as a systems analyst in a UNIX environment.

Objective

Paralegal position that requires expertise in legal research, Trusts and Estates, and Patent Law, as well as knowledge of Lexis and Westlaw.

EDUCATION

For some of you, this section will be a major selling point and should be placed at the top of your resume, just below your objective or summary statement. However, if you already have a great deal of professional experience in your field, the experience section would come first. You might also want to de-emphasize education if your degree is irrelevant to the field you are entering, or could in some way be considered a liability.

The core of the education section consists of the name of the institution you attended, the city and state in which it's located, the name of the degree, diploma, or certificate you received, your field of study, and the month and year of graduation. After you've been out of school a while just listing the year is fine.

Education

Northwestern University, Evanston, IL
B.A., English, May 1996

You can also list your minor and any other additional concentration of coursework that would interest an employer. And for those of you who financed all or part of your education, you can add a line to convey this fact, such as, "financed 75 percent of college expenses through part-time work as a waiter, bartender, and messenger." This demonstrates to employers that you are multidimensional and have a strong work ethic.

Education

New York University, New York, NY
Bachelor of Arts, Anthropology, December 1995
Minor: Sociology

Additional concentration in European History
• Financed 75 % of college costs through part-time work.

You Went to Whatchamacallit University?

The order in which you list your school and degree depends on what makes you most marketable. If you went to a highly regarded school that you think might open some doors then list the name of the institution first. On the other hand, if you went to a no-name school where you received a highly marketable degree, then list your degree first. If you went to a no-name school and received a no-name degree, then it really doesn't matter which comes first. Whatever you decide, it is best to consistently follow that sequence throughout your education section.

Multiple Degrees

If you are listing more than one degree, you have the option to begin with the one that is most relevant to your objective. And if you hold a prior degree that you feel is completely irrelevant then you have every right to leave it out. For those of you pursuing a graduate degree, it is usually a good idea to indicate your thesis or dissertation topic if you have one, as well as a brief statement describing your research or hypothesis.

Education

University of Virginia, Charlottesville, VA
Master of Arts, Sociology, May 1996
Thesis Topic: *The Effects of Teachers'
Expectations on Student Performance in
Elementary School.*

Princeton University, Princeton, NJ
Bachelor of Arts, Sociology, May 1994

Study Abroad

More and more American organizations consider it an asset for their employees to be globally minded and multilingual. For those of you who have participated in overseas programs, make sure that you describe them on your resume.

Education

Boston University, Boston, MA
B.A., Political Science, May 1996
BMT, Jerusalem, Israel, Junior Year Abroad,
1994–1995

Gained a deep appreciation for Israeli culture and history through a mixture of formal education and extensive travel. Spent six months living and working on a kibbutz.

Should You List Your GPA?

Seventy-three percent of the hiring professionals we surveyed encouraged recent graduates to list their GPA on their resume. Why such a high percentage? Establishing a GPA cutoff is a convenient way to trim down the applicant pool. GPA, however, is much less of an issue for graduates who have been out of school for a couple of years, as well as for graduates who are pursuing the non-corporate route.

Our opinion is that if you're a very recent grad, and you believe GPA is relevant to your field, and yours happens to be high—3.3 or above—then go ahead and list it. Alternatively, if you received any academic honors or awards (e.g., Dean's List, Phi Beta Kappa), you could list those instead of your GPA. When listing honors and awards, try to stress those that are most relevant to the job for which you are applying.

Education

University of Virginia, Charlottesville, VA
Bachelor of Arts, History, May 1996
Overall GPA: 3.4

Honors

Racoosin Scholar—participated in annual overseas excursions, attended guest lectures, coordinated annual community service projects.
Dean's List (four semesters)
National Honor Society

RELEVANT COURSEWORK

If academics are your strong suit, you might want to mention a few of the classes you've taken that are particularly relevant to your career objective. Prioritize your list of classes in order of their relevance to the employer. Stick to listing classes in which you've performed well and that are not typical requirements for your major. For example, you might want to list the seminar you took in Economies of the Third World. If you've taken intro, intermediate, and advanced courses in the same subject area, only list the advanced course, as it will be assumed that you took the prerequisites. Also, you can take some creative license with the names of the classes you've taken, as the official course names at many universities are often not very elucidating. For example, you could modify the title "Calculus III" to read "Advanced Calculus." Finally, it is advisable to describe distinctive class accomplishments if they are particularly relevant to your career goals.

Education

Bachelor of Science, Mechanical Engineering, May 1994
University of the Philippines, Manila

Relevant Courses

<u>Machine Design</u>
Constructed paper bridges capable of supporting 25 pounds.

<u>Turbo Pascal</u>
Wrote a computer program to calculate the dollar's equivalent in 15 foreign currencies.

EXPERIENCE

The experience section is the heart and soul of your resume. It can make or break you. In this section you are attempting to answer the employer's question: "If I hire you today, what can you do for me tomorrow?" To do this adequately, you'll need to offer concrete examples of your skills, and how you've used them to solve problems. Before you begin to write, arrange your accomplishments in order of their relevancy to your target employer.

If your experience section will be comprised of both paid and non-paid positions, then you might as well just call it "Experience." On the other hand, if it consists entirely of paid employment, then you have the option of calling it "Professional Experience." You could also categorize your experience by skill or field, in which case you would use the name of the skill or field being stressed as the main heading (e.g., "Marketing Experience" or "Photography Experience").

Before you begin to write, arrange your accomplishments in order of relevance to your target employer. Use the power verbs we introduced earlier to give your prose a little bit. For example, instead of using passive constructions like, "Responsibilities included selling raffle ticket," or "Duties consisted of designing logos," you could say "Sold raffle tickets," and "Designed logos." Remember to use the verb tense that accurately reflects when the activity took place.

In addition, use adjectives to spice up your writing and give a strong sense of your accomplishments. For example, instead of saying, "Counseled students and alumni," you could say, "Counseled over 1,000 students and alumni annually," or instead of "Resolved customer disputes," you could say, "Resolved customer disputes in a diplomatic and sensitive manner." Finally, keep your descriptions belief and to the point. There is no need to burden the reader with too many superfluous details. Besides, if you put everything in your resume, you'll have nothing new to say in the interview.

Why Is This Job Different Than All Other Jobs?

As you write your description, consider the following questions:

1. What Did You Accomplish or Achieve at Each Position?

This is the place to show that you're a go-getter. If you're drawing blanks trying to answer the question above, then ask yourself the following: What distinguishes you from your colleagues? Are you consistently praised by your boss for the way you perform certain tasks? Do your coworkers ask for your advice or opinion about how to carry out certain projects? Have you been designated to train new employees in certain procedures? Have you made any recommendations to you boss that have been adopted or put into use? Have any of your ideas regarding policy or procedure been implemented?

2. What Were Your Major Job Responsibilities?

In other words, what did you do all day long? When possible, try to indicate how well you performed your responsibilities. Just listing the duties of your job will put your reader to sleep (e.g., responded to customer inquiries in a courteous and sensitive manner).

3. What New Skills or Knowledge Did You Acquire on the Job?

This is particularly relevant for describing an internship or volunteer experience where you mostly played an apprenticeship role. While you may not have had many major responsibilities, you still may have developed new abilities, improved others, and learned the ins and outs of a new field. You might want to mention that you attended staff meetings, learned how the organization operates, became fluent in the lingo of the field, and proved administrative and technical support to staff, management, and executives. The point is to show your prospective employer that you're not completely wet behind the ears.

What Qualifies As Experience?

Just about anything. You can include full-time, part-time, and seasonal paid employment, volunteer work, internships, consulting, freelancing, military service, raising children, and extracurricular activities. Just make sure that the employer is clear on the capacity in which you were employed. You wouldn't want someone to think that you were a full-time staff member when in actuality you were volunteering only five hours a week.

Which Information Should You Include?

At the bare minimum, you need to include the name of your employer, the employer's location (city and state, or country if it's overseas—unless it's obvious), your job title, dates of employment, and a description of what you achieved. You might also want to include the name of the division or department within the organization, if it's relevant, as well as a brief description of the organization. What products or services does it provide? How large is it? Is it domestic or international?

PRESENTATION

Nearly three quarters of the employers we surveyed preferred applicants to "bullet" their job descriptions. The only down side of using bullets is that they take up more space than paragraphs and are not scanner friendly (more on this later). If you do use bullets you might want to try a theme-oriented approach in which each bullet would address a particular skill area. In this way, all of your accomplishments pertaining to customer service for example would be clustered together beside one bullet.

Bullets Organized By Themes

Social Service Experience

1993—Present

Substance Abuse Counselor/HIV Program Coordinator, Lafayette Medical Management, New York, NY

- Managed a caseload of 70 clients currently on methadone maintenance. Provided individual and group counseling—focus on issues such as goal setting, employment, education, nutrition, health care, and hygiene.
- Created the HIV Counseling Program, which services over 200 participants. Coordinated weekly rap sessions, arranged guest lectures and staff training, organized various group activities, distribute condoms and safe sex literature, and conducted pre- and post-HIV test counseling. Supervised two assistants.
- Prepared monthly, quarterly, semiannual, and annual reports based on case reviews. Monitored the results of weekly toxicological/urine profiles and took action as necessary. Conducted intake interviews with newly accepted program participants.

DOES ANYBODY REALLY KNOW WHAT TIME IT IS?

Listing dates is a regrettable necessity unless you want to make it
obvious, you're trying to hide something. Many recruiters we've
spoken with claim that dates are the first thing they look at. Nevertheless, you still have some leeway as far as how conspicuous the
dates appear. If your career progression has been logical and
steady, and you have no major gaps in your experience, then you
can list your dates of employment in a prominent location. However, if you've had a series of short-term jobs, taken time off to
study in a Tibetan monastery, or been out of the work force for a
long time, then dates become your enemy and your task is to de-
emphasize them.

Covering Up Gaps

Although it is quite common to list the month and year of one's
employment start and end dates, at times it is more advantageous
to list only the year. For the sake of argument, let's say that you
started working at Taco Bell in June of 1995 and left your job in
February of 1996. In July, you started a new job at Banana Republic
where you are presently employed. By using the "year only
method," the five month gap will vanish as your resume will reflect
that you were at Taco Bell from 1995—1996 and at Banana Republic
from 1996—present.

ODD JOBS

If you held a variety of odd jobs throughout college that don't
really require individual descriptions, you could lump them all
together under one heading such as "ADDITIONAL EXPERI-
ENCE." At least in this way you are demonstrating to the employer
that you have worked steadily while going to school, and have been
exposed to a wide range of experiences. You also are conveying a
positive impression about your work ethic.

Additional Experience

1993—Present
Worked an average of 20 hours per week while attending classes full-time. Held a variety of positions, including waitress, word processor, caterer, and entertainer at children's parties.

ACTIVITIES

For all you current students and recent graduates, here's a chance to show your prospective employer that college is about more than just books and beer. This is a chance to demonstrate that you've had a well-rounded college experience, enhanced by involvement in a variety of school and community clubs, organizations, and athletics. What's so great about that? It shows that you have developed certain abilities and personal qualities that will make you an asset to any organization.

If you choose to create a separate activities section, then you should describe each activity just as you would a job. Focus on accomplishments, results, and the development of new skills, especially those that are relevant to your job target. If you were in a club or organization, list its name along with your title or affiliation. If you've held elected office, definitely mention this, as being elected implies you've been able to elicit the support and confidence of others. Also note whether you've received any honors, awards, or official commendation as a result of your extracurricular involvement.

> Activities Connections, Alumni Mentor Program, Participant
> - Regularly met with an alumnus to discuss academic, career, and business issues.
> Society for Creative Anachronism, Treasurer
> - Oversaw the club's annual budget of $5,000. Science Fiction Club, Vice President
> - Coordinated the publication of the club's annual magazine.

SKILLS

This section provides you with an opportunity to tell your prospective employer about your "hard" skills—speaking a foreign language, programming a computer, utilizing various software packages, operating a video camera, etc. Even if you've already mentioned some of these skills in your position descriptions, the skills section offers a neat summary where an employer can see the whole package at a quick glance. List your skills in order of their relevancy to your target employer. If a skill has no relevancy, then leave it out. Also, when possible, qualify your level of proficiency for the skill listed (e.g., fluent in French or basic knowledge of C++).

Skills

Familiar with Microsoft Word and WordPerfect
Conversational Italian

PROFESSIONAL AFFILIATIONS OR MEMBERSHIPS

This category is generally most appropriate for graduates who have already established themselves professionally and are active members of one or more professional associations (e.g., The American Psychological Association). Including this category demonstrates that you are committed to your field, and are interested in developing professionally.

Professional Affiliations

American Counseling Association
Career Development Specialists' Network
Career Resource Managers' Association

PROFESSIONAL DEVELOPMENT OR CONTINUING EDUCATION

This is a perfect section in which to list all the workshops, seminars, and classes you've attended that were not part of your formal degree program. For example, if you were employed at a large organization, perhaps you took advantage of training that was offered in areas like conflict resolution, creative problem solving, or crisis management. Or maybe you sought out adult education classes on your own to keep abreast of what's going on in your field. The point is that you have taken the initiative to enrich yourself, acquire new skills, and build your knowledge base—achievements worth mentioning.

When listing classes, the main thing is to indicate the subject being studied. When you took the class and where is less important. However, if the course was offered by a world renowned expert, or at a well-known institution, then feel free to list this information.

PROFESSIONAL DEVELOPMENT

A Neurodevelopmental Approach to Baby Treatment—5-day course

Neurodevelopmental Treatment of Children with Cerebral Palsy—8 week course
Alternate Systems of Communication for the Person with Neuromuscular Disorders

LICENSES/CERTIFICATIONS

It is essential to list this information for nurses, social workers, real estate brokers, stock brokers, guidance counselors, teachers, and a host of other professionals whose fields are governed by licensure.

Licenses/Certificates

New York Gaming School, Certificate of Completion, 1980
New Jersey Gaming Commission, Key Casino Employee

PUBLICATIONS

If you're going after a job in academia, journalism, or publishing, it's a good idea to list your publications. Be selective, though, as you can always submit a complete list at the interview. Include the names of any coauthors, the title of the article/book, the name of the publication, the name of the publisher (for books only), and the date of publication.

Selected Publications

"Literature Adds Up," a chapter within the book, *Fact or Fiction: Reading and Writing Across the Curriculum*, The International Reading Association, 1992.
"Falling in Love with the Subject—Romance in Education," *The Holistic Education Review*, Spring 1991.
"Incorporating Video into the Curriculum: A Teacher's Perspective," *Video and Learning Newsletter*, Winter/Spring 1993.

EXHIBITIONS

This category is for all you fine and commercial artists and craftspeople who have shown your work at galleries, festivals, museums, and other exhibition spaces. As with everything else on your resume, lead with your strengths and be selective. You don't have to list your entire exhibition record, just the highlights. Start off with your most impressive solo exhibitions and work back through your group exhibitions. Make sure you list the name and location of the exhibition space. You may also want to list the title of the show, the medium of the work (especially if you work in more than one) and the year of the show. Also indicate under a separate subheading whether any of your work has been purchased for the permanent collection of a museum or private collector.

Solo Exhibitions

1993   Crawford and Sloan Gallery, New York, NY
        "Romantic Visions"
1992   Fotozeller, Berlin, Germany
        "Peace on Mars"

MILITARY SERVICE

Feel free to describe your abilities as a leader and decision maker. If you served as an officer, indicate your most significant accomplishments and responsibilities.

Military Service

1980–1984   Achieved the rank of Captain in the
             Israeli Army
             • Commanded 50 soldiers and 5 officers

WHAT NOT TO INCLUDE ON YOUR RESUME

Don't list height and weight, references, race, ethnicity, religious or political affiliations, marital status, the names and ages of your children, and the reasons why you left each job. Also don't staple a photo of yourself to your resume.

RESUME DESIGN & LAYOUT 101

You'll need to have the following at your fingertips: a draft of your resume, a computer equipped with word- processing software, several sheets of 8 1/2 x 11 paper, and a printer. Remember to always save your work on your own disk, especially if you're doing your resume in a computer lab where they usually trash everything on the hard drive by the next business day.

MARGINALLY SPEAKING

The first thing you're going to do is set your margins (which serve as a built-in memo pad for employers). Set your margins at 1" on all four sides. If you need extra space they can always be decreased later to a minimum of .5", just make sure you keep them even.

FONTARAMA

Your next step is to select a typeface, of which there are two basic kinds—serif and sans serif. A serif typeface, such as Palatino or Times, is characterized by letters that have small finishing strokes, affectionately referred to by the non-design crowd as curlicues. In contrast, the letters of a sans-serif typeface, such as Helvetica or

Futura, have no such finishing strokes. Most graphic designers agree that serif typefaces are best for the body of the resumes while sans serif typefaces are more effective for category headings. When choosing a typeface consider the following—readability, attractiveness, and appropriateness. Are the letters and words easy to distinguish? Do most people find the typeface pleasing to the eye? Does it convey an image of professionalism? Remember, you are not printing a party invitation. Some of the more popular typefaces that are suitable for resumes are illustrated below:

Times

New Century Schoolbook

Palatino

Bookman

Garamond

Helvetica

Futura

Size

Type size is also referred to as point size (72 points = 1 inch). Depending on the typeface being used, you will probably want to go with a point size between 9 and 12. The only way to figure out which size is best for a given typeface is to print a few lines of text and see how it looks. We recommend using three different type sizes—one for the basic text, one for the category headings, and one for your name. The headings should be about 2 points larger than the main text, and your name should be about 2 to 4 points larger than the headings.

Consistency

Although there are thousands of ways to lay out a resume, you should adhere to a few basic rules. Since employers will be scanning your resume (in some cases at high speed), you need to be consistent with where you place the information they are seeking. The reader will not be patient if their eyes have to zig all over your resume in order to decipher your qualifications. Generally, it is easiest if your main categories are justified to the left, and the supporting information is indented below. Another option is to set up columns so that the category headings and dates of employment are on the left side and the body of the text is on the right.

EXPERIENCE

Avon Products, Inc. 1993—Present

Marketing Intern

Provided administrative and technical support to the Planning, Analysis, and Research team. Assisted with the coordination and moderation of focus groups conducted nationwide; handled logistics, collected qualitative data to be used in forecasting.

EXPERIENCE

9/93–Present Admissions Ambassador
New York University, New York, NY

Conducted campus tours for up to 25 prospective students and their parents. Responded to phone inquiries regarding admissions and specific academic programs. Represented NYU at open houses.

SPACE—THE FINAL FRONTIER

Now that all of your qualifications have found a home, give your resume the once over and look at the spacing. Is it too cluttered? Are there gaping holes of white space that you could drive a truck through? Is it obvious where one category ends and another begins? Blank space is crucial if the reader is going to be able to make sense of your resume. The greatest amount of space should come between major categories. There should also be space between the end of one job and the beginning of the next, and a smaller space between your employer information and the beginning of your job.

GET GRAPHIC

Now it's time to add some finishing touches. There are five main text embellishment techniques to consider:

bolding

CAPITALIZING

• bulleting (you can substitute dashes, diamonds, boxes, arrows, checks, pointing hands, or asterisks for bullets),

rule lines

---

italicizing

All of these will add distinction and emphasis to your text in varying degrees. <u>Underlining</u> often has a nasty habit of slicing through the lower half of g's, q's, p's, y's and j's, but adding a <u>ruled line</u> of various thicknesses below your name or category headings can look really sharp. CAPITALS take up a lot of space and should be used sparingly. Bullets (•) work best for highlighting individual accomplishments. **Bold** print is most appropriate for category headings and other information that requires major emphasis. *Italics* lend a softer touch, but also are effective for highlighting key information.

Whichever graphic devices you use, make sure that you are consistent. If you italicize your first job title, then every job title on your resume should be italicized. Also be careful not to use the same graphic technique for adjacent items. For example if you bold both your job title and the name of your employer, neither item will stand out. You need contrast to make a word pop off the page.

APPLICANT TRACKING SYSTEMS

Now that you've learned all the tricks of the trade, we're going to throw you a little curve ball. Recent trends indicate that in order to save time and money, many large organizations, including AT&T, Microsoft, Nike, MCI, and American Express, are increasingly adopting computer-based applicant tracking systems to review the resumes of prospective employees. According to James Lemke, Manager of Employment and Human Resources Information Systems at UCLA, "...chances are if you are sending a resume to a company or institution that employs more than 1,000 people, a computer initially reads your resume." The fact is that computers, as opposed to their human counterparts, can sort through thousands of resumes in the blink of an eye, and select those that meet the criteria the employer has specified. Pretty cool, huh?Getting Past the Electronic Gatekeepers

Your first step is to find out if the organization you're approaching is using an applicant tracking system. Their human resources department should be able to give you this information. If so, then your resume may need a major overhaul to guarantee you a shot at an interview.

Let's assume that you're applying for a position with an organization that uses an applicant tracking system. The first thing that will happen to your resume after it has been yanked by a clerk from its beautiful matching envelope, is that it will be fed to a scanner, an electronic device, which will translate your resume into ASCII, a code that the computer can read. At this point, (we hope), a clerk will check the resume on-screen to make sure it's consistent with the printed one, because while most scanners are perfectly competent, they have also been known to foul up every once in a while. If the scanner misinterprets your resume and the clerk, misses the mistake, your resume is probably a goner. For this reason, it can never hurt to send more than one copy of your resume to an organization that is going to process it electronically.

A recent study by Peat Marwick L.L.P. reported that nearly 50 percent of all medium-sized and large organizations use applicant tracking systems for storage and retrieval of resumes.

Assuming both the scanner and clerk do their jobs well, your resume will then lie dormant in a database until it is roused from deep sleep by a computer search. During the search, the computer will be examining all the resumes in the database at blinding speed to see which ones satisfy the most criteria (i.e., keywords) that the folks doing the hiring consider to be most important. The keywords that guide the search represent varying types of skills and experience (e.g., B.S. in Biology, cell cultures), and are generally phrased as nouns. The resumes with the most keyword matches will rise to the top. All the other resumes that were not selected will remain until another search is conducted later on.

TAKING YOUR RESUME ON THE ROAD

Now that you've completed your resume, you need to make sure that it is completely, and we mean completely, error-free. One little mistake and all your hard work could be for naught. Enlist a couple of good proofreaders to give your resume the twice over, and only after it has received their seal of approval should you even contemplate having it printed.

PAPER

Now that your resume is error free and ready to print, you'll need to pick out paper and envelopes. You can't go wrong with a box of basic 24 pound 100 percent cotton fiber paper. Just make sure that it's 8 1/2 x 11 in size, and that it's laser friendly. Textured papers are fine as well, so long as the texture isn't so pronounced that it overpowers your text or your printer. Patterned papers, on the other hand, such as parchment, are distracting to the reader and are not recommended. Stick with neutral colors—white, off-white, ivory, light beige, and pale gray are all perfectly acceptable. The advantage of white is that it reproduces well when being either faxed or photocopied, whereas colored paper tends to come out with a muddled look. Pure white, though, is highly reflective and tends to be harsh on the reader's eyes.

According to Resumix, the creator of one of the most popular applicant tracking systems in the country, you should adhere to the following guidelines:

1. Use white paper.
2. Include nouns on your resume that are likely to match the keywords selected by the employer (e.g., direct marketing, desktop publishing, retail sales).
3. Since the computer will assume the first item on the page is you, make sure you place your name at the top. Also, if your resume is longer than one page, place your name at the top of subsequent pages.
4. Use type between 10 and 14 points (with the exception of Times 10 point, which is too small).
5. Don't use italics, underlining, graphics, shading, horizontal or vertical lines, borders, brackets, or parentheses.
6. Use a standard sans-serif typeface, such as Helvetica or a serif typeface, such as Palatino. A classic font like Times is the best choice
7. Don't fold or staple your resume. Use a 9 x 12 envelope to ensure your resume arrives flat.
8. Laser print your resume. The better the print quality of your resume, the less likely the scanner will have difficulty reading it.

PRINTING

For the best resolution and quality, laser printing is the way to go. If it's too costly for you to have all of your resumes laser printed, you could make photocopies, as you need them, from a laser printed original. Just be sure to tell the folks at the copy shop that you would appreciate it if they give the glass on the machine a good cleaning before printing your resumes. Also have them show you the first copy in the run before they print the rest of the job. This will allow you to make sure that your resume is properly aligned, and free of spots, streaks, and any other imperfections.

Never print more resumes than you are ready to send out at one time. Probably 10-15 is a reasonable number unless you are attending a large career fair or other special event. If you had any notion of doing a mass mailing, drop it. Mass mailings have been proven to be highly ineffective. Dump a hundred or so assembly line re-sumes and cover letters into the mail box and you might as well throw them in the trash. You will obtain much better results by individually tailoring your resumes to meet the needs of each pro-spective employer. Finally, printing up your resume in small batches makes sense since it will allow you to incorporate the sug-gestions of employers, counselors, and contacts for future versions.

ENVELOPES

Using envelopes that match your resume paper is a nice profes-sional touch; however, white envelopes will always do in a pinch. If you really want to impress your prospective employer send your resume and cover letter (don't worry, the next section will give you all the dirt on writing cover letters) in a large envelope (9" x 12" is perfect). By doing so, you won't have to fold your resume, which means it not only looks sharper when removed from the envelope, but will also lie flat if placed on a scanner.

Whichever type of envelope you use, it is important that you print the recipient's address legibly and correctly, otherwise your resume may never reach its destination. Also, don't forget to in-clude your return address on the envelope.

GETTING YOUR RESUME INTO THEIR HANDS

The only thing left to do is make sure your cover letter and resume reach your prospective employer in a timely fashion. There are several ways to accomplish this: via mail, e-mail, fax, courier, and hand delivery. The method you select should really be contingent on (a) how badly you want the job, (b) how long the job was posted before you heard about it, (c) how much of a rush the employer is in to fill the job, and (d) the personality type of the prospective em-ployer.

In most cases, if the position was advertised, the ad will state the preferred method of resume submission. Follow the directions to the letter.

When You Need Speed

For the ultimate in speed, faxing or e-mailing is the way to go. First, call the organization and find out if they will accept either. If so, terrific, but always send a hard copy through the mail just to be sure. If the organization won't accept a fax or e-mail, you always have the option of sending your package via Federal Express or some other courier service. You also have the alternative of hand delivering your letter and resume, provided the employer is within close proximity. This approach has the added benefit of enabling you to get a peak at your potential place of employment, as well as the opportunity to take a gander at some of your prospective colleagues in action.

FORMATTING A RESUME FOR E-MAIL

When e-mailing your resume, you no longer have to worry about picking out a beautiful typeface, fancy paper, or matching envelopes. Instead, you have another whole set of headaches to contend with.

Although you'll be creating your resume on your word processor, you'll be saving it and sending it in ASCII format, which is plainer than vanilla, so you'll have far fewer options for making your digital resume attractive as compared with what you can do to a paper resume. Basically, your graphic enhancements are limited to all caps, asterisks, dashes, and whatever other basic symbols you have on your keyboard. Also, you'll have to be careful not to exceed the character limit per line, which is imposed by your e-mail program (check the program for the exact number of characters, although you can expect it to be close to 65), otherwise the text that you thought would fit on one line will actually wrap around to the next.

Sample Resumes

Please turn to the Appendix in the back of the book to get a look at some sample job-winning resumes, all of which have been adapted from those of real-life job hunters.

COVER LETTERS

At minimum, the cover letter serves as an introduction of you and your resume to the reader. It summarizes your background by highlighting particular skills (as we discussed in chapter 1), and explains *why* you are sending your resume. It's also a way to state your job objective, if it is not listed on your resume. More importantly, though, a cover letter is a powerful tool, subtly but effectively enticing the reader to want to meet you.

That's not to say that every employer places equal importance on the cover letter. Some never even read them. Others might read the letter only to see if the applicant has any writing skills before tackling the resume. So, although we can't guarantee that everyone who receives letters from you will place equal importance on them, why not make the most of this potentially powerful marketing tool?

FROM TARGET TO BULLSEYE

The first thing to deal with when writing cover letters is to figure out who is at the receiving end of the letter. It is essential that you personalize each cover letter. "To whom it may concern" just doesn't cut it, unless you are responding to a blind ad where no name is given and only an address is listed.

In some cases, your target reader may be obvious. You may have received the name of the individual through a personal acquaintance or current job advertisement. In other cases, however, you may be sending out cover letters and resumes to organizations that have not posted a job but are of interest to you anyway. If sending such an "unsolicited" cover letter and resume, it is crucial that you call the organization and obtain the name of the appropriate contact person. Also, if you're getting your contact names out of trade publications or from what appear to be outdated job ads or organizational materials, it's always wise to call the organization to verify the name of the contact person. You may also need to call to ask for the correct spelling of the names ("Is it Stengle or Stengel???") as well as accurate job title. Misspelling a name or listing the wrong job title could be your ticket to the "circular file.".

In larger organizations, find out the name of the appropriate people in both the department where you'd like to work as well as the human resources or personnel department. Why duplicate your efforts? Well, the director of the department is more aware of hiring needs for that office and also has a more vested interest in possible job candidates. In the human resources department, they may be reviewing thousands of resumes and cover letters for all departments in the organization, so there's more of a chance that your materials will be filed away, (never to be found again.) They are, though, the ones responsible for recruiting candidates, so you still need to send them your letter and resume. By covering both bases in this way you are assured that all appropriate people have seen your "stuff." Be sure to put a "cc" at the bottom of each letter (e.g., "cc: Human Resources" on a letter to the Director of Marketing) so that everyone knows who else has a copy.

TONE AND FORMAT

The tone of the cover letter should reflect the style of the organization you're writing to, somewhere on a spectrum from casual to formal. In general, a straightforward, concise approach is more effective than a gimmicky, unnecessarily long one. As for the length, it should not exceed one page unless a "detailed" or "extended" cover letter is requested. If you do exceed one page make sure that all of the information you are including is *absolutely* necessary.

With format, you have a couple of choices. You should use the standard business layouts—either indented or block format. An example of each follows:

INDENTED FORMAT

Your address
Date

Name
Title
Organization name
Organization address

Dear Dr., Ms., Mr.:

Opening paragraph (Why are you writing? Are you responding to a job ad?)

Middle section (What do you have to offer? In what way will you be an asset to the readers organization?)

Concluding Paragraph (Summary; Propose the next course of action)

Sincerely,

Your name (typed)

enclosure

Block Format

Your address
Date

Name
Title
Organization name
Organization address

Dear Dr., Ms., Mr.:

Opening paragraph (Why are you writing?)

Middle section (What do you have to offer?)

Concluding Paragraph (Summary; Propose the next course of action)

Sincerely,

Your name (typed)
enclosure

Aesthetics

Make sure you have centered your cover letter on the page and that there are adequate margins all around (at least one inch). If your letter is very short, use 1.5" margins on the left and right. Type your letter on good quality paper—not xerox paper. Try to use the same type of paper, both in weight and color, as you used for your resume. Don't feel, however, that it's necessary to laser print your cover letter if you don't have access to a computer, simply because you have done so with your resume. The cover letter should be typed on a typewriter or printed on a letter-quality printer, and should be similar in font size and style to that of your resume. It should be single spaced (or 1.5 spaced if very short), and have a space between paragraphs.

If there is one rule that we'd like to shout from the rooftops, it is this: *There should be no grammatical errors, misspellings, or typos in your cover letter!!* Similarly, don't use white-out and don't cross out any letters or words. If using a computer, use the spell check function and have several people proof your cover letter. You'd be pretty embarrassed if you used "form" rather than "from" when writing "I moved to New York form Chicago." The quickest way to have yourself eliminated from the competition is by committing these errors. You'd be surprised, too, how something as simple as a clean resume and cover letter can put you at the top of the candidate list.

WHAT TO SAY IN YOUR LETTER

Now let's get to the meat of the matter—what do you put in the cover letter? First, be aware that you need to tailor each letter to the target reader and prospective job. Mass produced cover letters can be easily identified by their vague tone, so take time to personalize each letter. It's easiest to think of the cover letter as having three parts: Opening Paragraph, Middle Section, and Concluding Paragraph. Let's take them one at a time:

Opening Paragraph

In this paragraph, you need to give the reader some idea of who you are. This is not the time to document your life; an employer is not interested in what you've done since you were five years old. Instead, briefly mention whatever is relevant. This may be the school you'll soon be graduating from or your present employment situation or past experience. You will also need to specify why you are writing (i.e., I saw your advertisement in the *New York Times*... Your organization interests me because... Ms. Karen Sims suggested I contact you... I will soon be moving to...). You can also mention here that you have enclosed a resume. Order all this information in any way that feels comfortable for you and flows well.

Middle Section

The middle section is usually one to two paragraphs. There is a general rule that we have found to be quite effective when trying to decide what to include in this section of your cover letter. Whether you are responding to an ad where specific skills are listed as job requirements or whether you are sending an unsolicited inquiry, *determine the three to four skills that would be necessary for that job and show how you have acquired those skills.* You may need to review your skills package at this point (from chapter 1). The trick here is to not simply to restate what is included on your resume. Think of your resume as an objective, detailed presentation of your assets and think of your cover letter as a strategic highlighting of those selling points.

Now let's take that a step further and show a more subjective slant to those assets. For instance, if you have listed on your resume that you "Oversaw entire business operation during owner's absence," you may want to add to this in your cover letter by stating that you "demonstrated organizational and managerial abilities while troubleshooting problems and overseeing a staff of five when the owner was away from the office."

Let's look at another example. Where you may have included the statement "Developed relations with community service agencies" on your resume. You could elaborate by further highlighting certain skills. For instance, in your cover letter you might state, "I fostered relations with over 100 community service agencies through site visits, and honed my communication skills by interacting with diverse populations.".

While presenting yourself in this positive light, you should also demonstrate your knowledge of the organization to which you are applying. You can do this by spelling out how your assets relate to the company's products, services, and goals. Showing that you have done your homework and personalizing your letter in such a way can only strengthen your candidacy for a particular job.

Another issue you might have to address in the middle is salary. Job advertisements or listings will often ask that you include salary history or salary requirements in your cover letter. Requests for salary requirements or history are the most often ignored parts of a classified ad. They wouldn't ask for it if they didn't want it, and your resume is likely to end up being tossed if you don't address the issue. As we'll discuss in chapters 8 and 10, you want to avoid discussions of specific dollar amounts whenever possible so that you don't state a figure that's lower than the amount you could have gotten. By asking you to talk salary in a reply to an ad, the employer is getting the upper hand in future negotiations, but unfortunately you can't entirely avoid the question.

If the ad asks for salary *requirements*, try stating a broad range that you're looking for, like "upper teens to mid-twenties." Or, if you don't want to have to end up taking upper teens, say "in the $20,000s." And to be even safer, you can avoid stating figures all together and say something like "I am aware of typical salaries for paralegal positions and am comfortable with figures in that range."

If you're asked for salary history (rare for entry-level positions since you don't really have one), avoid listing each job you've held and giving exact figures. Instead offer, "I am currently earning in the $30,000s and do not consider salary to be my primary motivator in changing jobs. Once we've had a chance to meet and assess the value I could add to your organization, I will gladly discuss my salary needs."

Concluding Paragraph

You can begin with a summary statement here, indicating that you are confident that your background makes you a strong/competitive candidate for the position or for their organization in general, if you don't know of a specific opening. You will also want to thank them for their time and consideration. Most important for this section, though, is to propose a specific plan of action at the conclusion of your cover letter. For instance, you might state that you will contact them in about a week to ensure receipt of your resume and to see if you can arrange an appointment to discuss the position further. Or, if conducting a long distance job search, you should include dates when you will be visiting the area and would be available to interview. Basically, you should be as assertive as possible in the closing without being pushy, especially if you've initiated the contact yourself. If responding to a blind ad, or one that clearly states "No calls," then you usually have to be more passive in your closing and wait for them to respond.

SUREFIRE TIPS FOR EFFECTIVE LETTERS

- Tailor your letters as much as possible to the reader and the industry as a whole

- Talk more about what you can do for the reader than what they can do for you—tell them how you will add value

- Convey focused career goals

- Say nothing negative

- Always be honest but not too modest

- Use lists of bulleted points or sections delineated with bold or underlined headings rather than long paragraphs

- Cut to the chase—don't ramble

- Don't say anything that you don't back up with evidence

- Talk about problems you've solved in the past for other employers or organizations

- Consider cultural differences if you know the target reader; some cultures are more formal than others.

- Make the letter visually appealing

- Get others' opinions of your letter before sending it out

- Keep a notebook of all letters your send out with a log of follow-up efforts

TESTING, TESTING...

We've included a number of examples of cover letters for a variety of situations. So, although you may never *enjoy* writing cover letters, we hope at least we've made you more comfortable with the process!

Letter for an Informational Interview—Personal Referral

14 Old Bass Street
Los Angeles, CA 77254
(415) 581-9922
July 10, 1997

Mr. Sid Smith
4116 South Street
Los Angeles, CA 77254

Dear Mr. Smith:

You may recall meeting my parents, Lisa and Michael Pringle, at The Mayor's Ball last month. I believe that they spoke to you about my interest in radio and my work as a dj for WBBR, a public radio station in Los Angeles, CA. I am graduating from UCLA this May and am beginning to explore my career options, both in radio broadcasting and programming.

I would appreciate the chance to speak with you or any colleagues you could recommend. I am not requesting a job interview at this point, just the opportunity to meet with someone who is knowledgeable about careers in radio. I would like to identify the best match for my skills and experience and determine the feasibility of finding a job in Los Angeles.

I have enclosed a resume to give you more information about my background and will contact you soon to see if we could arrange to meet. Thank you for your time.

Sincerely,

Lesley Pringle

Internship Inquiry

April 4, 1996

Laura Hintelmann
Actors for the Arts
P. O. Box 30027
Chicago, IL

Dear Ms. Hintelmann:

I enjoyed speaking with you last Friday about internship opportunities at Actors for the Arts. As a junior at the University of Chicago, I am hoping to pursue a career in the arts. I am interested in the summer internship assisting Joe Pearce, as we discussed.

The opportunity is of particular interest to me because it offers the chance to gain experience in all aspects of artist management. In addition, I would welcome the chance to work for a nonprofit organization since I have been very involved in community service throughout college.

As an actor and producer for my college theater group, I have gained experience in both the performing and business sides of theater. I have also done temporary office work for the past two summers, so I can effectively carry out the duties of an assistant.

I will be available to work after June 6th and am flexible in terms of days and times. Thank you for your time and consideration. I will contact you later this week to see if we can arrange a time to meet. Please call if you have any questions.

Sincerely,

Karen Reed

Unsolicited Letter for a Long Distance Search—Entry Level

Timothy Michaels
114 River Road
Rye, New York 11111

September 8, 1995

William Stephens
Director, Marketing
Southern Trust Bank
230 Peachtree Street, Suite 450
Atlanta, GA 11111

Dear Mr. Stephens,

As a recent college graduate with experience in finance and sales, I am writing to express my interest in any entry-level marketing positions available with Southern Trust Bank.

Since graduating from Syracuse University in May of 1996, I have gained valuable knowledge in banking and personal finance by working for Sussex Savings Bank on Wall Street. I have been exposed to the daily grind of big business as well as the intimate climate of bank-client relationships.

During my college years, I achieved success in both academics and leadership, the highlights of which are:

- Awarded the Dean's List five times

- Inducted as a member of the Golden Key National Honor Society

- Developed strong interpersonal and decision-making skills as President of the Young Business Leaders Association.

- Excelled in marketing courses with many "real-world" team projects.

I was involved in numerous extracurricular activities both on campus and in the community. I assumed leadership positions which allowed me to develop strong interpersonal and decision-making skills.

I plan to move to Atlanta and will be spending a week there next month. I will call you in a few days to see if it would be convenient for you to meet with me during that time. Thank you for your consideration.

Sincerely,

Timothy Michaels
enclosure

Unsolicited Letter—Career Changer

Jane Pinchot
4000 High Street
Brooklyn, NY 11111
(718) 555-5555

July 8, 1997

Scott Josephs
Media Planning Director
Cityscape Communications
2120 Madison Avenue
New York, NY 11111

Dear Mr. Josephs:

Alexis Moser of Stevens & Tate suggested I contact you about the expansion of your media services department. I met Ms. Moser at a recent meeting of Women in Communications and was telling her about my interest in making the transition into media planning from my current research role at Columbia University. She, along with others I have spoken to in advertising, seemed to think that my experience could be of value to an ad agency's media department.

You will see from the enclosed resume that my work involves many activities that translate well to media planning, including:

* Target potential donors by understanding "consumer" mentality and using innovative research methods.

* Work closely with the university's public relations department to promote a positive image of the school, based largely on feedback I collect during my fundraising efforts.

* Successfully meet the demands of multiple managers in a fast-paced environment.

While these responsibilities are comparable to the process of media planning, I am also taking a continuing education course in Media Strategies for Advertising at New York University to learn the specifics of your industry. This course has strengthened my interest in working as a media planner and is providing me with the hands-on skills I need to transition successfully into a dynamic agency like Cityscape.

I would welcome the opportunity to meet with you (regardless of your staffing needs at this time) to discuss how my qualifications might be of use to your department in the near future. Thank you for your consideration. I will call you soon to follow-up.

Sincerely,

Jane Pinchot

Job Fair—Long-Distance Job Search

September 12, 1997

Jason Stone
Director, Creative Development
WebWorld, Incorporated
200 Hudson Street
Portland, OR 11111

Dear Jason,

Thanks so much for taking the time to speak with me at the Portland Info Tech Job Fair yesterday. I'm sure you met quite a few people there, so to refresh your memory, I was the one involved in the new multimedia projects at Interactive, Inc. You mentioned that WebWorld might have a need for website designers in the near future, so I'd like to set up an appointment with you to continue our conversation in a less hectic atmosphere than we had at the job fair.

I've enclosed a copy of my resume for you so you'll have a better idea of what I have to offer, including:

• Developed two new highly successful CD-ROM product lines at Interactive

• Proficient in all major graphics applications and cutting-edge animation software.

• Created over 20 websites for freelance clients including small businesses, educational institutions, and individuals.

I'll give you a call in a few days to see when we can get together.

Thank you,

Amanda Elliot

Responding to a Classified Ad

12 Plimstock Lane
Tucson, AZ 11111

Molly Rivera
Manager, Human Resources
Midwest Securities
8105 Aston Avenue
Fifteenth Floor
Tucson, AZ 11111

June 15, 1996

Dear Ms. Rivera:

Having graduated from college in May with a major in business and
internship experience in a brokerage firm. I am very interested in the sales
assistant positions advertised in the June 13th *Tucson Chronicle*.

Through an internship last summer with Dean Witter in New York, I
gained exposure to a variety of financial products and developed strong
client relations skills. I also became proficient in processing orders and
meeting the needs of brokers in a fast-paced environment.

I was impressed with the reports of Midwest's recent growth as reported
in the *Wall Street Journal* and I would welcome the opportunity to be an
asset to such a successful team.

I look forward to meeting with you to discuss my qualifications further.
Thank you for you consideration.

Sincerely,

Melissa Allen
enclosure

ASSEMBLING YOUR PORTFOLIO

If you thought portfolios of sample work were for artists only, think
again. One of the best ways to distinguish yourself from other
candidates for a job in any field is to put together a collection of
materials that reflect your accomplishments and potential.

In chapter 1, we said that you're being hired for both the skills
you already have (the I Know Skills) and for your potential (the I
Am and I Can Skills). By presenting samples of your work and
"testimonials" from people who've known you, a portfolio provides tangible proof of those skills and capabilities. Putting it all

together in one folder or loose-leaf notebook also demonstrates your organizational abilities and shows that you can make an effective, professional presentation.

A portfolio can include any or all of the following materials: writing samples; materials relating to projects you've done at school or work; letters of recommendation; a reference list; and academic transcripts. If you do happen to be an artist of some sort, then your portfolio will, of course, include samples of your artwork almost exclusively. The strategy behind good art portfolios is beyond the scope of this book; you're better off turning to professors and professional architects, fashion designers, photographers, graphic artists, or anyone who can advise you on what they would want to see in your portfolio.

For non-arts jobs, you'll rarely be asked specifically for a portfolio, but having one on hand at a job interview can impress a prospective employer and really distinguish you from the crowd.

Can You Write?

Sometimes you'll see a job listing that asks you to send a brief writing sample with your resume. Deciding what "brief" means can be a nightmare. Generally, no one wants to read more than about three to five pages, unless they specified another length. No one wants to read your ninety-page thesis on the mating habits of Peruvian newts.

An appropriate sample could be an excerpt from a class paper or an article from a school or local newspaper or magazine. It's ideal if the subject matter of the sample is relevant to the job, so if you're applying for a position with a public policy think-tank and you've written a paper analyzing the controversy over prayer in schools, then by all means use it.

Try to determine if the employer is more interested in your actual writing ability or simply in how you think. If it's writing ability they're after, then the subject of the sample is a little less important. On the other hand, if they're looking for how you use your mind and express your thoughts, then make sure the content of the work is related to the job or the organization. You can include several writing samples in your portfolio and choose the one or two that you want to show to any given employer.

What Have You Done for Me Lately?

If you have been out of college a while and working, then you've undoubtedly been involved in projects that can be represented on paper. Work samples can include anything you've designed, organized, or generally been responsible for, such as business correspondence (which could also be used as a writing sample), training manuals, marketing plans, company newsletters, computer programs, or reports.

Be aware that in many organizations, the work you produce while there remains the property of that organization after you leave. You must therefore be very careful when presenting samples of your work from a past employer. If you're still working for the organization, keep in mind that some of your work is confidential. You can't be giving away trade secrets, for example, about how to market the latest toothpaste. You may still be able to use these materials if you black out or omit any confidential areas, leaving the essence of your work intact. Whatever you do, remember that a prospective employer will evaluate your sense of discretion as much as they'll evaluate the samples.

Seal of Approval

Whether you're putting together an extensive portfolio or not, letters of recommendation are a must. Almost every prospective employer will want to see a letter or two attesting to your experience, accomplishments, and character. Depending on your level, these letters can be from teachers, professors, previous or current supervisors, or people attesting to your personal qualities, usually referred to as "character references." It's helpful to have letters from a combination of academic, professional, and personal referrals.

Many college career centers or deans' offices keep files of these recommendations for current students and alumni and will mail them out to prospective employers or graduate schools when requested in writing. This is a useful service since some jobs require that your letters be sent blindly, i.e., directly from the person writing the recommendation or from a neutral third party such as the college career center. This way, the letter is given more weight because the person was able to write it more without you being able to see it. In reality, many people writing recommendations give you a copy on the sly anyway because they're happy for you to see the glowing praise they've given you. You can then make copies of these letters and use them with prospective employers who don't care if the letter comes directly from you. Never give away your original copy!

In selecting teachers or professors from whom to request recommendations from, try to find ones who know you well enough to comment on you in some depth, either from classes you took with them or research or teaching assistantships you may have held.

Recommendations from employers are typically from supervisors at summer jobs, internships, part-time jobs, and, of course, full-time jobs. In some cases, the official supervisor for your position didn't actually observe your day-to-day performance. If that's the case, the recommendation can come from someone who may hold a lesser title but supervised you more on a regular basis or maybe on a special project. This strategy can also work for those tricky situations where you didn't get along with one of your bosses and are worried about what kind of letter they'd write. Just be sure to avoid peers or coworkers who did not have any authority over you.

The one time you might get recommendations from peers is when a personal or character reference is requested. These references can come from almost any individual who knows you well but is not a member of your family. In some cases, the employer requests that the recommendation be from a peer—perhaps a classmate or friend. These letters should typically address your personal qualities such as honesty, focus, integrity, and determination.

RECOMMENDATIONS FOR GETTING RECOMMENDATIONS

Many people feel uncomfortable asking for recommendations. Am I bothering them? What if they say no? It's natural to worry about these things. Here are some tips for making it easier.

START EARLY

Ideally, you want to ask professors or employers for recommendations as soon as possible after finishing the course or employment stint rather than waiting several months or years later when you're applying for a job. You want your achievements to be fresh in their minds. When a lot of time has passed, they might be a little fuzzy on the details and write a weaker letter. If you do find yourself needing a recommendation from someone you haven't talked to in ages, it's still okay to ask. You might be pleasantly surprised that they actually remember you. Professors, in particular, are used to getting requests years after you graduate. Writing recommendations is a significant part of their job, so it doesn't come across as an odd request to them.

Don't Rush Them

Give the person plenty of time to write the recommendation. Even people who worship the ground you walk on will write a less than stellar recommendation if they don't have enough time to put into it. People have busy lives, and there is nothing more aggravating than a person rushing in, asking for a recommendation letter, and then saying, "By the way, can you write this by tomorrow?" Not only might it cause them to do a sloppy job, it can also cause resentment, which could be reflected in the tone of the recommendation. If you really do have to have it tomorrow, then you'll need to give them at least a basic format to work from so they don't have to start from scratch, as we describe in the next tip.

Don't Take Anything for Granted

Take the initiative to give the person recommending you some specific things to include in their letter. Remind them of the basics like what class(es) you took, grades you got, or special projects you did. In the case of an employer, refresh their memory about your job responsibilities, title, and dates you held the position. For a really powerful letter, highlight for them not only the basics of what you accomplished on the job or in class but also suggest how you distinguished yourself from others in the class or same position. Think about the competencies and skills we mentioned in chapter 2 that employers are looking for and remind your recommender how you demonstrated those qualities.

Writing Your Own Letter

Sometimes, a professor or employer will go so far as to ask that you write your own letter. This happens more often than you might think. If they really do want more than just an outline like we described above, then you will find yourself in that awkward position of having to blow your own horn. This is no time to be modest. If you're uncomfortable with that, try to detach yourself from the process and pretend you're writing about someone else.

Start by developing an outline of your assets with evidence of your accomplishments, then expand it into a real letter. Ideally, you don't want to be fully responsible for the complete finished product that they just sign. Ask if they wouldn't mind looking it over to add a few words here and there about their own impressions of you before the final draft is complete. This is especially important if you suspect you haven't given enough of a sales pitch for yourself. If they can't take the time to add their personal touch, then at least have some other people, perhaps from your Support Team, look it over to make sure you didn't sell yourself short.

YOUR FAN CLUB

In addition to having some letters of recommendation on file, you'll need to have a list of references available. The list typically becomes necessary when you get well into the interview process and are in the running for an offer. At that point, you will probably be asked for the names, phone numbers, and possibly addresses of at least three people who can speak about your qualifications and verify your employment history. While three is the usual number requested, it's helpful to have up to five on your list, in case some can't be reached or so you can pick and choose who to use.

The people on this list may be the same ones who write letters of recommendation, or they can be others. In selecting your references, use the same criteria for compiling the list as you did for requesting letters. It's very important that you talk to your references before including them on the list—both to ask them permission to do so and to warn them that they might be getting calls or letters from organizations you interview with.

The format of the actual list should follow that of your resume in that you should ideally use the same color and weight of paper as well as same type style since the list and resume will often be mailed or handed to someone at the same time. Start by putting your name, address, and phone number at the top of the page as you did on your resume and label the page "References." Then list each reference, giving their first and last names, job title or academic title, name of the organization or school where they work, office address, and phone number. It's also helpful in some cases to write a brief sentence or two clarifying your connection to this person, as we've illustrated in the sample on the next page. This is especially important if the information on the list doesn't directly correspond to experiences on your resume.

JOE BLOGGS
230 Baldwin Road • Stockton, California 90210 415/555-5555

References

Dr. Sue Smithers
Professor, Dept. of Oceanography
Water University
123 Ocean Court
Sea Island, CA 90222
(415) 777-7777
Supervisor of research assistantship, 1993–1994.

Dr. Gene Henry
Dean of Students
Water University
123 Ocean Court
Sea Island, CA 90222
(415) 777-7778
Worked with Dr. Henry as member of Student-Faculty Curriculum
Development Committee, 1993–1994.

Mr. John Smith
Owner, Smith Deli
476 Layland Drive
Catalina Island, CA 91111
(415) 222-5566
Immediate supervisor in summer job, 1990–1994.

Ms. Helen Drew
President
Deep Sea Explorations
111 Conch Shell Road
Marina Bay, CA 90000
(415) 444-4444
Ms. Drew was formerly Senior Research Associate with the Marina Bay
Aquarium. Worked with her as Research Assistant 1994–1995.

PHONE TACTICS

You probably think that it's pretty self-explanatory, but people
often overlook the importance of phone strategies when conducting
the job search. Which strategy you use will largely be determined
by the reason for your call. Remember, though, that your phone
tactics are just as important as your other job search strategies and
deserve as much attention.

GETTING BEYOND THE GATEKEEPERS

It is often assumed that the potential employer is the most important person you speak to when making phone calls about job
contacts. Few people realize the importance of establishing rapport

not only with the boss but with the people who can connect you with the boss, such as administrative assistants or receptionists. Keep in mind that your interaction with this person can mean success or disaster in actually reaching your contact. Be professional and courteous.

Let's take the case of Abigail Smuthers, who attempted to call a potential job contact, Ms. Kelly Knots, at RCA Records. Abigail conducted a direct mail campaign (see chapter 5), carefully researching her target companies, and through it sent a resume and cover letter to Ms. Knots. A week later Abigail followed up with her prospective employers. She phoned Ms. Kelly twice leaving her name and number, but her calls were not returned. In her third attempt to make contact, Abigail coldly said to Ms. Kelly's assistant, "Are you sure she's been receiving my messages?" The assistant was quite insulted by the comment and relayed the conversation to Ms. Knots. Disturbed by the behavior, Ms. Knots called Abigail and curtly informed her there were no positions available with RCA. Remember, the gatekeepers can directly impact your success in reaching your potential employers and securing employment.

Frigid Responses to Cold Calls

If you are making an unsolicited contact or a "cold call" and your contact is unable to take your call, do not leave your name. Instead, ask when would be a convenient time to call back when that person would be available. Don't leave a lengthy message with the receptionist regarding the purpose of your call. And simply leaving your name for a person who is extremely busy may put you at the bottom of the priority list for returned phone messages. If you are returning a call to a potential employer who has contacted you, however, it is appropriate to leave your name, telephone number, and time when you can be reached.

When Is the Best Time to Reach You?

If you call contacts with whom you have previously had contact and they are not available, leave a time when you will be home. Nobody likes playing phone tag, least of all a busy potential employer. Initiate a block of time when you know you'll be available. Also, make sure that there's no loud music or blaring television noise when you are expecting phone calls.

Answering Machines

Answering machines are an absolute must for the job search. The message you have on your machine is just as important. When getting calls from friends and family, it's fine to have an excerpt from your favorite song on your answering machine, but, when conducting a job search, employers don't want to hear the latest hot band (or any other music, for that matter) wailing in their ear. Now is the time to have a clear, professional message on your answering machine. No music, no poems, just your name and number will suffice.

WORKING NINE TO FIVE

Although there is no "best time" to reach a potential job contact, there are some times that are better than others. First thing in the morning (sometime between 9:00 A.M. and 10:30 A.M.) is a time when people are usually just getting to the office and can more often be found near their desk/office. Also, later in the day, between 4:00 pm and 5:30 P.M., is a time when things generally start to slow down (although not in all professions!), and you may have more success speaking directly to your contact.

MAKING CONTACT WITH YOUR TARGET

So you've finally made it through the person answering the phone and are about to speak with the your targeted employer. Now what? Remember, you don't have a lot of time to get your point across (employers can be very busy people), but you want to cover some important details. You should be clear about your reason for making contact. Again, this may seem rather obvious, but many people find themselves stammering and stuttering when they (surprise!) find their contact person on the other end of the phone. In many instances this may be your first verbal connection with potential employers, so you want to sound self-assured and clear about your purpose. Because you do not have a great deal of time, you want to "hook" them with your succinct sales pitch.

YOUR SALES PITCH

Before making phone calls, whether it be for informational interviews or in response to job advertisements, you need to formulate a sales pitch. In essence, your sales pitch is a clear, concise description of you, your reason for calling, and what you are seeking through the phone call. Have a copy of your resume handy in case you need to refer to it, as well as paper and pencil for writing down any pertinent information. You may be asked to describe a past job or schedule an interview while on the phone. Your pitch should include:

1. **State your name.** (Rather obvious, we hope.)

2. **Your purpose for calling.** You want to make clear here why you have made contact. This can include statements such as:

   "I sent you a resume in response to your advertisement and am following up to see that you received it and to see if we should schedule an interview..." or

   "My Uncle Don suggested I contact you..." or even

   "I saw your name in the alumni contact files at school and am very interested in pursuing a career in the fashion industry. I was hoping we could schedule an informational interview, provided your time permits."

You need to set the groundwork for what is to follow, which includes:

3. **Why it would be to the employer's benefit to speak with you further.** Think about it. You need to sell yourself here. Why are you an appropriate person for a job with XYZ company? What skills can you offer? Your main goal is to get your foot in the door. Your response should be concise and to the point. For example, "I feel that my seven years of sales experience at Kitt and Company and my two years in management make me a competitive candidate for a position in Product Management." Another approach could be "My internships at The Legal Aid Society and The American Civil Liberties Union have allowed me to hone my research skills and increase my practical knowledge of the legal field. I am confident that these skills would be helpful in a position as a paralegal at your law firm." Yet another pitch might sound like, "I have been carefully following the growth of Anderson Consulting, and feel my leadership experiences at Columbia University coupled with my internships at Citibank and Goldman Sachs have given me knowledge that could further add to the success of the company." Again, you are selling *yourself* as the product here, so have your sales pitch prepared. Carefully think out what you want to say and, as corny as it sounds, even do a practice run before initiating your call.

5

The Places You'll Go to Find the Jobs

PLANNING YOUR JOB SEARCH STRATEGY

True or false?

- Networking is always the best way to get a job.
- I won't find an entry-level job through the newspaper.
- Employment agencies only place secretaries.
- I'm at a real disadvantage if my parents don't have a lot of contacts.
- The more places I send my resume, the better my chances of getting a job.

Believe it or not, all these statements are false. They're too extreme and can be misleading as you plan your job search strategy. They also happen to be actual statements we hear real-life job seekers make all the time. The problem with blanket statements like the list above is that they result in cookie-cutter job searches, which can't account for the experiences of all job seekers. In other words, they might not be meaningful to *you*.

Instead of trying to find the last word on job search, consider all job-search methods as potentially effective, then mix and match them into a strategy that's tailored to fit your goals and your resources.

A job search strategy must be diversified, balanced, personalized, and based on a quality-over-quantity philosophy.

Let's look at each component of this definition to see what it means for your campaign.

DIVERSIFIED AND BALANCED

We suggest using many job-finding techniques concurrently during your search. You might, for example, put most of your efforts into networking, but also answer an occasional newspaper ad, send some broadcast letters to companies on your Hit List, and maybe sign up with an employment agency. As long as you stay organized, keeping track of all the irons in the fire, the diversified approach can be quite effective.

PERSONALIZED AND TAILORED

A job search strategy should be tailored to fit the type of job you're aiming for. Some career fields or industries, like television, film, and radio are just about impenetrable without active networking. If, on the other hand, a position with an elite management consulting firm is what you're after, then your best bet is on-campus recruiting for undergrads or MBA candidates. By doing some preliminary research through people, computers, and libraries, you can find out which strategies work best for your career goals.

Also consider personalizing your search to fit your own resources. If you have endless personal or family contacts in a given field, then it's not a bad idea to focus most of your efforts on networking with these people and avoid having to do direct mailings or using other sources. If writing persuasively is a strength but cultivating a network terrifies you, then you'll want to concentrate more on an effective written campaign to get interviews. Whatever your own strengths and resources, use them to your advantage whether or not that method meshes with what others claim is "the only way to find a job."

QUALITY OVER QUANTITY

During the course of your job search, it's inevitable that someone will ask "How many resumes have you sent out?" Never mind that the direct mail approach they're advocating is rarely the best way to go, the quantity issue they're emphasizing is the real problem with that question. You're much better off spending time carefully constructing one letter targeted to one classified ad or ten letters tailored to ten companies on your Hit List than you are dashing off responses to twenty ads or doing a merge mailing of one generic letter to two hundred companies.

The whole aim of a job search is to make yourself more than just a face (or resume) in the crowd. Mass mailings won't do it. Neither will shaking fifty hands at a networking meeting instead of having in-depth conversations with two people. Don't be afraid to limit your contacts as long as you're not just being lazy but are genuinely putting your best effort into the quality of a smaller quantity of approaches.

THE GRASS IS GREENER ON THE OTHER SIDE—OF THE COUNTRY

Whether you're looking for a job in Missoula, Montana or Timbuktu, Mali, the way you'll find it is basically the same. If you're looking for a job long distance, it's extra important that you know what you want. You're not likely to get away with the unfocused, passive approach. Your college career center in Boston isn't going to have a lot of job listings for positions in Timbuktu (though you never know!). They might not even have any for L.A. Since you can't just use the "cafeteria method" of browsing through job listings or signing-up for on-campus recruiting (a method explained in the Campus Resources section of this chapter), you have to uncover the opportunities more actively and aggressively.

The first thing to do is to decide why you want to go where you're going. Are you moving to Seattle just to get away from your parents and "find yourself" over endless cups of café latte or because the environmental science opportunities are better there than in Brooklyn? Having a mission will determine which resources make sense for your search.

A second big issue with long-distance searches is finding those resources. Your college career center library might not have directories of companies in other cities, and your local paper rarely lists job openings outside of the region it covers. For a long-distance search, you'll find you have to make use of a broader range of the electronic and print resources described in Compiling Your Hit List to target people and organizations at your destination. If your search is overseas, be aware that there are many excellent guidebooks for finding a job in other countries. We've listed some of these in the resources section of this book.

The final point to note with long distance searches is geography, which poses obvious logistical difficulties and not so obvious image problems. By image problems, we mean how seriously will an employer in another state or country take you? You must do everything you can to convey a commitment to relocating, so that the employers you contact will take you seriously. Avoid phrases like "I'm looking into the possibility of moving to Chicago." If you're contacting companies in Chicago, then you'd better have already "looked into it" and decided you do want to live there. Then you can say "I plan to relocate to Chicago..." and they'll be willing to spend some time with you.

To further project a focused image, plan a trip to your desired location to interview before moving there. If finances and distance allow, schedule a week or two in the new location and try to arrange as many appointments as possible—both real job interviews and exploratory or informational ones—before going. For those people you can't get an answer from before departing, allow some open time in your itinerary to have an impromptu meeting once you're there. Unless they're extremely busy, few people in Atlanta, Georgia will turn you down when you call and say "I'm in town all the way from Portland, Oregon and would appreciate the chance to meet with you at your convenience during my ten day stay here." Even if there aren't any openings, you're likely to get a courtesy interview, which could lead to a job in the future, or at least a referral to another person to meet with.

"If opportunity doesn't knock, build a door."
Milton Berle

CULTIVATING YOUR NETWORK OF CONTACTS

You have probably heard the term "networking" a thousand times, as it is the "buzz word" in the world of job search. You may have also heard it called by a variety of other names, such as schmoozing. Whatever you call it, networking is one of the most important components of the job search. Think about it. The more people you know, the more information you gather, and the more you are "out there," the better your chances are for finding employment, provided you do it the right way.

"It's not who you know or what you know, it's whether who you know can use what you know."
Manley Walker

WHY YOU SHOULD NETWORK

Why do you have to meet with your Uncle Henry's friend in the business? Why can't you just read up on a particular career field and be done with it? Networking can serve a number of purposes beyond the obvious:

- To get you advice about your job search strategy
- To find information about a particular company
- To learn how your skills are relevant to a certain industry
- To find out what a particular job might involve
- To research trends in your field of interest
- To uncover hidden job openings or create new ones

Ultimately, you hope that networking will lead to consideration for job openings, whether it be with Uncle Henry's friend or with some other contact, but don't walk into a networking meeting expecting this to happen.

YEAH, BUT WHO THE HECK DO I KNOW?

You might feel your list of personal contacts is too short; or, you might not even know *one* person in the field in which you want to work, so you figure you're done for. Don't despair, you are probably more prepared than you think.

Even when starting with limited connections, you can network successfully. The trick is to delve beyond the first layer of contacts. Let's say, for example, you want to get into publishing. You've asked your mom, your sister, and even your obnoxious cousin Barry if they know anybody who works in publishing and they don't. What do you do next? You delve beyond the first layer.

EXPAND THAT FIRST LIST BEYOND YOUR IMMEDIATE CIRCLE

Ask professors (both present and past), ask colleagues, even ask your dentist. Ask anyone you come in contact with in your daily routine. We wouldn't suggest stopping strangers on the street, but you'd be surprised at how the most tenuous of acquaintances are willing to give you names of people to talk to. Below is a list of sources for contacts:

- **family/extended family**—Use your parents, guardians, siblings, grandparents, aunts, uncles, and/or cousins as possible resources.

- **friends/acquaintances**—This category includes friends, friends of friends, and neighbors.

- **coworkers and employers past and present**—Obviously, you have to be careful if you do not want your present employer to know you're looking for another job, but past and present colleagues can be good sources of networking information.

- **teachers and professors past and present**—Particularly if you have/had a good rapport with them, educators can be excellent sources for contacts.

- **alumni/ae of your high school(s) and college(s)**—These contacts can be extremely helpful. Of course, getting in touch with them is contingent upon the quality of your high school or college's career centers and/or alumni affairs offices. Many schools will have their graduates categorized by career area and by geographic location, so if you are considering moving to another city or state it may be helpful to find out if there are alums in that area.

- **counselors/advisors in your high school(s) or college(s)**—This category could include career counselors, deans, and college activities officers.

- **clubs or organizations to which you belong**—Think about it, were/are you a member of the Women's Cooperative, Economics Club, or Student Government? Or, if you're out of school, do you belong to the Alumnae Organization at your school?

- **health clubs or sports teams**—Past or present, people in these organizations, (yes, even the woman who keeps bumping into you in aerobics class) may have contacts in your field.

- **churches/temples/other religious organizations**—these organizations can be a rich resource, offering a wide variety of contacts in different career fields.

- **your doctor, dentist, and anyone else who works with you and other people**—Yes, even while getting a trim, ask your hairdresser or barber about possible contacts!

- **people you don't know but who do work that interests you**—Try writing a letter to someone you read an article about or whom you found listed in a directory of professional organizations. It may feel weird to do this, but many people enjoy the attention and recognition, or may simply be interested in helping out. Check out *The Encyclopedia of Associations,* which lists thousand of professional associations. You can also check with your local Chamber of Commerce for similar information in your immediate area.

BOTH QUALITY AND QUANTITY MATTER

You won't win the lottery or get a job simply by being the first among your friends to accumulate 1,000 contact names. While the number of connections you make is certainly important, never let the quantity of contacts take precedence over the quality of contacts. Be sure that every contact is made with courtesy and tact, and make sure that your strategy is appropriate. Be prepared with specific questions. People can be most helpful when they know precisely what you need. Meet in person whenever possible. People are more likely to help when they can attach a name to a face. Also, be sure to follow up with your contacts, thanking them for their assistance or keeping them abreast of your plans. They may then serve as future contacts for you.

INFORMATIONAL INTERVIEWS

One of the most effective ways to network is through what is often called an *informational interview.* These are usually limited to one meeting and require you as the interviewer to be prepared (i.e., research!). An informational interview is *not* a job interview and shouldn't be used to ask for a job (although it may ultimately lead to one). Rather, it is a way to discover paths to particular jobs.

To start with, you should target people who are in career fields that interest you. (Your possible contacts can be found through the strategies listed in the networking section above.) For instance, contact your high school or college career center or alumni affairs office for a list of graduates in a particular career area. Once you have acquired a list of names, initiate contact through either a phone call or letter. When contacting prospective interviewees, explain that you are considering entering the career field in which they work and would like to talk to them for information and advice.

STRUCTURE OF THE BIG MEET

Informational interviews are typically 30 minutes to one hour in duration, and you should request an amount of time in that range when contacting people. The interviews themselves can be conducted in several locations, but we suggest that you ask the interviewee which arena he would prefer. It's ideal to meet at the interviewee's workplace so you can get a peek at the work environment. This allows you to get a more complete picture of the climate of the office and industry. If, for some reason, that is not possible, you can also meet at some other mutually convenient location. Either way, you should be punctual, arriving about five to ten minutes before the interview is to begin. If a personal interview is not feasible, interviews can also be conducted by telephone. If you mutually decide to conduct a phone interview, you should initiate the call (unless the interviewee asks to do so). Be prepared with a copy of your resume and a list of questions when calling.

Now That I Have the Interview, What Do I Do?

Preparation for the informational interview should involve some knowledge of the field and the interviewee's organization, being clear about your purpose for conducting the interview, and being equipped with intelligent questions. Below is a list of related questions for you to consider when preparing for an informational interview:

Educational Preparation:

- How did you get into the profession?
- What degree/academic training is needed for a job in the field?
- Is any other prior experience required?
- What preparation would you suggest for someone interested in entering this field?

Interviewee Dirt:

- What do you like most/least about your job?
- What are your major duties or responsibilities?
- What is a typical day/average week like in your job?
- How many hours per week do you or your colleagues work?
- What skills and abilities do you find are most important in your work?
- What are some of the problems you encounter in trying to accomplish your goals?

Employer Dirt:

- What is the size and geographic locations of your organization?
- How does this position fit into your organizational structure?
- With whom in your organization do you have the most contact?
- What do you think about the way the organization operates?
- Is there currently a demand for employees in this field?
- Where are the windows of opportunity within the profession?
- How long does it take to move from one step to the next in this field? What are the salary ranges for the different levels in this field?

Advice for You:

- Do you have any special advice for someone entering this field?
- How is my background suited for a job in this field?
- Do you have any feedback on my resume or cover letter?
- What approach do you suggest I take from here?
- Could you suggest other people in the field with whom I could speak?

You may bring a list of some of these questions to the interview, but try to keep the tone of the interview conversational. This is not a military investigation; you do not want it to appear that you are simply rifling off questions at the interviewee. As you may have noticed, most of the questions listed above are open-ended, encouraging more of a dialogue. The informational interview should be treated as a serious, businesslike meeting, even if you are speaking with someone you already know. Remember to dress professionally for the interview, wearing something that is appropriate for the career field. Bring several copies of you resume in case the interviewee wants one or would like to forward one to somebody else.

What if the Tables Turn?

Now, all of this advice is swell, but what happens if the interviewee turns the tables and starts interviewing you? As we've warned, you should do your research before conducting informational interviews, and that also includes self-examination. There are some general interview questions you should *always* be prepared to answer or discuss, even if you are just beginning your informational interviews or your job search as a whole. These questions may include, but are certainly not limited to, the following:

- How did you become interested in this field?

- What skills could you bring to this field/job?

- What have you learned from your other job experiences that leads you to this field?

- How did you choose your college major?

Being able to answer these broad questions shows that you have put some thought into the career decision-making process.

Names, Names, Names

After you have conducted an interview, ask the person you've met for names of other people who might serve as possible resources. If you make it a point to always leave an informational interview with another name, your networking circle just got that much bigger. Interviewing more than one person in a career field also ensures that you do not get a "slanted view" of a particular job—all the better when you're making decisions about your career.

SHADOWING EXPERIENCES

Informational interviews are usually a "one shot deal." If you are interested in gaining even more in-depth information about a particular job, try the *shadowing experience*. No, we're not talking about following around your potential job contact in a raincoat and sunglasses. The term "shadowing" in this case refers to spending one or several days following a person through a typical work day(s). It allows you as the shadower to gain a glimpse at "a day in the life" of a particular career. For instance, let's say you were interested in advertising and your mother has a friend who is in fact an advertising executive for a well-known firm. Through the shadowing experience, you might be able to get a more intensive view of what a job in advertising actually involves. Not only can you ask questions, you might be able to sit in on a research meeting about a particular product, and come in contact with more than one of the key players at a given organization. Networking at its best!

To set up a shadowing experience, you can call or write to your contact. You can also preface such an experience with an informational interview. In any case, you should explain to your contacts that you are considering entering the career field in which they work and would like to shadow them for a short period of time. This task can be accomplished in half a day, one whole day, or two to three full days. It is best to ask your contacts for the specific format and schedule that would best suit them. You should be warned that shadowing may be difficult in some professions, such as psychology or law, where there is a large amount of client contact and where client confidentiality is important. Here again, it is best to ask your shadowing contact persons what is most appropriate.

Be Equipped and Prepared!

You should bring several copies of your resume to the shadowing experience. You may be introduced to someone where offering a copy of your resume would be appropriate. Also, bring a pad of paper and pen. You may want to note some observations or write down some key questions. While at the shadowing site, remain unobtrusive. Ask your shadowing contact if you can ask questions as the day progresses or if you should save them for the end of the day. Remember, you are there to observe your contact persons and interrupt their day as little as possible.

As with any of the other networking opportunities we've mentioned, the same rules apply: dress and act in a professional manner and don't assume that this experience will lead to a job. The main purpose of these experiences is to expand your networking circle during the job search.

Thanks for the Memories

A thank you note isn't just a pleasant thought if you can find the time, it is a *requirement* after an informational interview or shadowing experience (and all other interviews, for that matter). Your contact person has taken time out of a busy day to talk to you, so show your appreciation—and make sure you do so within forty-eight hours after the meeting. The thank you note should be concise and businesslike, referring to the meeting and perhaps a sentence or two about what you learned. You should also thank the interviewer for any additional contacts that were offered. (See the section on writing thank you notes in chapter 7 on page 212.).

Even if you claim to have the sharpest memory on the planet, keep a log of your meetings including with whom you met, when you met, how you were put in contact with that person, and when you sent your thank-you note. Although this may seem a bit over the top, it offers an organized approach to the networking process. As your list of contacts becomes more lengthy and your networking web more complicated, you will be glad that you were so methodical. It also allows you to keep in contact with your networking acquaintances, something that many of them would appreciate.

SURFING THE NET, SPINNING THE WEB

Recently, a number of factors have converged to bring Internet job searching to the fore. Personal computers, modems, and the software that makes them tick are not only more affordable than ever before, they are also faster and more powerful, making cyber communication a relative breeze. There has been a virtual explosion in the numbers of those who have hooked up to the Internet, with some estimates running as high as 20 million in the U.S. alone. In addition, many employers have finally caught on to the fact that there is an enormous pool of talented, technologically savvy job seekers just a mouse click away. They have also recognized that using the Internet as a recruitment tool is economically prudent since it costs far less to announce job vacancies online than it does to place an ad in a newspaper or contract with a headhunter.

Reality Bytes Again

While some job search experts claim that the Internet has revolutionized the way job hunting is done, we won't go quite that far. The Internet is certainly a useful tool, but definitely not a substitute for any of the other techniques, methods, or resources that we cover throughout this book.

Although you may not actually get hired over the Internet, it is nevertheless an excellent networking tool, providing you with easy access to vast numbers of people in your field of interest through mailing lists, newsgroups, bulletin boards, and chat groups. For those of you who are shy, anxious, or flat out terrified about face-to-face networking with strangers, online networking is a much less scary experience. The Internet can also be a huge aid to the job hunter who is researching prospective employers as it provides a gateway to enormous warehouses of information, making it easier than ever before to gather data on literally thousands of organizations.

So what are we really saying? Don't run out tomorrow and sign up for an Internet account just because you've heard a lot of hype about electronic job search. First, perfect the other strategies we've discussed throughout this book, then use the Internet as a complement to those. If you decide you would like to check out the cyberscene, start off by approaching a friend who's already online, or experiment from a free site such as the one at your local public library, or if you're still a student, at your campus computing facility or career center. Even if you don't find a job or develop any good employment contacts through the Internet, you'll have at least picked up another marketable skill which you can slap on your resume and discuss at an interview.

"The Internet is only part of the job search journey, not the destination. Where the Internet is most effective is as a networking and research tool. It allows you to break the ice with minimal anxiety, and find information in minutes that used to take days to find in a library."

John Aigner, Director, The Livelihood Center

Surf City, Here We Come

If you're already familiar with the Internet, using it as a job search tool should be a piece of cake. You're going to use all the same tricks you've already learned, but instead of chatting someone up online, looking for the coolest graphics you can find on the web, or downloading the latest games, you're going to focus on your job search. Just about everything you can do off-line regarding your job hunt you can also do online. You can network with pros in your field, research industries and employers, scope out job listings, post your resume and cover letter for review by employers, and get advice from career counselors. Just be careful to take notes on where you found the most helpful items. We strongly suggest you keep a list of e-mail and Web addresses, particularly those that you frequently access.

We Are Family

One of the great things about the Internet is that it really does have the feel of a close-knit community. More experienced users are often eager to help out newbies (the lame term for internet novices), so odds are that if you ask questions nicely you are likely to get helpful responses. Just don't ask any questions until you thoroughly read all the help and "FAQ" (frequently asked questions) documents that have been posted by the service or group that you're investigating.

Another plus of the Internet is that because for all practical purposes, you are anonymous when you go online. You don't have to contend with the prejudices, biases, and misconceptions that typically accompany a face-to-face meeting. You will eventually have to meet your future boss, but by that point you will have established a positive rapport through your online communications.

> *"The thing one needs to recognize... is that most of the jobs listed on the Internet are technology/engineering oriented. We tend to consider leads on the Net as just other eggs in the basket. In the end, it's whoever can personally sell themselves and network the best that gets hired. Still, it's mind-boggling to think of all the company information floating out there in cyberspace that was previously so hard to find!"*
>
> **Alexis Lucas, Director, Career Center,**
> **Boston University School of Management**

Hooking Up

If you're still a student, your best and least expensive option is to obtain an Internet account through your university. If you've already graduated, you basically have two remaining choices—signing on with a commercial service provider, such as America OnLine or Compuserve, or gaining access through a direct connection provider. Some cyberphiles claim the latter typically offers better service and faster connection times. The advantage of the big boys is that they provide special services, forums, and exclusive online events. They also tend to be less intimidating for online neophytes and technophobes. These services typically offer free trial packages with the purchase of new software, computers, or computer-related magazines, so you have nothing to lose if you want to try a test run.

Alternative methods of accessing the Internet include connecting through free sites at public libraries (beware of long lines and strict time limits), through Internet cafes or copy shops (watch those high hourly rates), or through your workplace (don't let your boss catch you).

THE WORLD WIDE WEB

The World Wide Web is the fastest growing sector of the Internet, and probably the most enjoyable to use since it supports graphics, sound, motion, and text. More importantly, the Web probably contains the most valuable information for the online job seeker. On the Web you can search through job listings, post your resume, and research prospective employers, all by just pointing and clicking your mouse. Navigating the web is relatively easy thanks to the development of hypertext and hypergraphics, which enable you to connect to multiple websites from a single page by clicking on a highlighted phrase or picture. Alternatively, you can type in the URL (Uniform Resource Locator) of the site you would like to access, and bingo, you're there. Beware, though, that some of the captivating graphics and images for which the Web is renowned can take an inordinate amount of time to materialize on your monitor, particularly if you are using a slower modem. In fact, use anything less than a 14.4 modem (although we strongly recommend 28.8) and you may find surfing the Web to be a wipeout.

Questions to Consider When Choosing an Internet Service Provider

- *How long has the company been in business?*
- *What kind of equipment does the provider have? Is it state-of-the-art?*
- *Does the service provide full Internet access? If not, which sectors are off limits?*
- *Is the software provided by the service easy to use?*
- *What kind of technical support is available and what hours does the "help desk" maintain?*
- *How much does the service cost? Are there any hidden fees or surcharges?*
- *Does the service enable you to mount your own home page on the World Wide Web?*
- *What modem speeds are supported?*
- *How many lines does the service have coming in? Is it easy to establish a connection?*

Perhaps the most frustrating part of using the World Wide Web is searching its massive warehouse of goodies to find what you really want. You'll need one or more search engines to make the most of what the Web has to offer. Some popular search engines include Alta Vista (http://www.altavista.com), Excite (http://www.excite.com), Infoseek (http://www.infoseek.com), Hot Bot (http://www.hotbot.com), Look Smart (http://www.mulwala.loosmart.com:8080), and Yahoo (http://www.yahoo.com). These vary in the number of URLs they catalogue, the extent to which they index an entire web site, what kinds of subjects they index, and how often they are updated. For a comprehensive list of the search engines currently available visit http://cuiwww.unige.ch/meta-index.html.

TPR'S LIST OF TOP WEBSITES FOR THE JOB SEEKER

JobWeb   http://www.jobweb.org

This is the home page for the National Association of Colleges and Employers, the umbrella organization which governs college career planning centers around the country. JobWeb was rated as one of the top 25 electronic recruitment sites on the Internet by Internet

Business Network and is a good place to begin your quest. In addition to offering job listings, company profiles, and a variety of other career-related information, JobWeb provides excellent links to job banks, databases, newsgroups and more.

Career Mosaic http://www.careermosaic.com

Features J.O.B.S., a searchable database containing thousands of job listings, Resume CM, a place where you can post your resume so it can be accessed by employers, and the Career Resource Center, where you can get tips on all aspects of the job search.

JOBTRAK http://www.jobtrak.com

JOBTRAK has formed a partnership with over 400 college and university career centers and claims to be utilized by over 250,000 employers. If you are a student or alum from one of the member schools (there is a list of member schools online) you can gain access to the more than 2,100 new jobs that are posted every day. JOBTRAK also features a Guide to Graduate Schools, listing of career fairs, and links to many other sites.

The Monster Board http://www.monster.com

Provides access to more than 50,000 job opportunities worldwide which can be searched by location, industry, company name, or keyword. You can also post your resume online to increase your exposure to potential employers. Other resources include employer profiles and a listing of career events such as job fairs.

Getting Past Go
http://lattanze.loyola.edu/MonGen/home.html

This site is geared to new and recent college grads, and provides assistance with resume writing, finding jobs, scoping out new locations, and keeping up with the Net.

Espan http://www.espan.com

This site was rated best in its class by Internet Business Network. It provides access to thousands of job listings, employer profiles, and an immense library of job search resources for both the job seeker and the human resources professional.

Online Career Center http://www.occ.com

This site offers a database of job listings searchable by industry and location, a database of job seekers' resumes which is searchable by employers, and company information and profiles.

CareerPath http://www.careerpath.com

You'll need lots of espresso to search the more than 105,000 help wanted ads from 25 newspapers across the country, including the

New York Times, Boston Globe, Chicago Tribune, Washington Post, and *Los Angeles Times.*

Taxi's Newspaper List
http://www.deltanet.com/users/taxicat/e_papers.html
Provides links to numerous newspapers throughout the world and the U.S. Helpful for the long distance job hunter.

Meta-Index of Non-Profits
http://www.philanthropy_journal.org
Provides comprehensive information on the world of philanthropy as well as an award-winning meta-index of nonprofit organizations.

Editor & Publisher Interactive
http://www.mediainfo.com/edpub
Links to over 600 electronic newspapers worldwide. Helpful for uncovering articles about potential employers.

You may also want to check out *NetGuide* and *The Net,* two monthly magazines that list and review new websites.

MAILING LISTS
Joining a mailing list is a little like subscribing to an interactive periodical that has no set publication schedule. You can read the letters, comments, or articles that other subscribers send in, as well as contribute your own remarks. The information comes to you as e-mail and may arrive on a daily, weekly, or monthly basis depending on how active the group is. Mailing lists tend to focus on a particular topic or subject area such as an industry. They can be used both as a networking and information gathering tool. To join a mailing list, you must subscribe by sending an e-mail message in the specified format to the appropriate list administrator. To find the lists that are most relevant for your job search, try using the following search engines located on the World Wide Web:

> http://www.nova.edu/Inter-Links/listserv.html

> http://www.liszt.com

> http://www.tile.net/tile/listserv/index.html

Extra! Extra! Read All About Newsgroups!
Despite their name, newsgroups are not encounter sessions for journalists. They are simply discussion groups, created and maintained by the people who use them. At last count there were over 20,000 of them accessible through Internet. Newsgroups deal with just about every subject imaginable, and for the job seeker can be an

excellent source of career-related information, job leads, and networking contacts.

Once you're on the Internet you can go directly to a newsgroup, if you know its address, or you can use DejaNews (www.dejanews.com), a search engine, to find the newsgroups related to your area of interest. In addition, the Career Mosaic Web site (www.careermosaic.com) features a sizable list of job search related newsgroups.

When you visit a newsgroup you'll have an opportunity to browse through all the messages that have been posted by the group's members (sometimes these number in the hundreds), download those that interest you, and if you like, post your own messages in response. If the group focuses mainly on your field of interest, you might even want to post your resume for the other members to review, or at least a general inquiry concerning the availability of jobs that might be appropriate given your qualifications.

Bulletin Board Systems

Bulletin Board Systems, also known as BBSs, are actually not part of the Internet, but since we're talking computers, this seems to be a good place to mention them. BBS is software that enables a computer to serve as a message board. As a user, once you dial up and log on to a BBS via your modem, you can post your own messages, as well as read those posted by others. You can also download files that have been stored on the system. Typically, each bulletin board has a particular theme, so it is likely that the people who visit have common interests. Thus, if you are able to find a bulletin board that focuses on your field of interest, there is a good chance you may be able to learn more about employment opportunities in your field and the companies that offer them. You can also network with potential employers and, if appropriate, post your resume for review.

MAXIMIZING CAMPUS RESOURCES

Your college or university career office can be a veritable Land of Oz on the Planet Job Search. Unfortunately, too few students and alumni make that trip down the Yellow Brick Road to take advantage of this amazing service. Some have been swayed by grapevine gospel that proclaims, "They only have jobs for business majors and engineers" or "They can't help me find a job five thousand miles from my hometown."

Having worked in six different campus career centers around this country, we find it particularly frustrating that this valuable resource is so often underutilized. Where else under one roof can you get counseling to choose a career direction, attend workshops on every technique related to job search, peruse listings of job openings (some listed exclusively with your school!), find names of people in many industries willing to help with your search, and interview with prospective employers without ever having to leave campus—all for free or at a very low cost?

Despite our obvious bias toward the value of these places, we do admit that some college career offices deserve their bad rap. Many are understaffed and stretched too thin with limited resources and services. When the career guidebooks on the shelf are from 1967 and all the job listings were filled two years ago, it's hard to have confidence in the office. These problems are usually through no fault of their own but may be due to budget cutbacks or lack of recognition from the university administration. Luckily this scenario is becoming increasingly rare, as career centers diversify, improve, and expand their services. Many are also embarking on "marketing campaigns" to make their offerings better known across campus and to convey a more accessible image.

As an undergraduate, you'll probably find that there is one central career office that serves students of all majors. Graduate and professional school students usually use satellite offices on campus that specialize in careers and jobs in that one field, or might use the same office as the undergrads. If you're an alum, check into services available to you, if any, either on-campus or long distance. Many offices work with alumni at no cost or for low fees. Let's look at the ways the career development office may be able to help, depending on its size, scope, and services:

JOB LISTINGS

Most career centers list full-time and part-time positions for students and graduates. These are sometimes posted in books to browse through or on viewing boards. It's becoming more common for jobs to be listed online as college career centers become technologically advanced and set up databases for use in the office or via e-mail from the comfort of your dorm room or apartment.

The quantity and quality of job listings depend on the office's job development efforts, and to a large part on the geographical location of the campus. If you want a job in San Francisco, but your college is in a small town in North Carolina, you might not find too many listings. Don't despair. As we told you in the Planning Your Strategy section, there are plenty of other ways to find a job long-distance, many of which can be found in the career development office.

If you are an alum living far from the area of your alma mater, inquire about any newsletters the career office publishes. Many have free or low-cost subscriptions available to newsletters listing jobs that are also posted on campus. You get the benefits of using your college career office without having to travel. Like any newspaper listings, though, there's no guarantee that these jobs will still be open by the time the newsletter gets to you, but you can still contact organizations that interest you to network for future openings.

ON-CAMPUS RECRUITING

When people claim that college isn't the so-called Real World, it's hard to argue with them when you look at something like a campus recruitment program. Think about it. All you typically have to do is go to an informational meeting to hear about the program, then look through a book of employers, picking out what you like as if it were a J. Crew catalog. By a certain deadline, you drop off copies of your resume to the Recruitment Coordinator. Then, if selected to interview, you sign up for a time slot. On the day of the interview, you put on a suit, mosey across campus, and do your stuff for perhaps as short a time as fifteen minutes.

How ideal. No cold calls to make, no cover letters to write (usually), no traveling to an office building. On-campus interviewing is such a convenient method of looking for jobs, we suggest you take advantage of this service if you're a graduating senior or in a graduate program that offers it. (On-campus recruiting is, unfortunately, rarely open to alumni.)

Now, before you get too excited, we don't mean to make this method sound totally easy or to imply that it's an automatic ticket to interviews and a job. It *is* a competitive and time-consuming process, which you can't afford to approach passively. You still have to write an effective resume and have the qualifications they're looking for to be in the running.

If you do have what the employers are looking for, and if you meet all the deadlines of the program and treat the campus recruitment staff with courtesy, then you have a good shot at getting a job through on-campus recruiting. If the employers involved in your school's program fit your interests, then by all means make use of this job search method while you still can.

INFORMATION SESSIONS AND CAREER PANELS

Don't think that job listings and the recruitment program are the only way to find jobs using your campus resources. As we've said before, finding a job requires a combination of approaches, with research and networking as integral parts of the process. Most undergraduate and graduate school career offices offer many different ways to learn about various types of jobs, career paths, and specific employers. The companies that participate in on-campus recruiting usually come on campus well before interview time to conduct an informational session. Whether you plan to participate in the recruitment program or not, attending these sessions is extremely useful for getting to know who and what's out there and where you might fit in.

A related event is what is often called a "career panel." Schools with strong alumni support may have alumni come on campus to discuss their careers in a particular field. The event is usually structured like a panel discussion with each alum making a presentation about his or her work, then a roundtable discussion or question and answer period typically follows. You might, for example, attend a panel discussion on environmental careers with an environmental scientist, a researcher from an environmental think-tank, a policy analyst from a government agency on the environment, and a manager from a waste management corporation. These events are great opportunities to find out all the ways one can build a career around an interest area and also to learn strategies for entering and advancing in a field. By following up with the participants after the event, you can also expand your job search network.

ALUMNI LISTINGS

Some career development offices have listings of alumni who have volunteered to serve as a resource for current students or other graduates. The names are often listed in books or computer databases you can look through in the office or are available by mail when you make a formal request for a search of alumni in a given geographical area and/or career field or industry. Occasionally, these listings are administered through the alumni relations office rather than the career center.

These generous colleagues of yours may be available for informational interviews by phone or in person and might even know of actual job openings or internship opportunities. Just because these alumni have offered to help, however, doesn't mean you can assume they'll get you a job. Like we discussed in the networking section of this chapter, relationships need to be cultivated carefully, slowly, and with common courtesy. You can't expect an alum to get you a job without even knowing you. Consider these people to be sources of information only, and you might end up pleasantly surprised when they turn out to be sources of jobs as well.

HIGH-TECH SERVICES

Some college and university career development offices have home pages on the Web that give you an orientation to the office. These pages usually include descriptions of services, office hours, calendars of special events, and how-to information on getting internships, finding jobs, conducting research, etc.

Depending on the office's budget and size of the school, you might find lots of technology to help you inside the career center as well. Some have databases of employers, library resources on CD-ROM like the Department of Labor guides to careers, or self-guided career counseling computer programs to help you find a focus. The value of this hi-tech approach over the human touch is still up for debate. If your school's career center isn't decked out like a pantheon to the gods of electronic communication, don't feel you're being slighted. As long as there are a few well-trained human beings around to help you, you *can* find a job without all the fancy technology.

CAREER INFORMATION LIBRARY

The library (as we mentioned in the Compiling Your Hit List section of chapter 3) is an essential place to start your job search. Guidebooks describing various career fields or job search techniques can often be found in a good college career center. If the office has an on-campus recruiting program, you're also likely to find company profiles, and annual reports, and even videos on companies or career fields. These libraries also often contain brief handouts called "Tip Sheets" or "Fact Sheets" which give you a quick education in some part of the job search process.

COUNSELING

So many students and alumni make frequent visits to their career centers to use the library or peruse the job listings, never realizing that their search would be a lot easier if they actually talked to somebody. Most career offices offer individual counseling sessions on a drop-in basis or by appointment. You can use these sessions for help with choosing a career, planning a job search strategy, writing resumes and cover letters, or preparing for interviews. You may also be able to learn about these topics in group workshops, where you have the benefit of seeing other students go through the same process and can get their input.

If you are a graduate not living near your alma mater, find out about any counseling available by phone. Some schools also have career representatives in various parts of the country who can advise you, often through the local alumni club.

Also, find out if your alma mater's career development office has a reciprocity arrangement with any colleges or universities near you. Some have ongoing reciprocal agreements, while others do so on an informal, ad hoc basis. The way it usually works is that a counselor (or perhaps the director) of your school's career office writes a letter to the career center of a college or university near where you live asking them to allow you admittance to their office. If the school near you agrees, then you have access to their services, usually on a limited basis.

Reciprocity arrangements typically give you permission to use the career information library and perhaps receive some counseling, often only on a "drop-in" or "walk-in" basis rather than in formal appointments. Some schools allow you to view their job listings (which is why you're really there in the first place), but many reserve the listings only for their own students and graduates. Even so, just having access to a career library to conduct research and having the chance to talk to a career counselor is better than going it alone.

Tips for Making the Most of Your College Career Center

1. It's Never Too Early or Too Late to Go
It doesn't hurt to stop in freshman year to find out about internships, put together a first resume, and plan ways to explore your career interests over the next few years. On the other hand, if it's second semester senior year and you're feeling well behind the eight ball, don't think it's too late to visit. You might have missed out on some deadlines, but you can always get advice on a postgraduate job search. As an alum, don't feel you're too old to go back to campus for help. In career centers where we've worked, we've seen alumni come in to prepare for post-retirement careers!

2. Take Initiative
Even though many career offices try to market themselves around campus, they don't always get the message out adequately. You might have to take it upon yourself to find out what they have to offer. Don't just sit around your dorm room or apartment saying "They don't have anything for me" or feeling intimidated by the stream of dark suited, eager interviewees marching into the office looking all focused and put together. The career office is for everyone. Go over and see for yourself. You might be pleasantly surprised.

Also, a note to students who believe that career offices can only help blond-haired, blue-eyed, heterosexual, American-born students with 3.9 GPAs: You'll be amazed at the range of resources available. Whether it's a book on the best companies in America for gays and lesbians, or a counselor specially trained in career issues for the learning disabled, or an alumni network for students of color, you won't know about all the great resources until you set foot in the place.

3. Don't Just Focus on Job Listings

Just as reading the classified ads in the Sunday city paper, is not the best way to get a job, passively browsing through a book of job listings in your campus career center is a pretty ineffectual method as well. Make use of the full range of resources available to you.

4. Hang Out and Make Friends

While college career centers are not in the habit of practicing favoritism, it's a fact that the students who are most visible to the staff of the career office are often the first to hear about jobs. Think about it—it's all about being in the right place at the right time and doing so with courtesy, tact, and patience. We don't mean you should be a pest and hover over desks annoying people. Just try to get to know some key people in the office. Usually, that's the person at the front desk, the job listing clerk (who might double as receptionist), at least one career counselor, and often the director.

5. Give Something Back

By "give," we don't necessarily mean money. This is not a suggestion to have Daddy endow a new building for the career center so that you can get a job. What we mean is help out and get involved wherever you can. Some offices have peer advisors who receive training from the professional career counselors to help other students with such things as resumes or practice interviewing. There is often a need for a student to operate video equipment for mock interviews, help students format their resumes at the computer center, lead discussion groups or arrange workshops in the dorms, or stuff envelopes with resumes for the on-campus recruitment coordinator. Whether you're an official part-time employee of the office through a work-study program or just offer to help out with special projects on a volunteer basis, you'll be on the inside track for jobs and will be doing something worthwhile for the office and your fellow students.

As an alum, ask how you can get involved in career panels, peer advising, or just being on a resource list. Not only is it a nice thing to do, it makes you visible to the counselors who can keep you in mind when they hear of interesting opportunities.

CAREER AND JOB FAIRS

The terms "Employment Fair," "Career Fair," and "Job Fair" are interchangeable terms used to describe an event where a large number of employers congregate to interview job candidates. The Job Fair may not be your idea of a good time, but it can be most helpful in your job search. Where else can you find upwards of 100 organizations in the same physical space looking for people to hire? Talk about not having to ruin the soles on your new interview shoes!

Career and Job Fairs are typically held by college career centers or a consortium of organizations with a particular focus or interest. There are not-for-profit fairs, business/financial service fairs, and minority career fairs, to name a few. The purpose of these fairs is to get the largest number of job candidates into the same room with the largest number of organizations with positions to fill. Pretty convenient, huh?

Because of the unique nature of the Career and Job Fair, you need to follow some just-as-unique steps to make yourself a successful job candidate at one of these events.

RESEARCH!

The only way to find out about these events is by doing your research. These events are usually publicized through college career centers, specific industry or trade association journals, and area newspapers. If you're still in school, stop by your college career center to see if any are posted and, if so, when and where they are to take place.

Also try to conduct research on the organizations to be in attendance. Be realistic here. If 100 organizations are scheduled to be present at the fair, don't feel that you must chain yourself to the library for four weeks prior to the fair to learn something about *every* company. If you can prioritize the companies, and really focus your energies on researching those that interest you the most, you may save some semblance of your sanity.

RESUME MADNESS

You should go to the job fair prepared. This means dressing professionally and bringing ample copies of your resume. How many? Well, first find out how many companies are to be represented at the event. This can usually be done by contacting the sponsoring organization of the fair. To be on the safe side, you should bring one resume for every represented organization. Chances are you won't be interested in every organization, but it's better to be safe than sorry.

Some job fairs have what is called a "resume drop" as you enter the fair. You submit one copy of your resume, which is scanned and then available to every organization at the fair. Even if you attend a fair with such a format, it never hurts to have hard copies of your resume available when speaking with an organizational representative or recruiter.

TIME IS OF THE ESSENCE

Get to the job fair early!! If you do, it's usually less crowded and you will have more individual time with organizational reps. Fewer people mean less competition for attention. A woman recently told us that she wholeheartedly believes that she received three interviews from attending a recent fair because she got there promptly at the time the fair was to begin. She was able to speak with representatives at length without interruptions from other attendees, allowing her time to "sell" her skills.

We also suggest the earlier part of the day rather than the later when people are fresher and more apt to want to talk. Very often people are all talked out at the end of these events!

INTERVIEWS

Recruiters may ask you to interview on the spot at career fairs, or they may ask you to come to their office at a later time. In any case, be prepared to talk about your interests and discuss your resume while there. If interested in boning up on your interviewing techniques, review chapter 6. Do remember, however, that the interviews at career fairs can be a slightly different bird. They are obviously not as private, and your surroundings may be somewhat chaotic. Remain focused and try not to become flustered by noise and interruptions.

FOLLOW UP

If you interview with any recruiters, determine the next course of action so you are clear what the next step will be (Will they be in touch? Should you phone them?). Whatever you do, don't forget to get a business card or other company information with an address and the name of the recruiters with whom you interviewed. Why? So you can follow up with a thank you note. In your thank you note you should remind them where you met. Try to make several specific references to your conversation so they might more easily identify you. You may also want to include another copy of your resume for their records.

Career Fairs can be a great way to target a large number of employers at one time. Use your time and energy wisely.

ANSWERING CLASSIFIED ADVERTISEMENTS

"You'll never find a job through the paper." That's the one piece of job search advice you're most likely to hear, whether you're a recent grad with a liberal arts major or the former CEO of a major corporation. The statement is common because it's frequently true, especially for entry-level job seekers.

The odds against getting a job from an ad are enormous. First of all, positions listed in the paper tend to require levels of experience and job-related skills that entry-level people haven't had a chance to acquire. If a company lists an opening in the paper, it's usually because they're looking for something really specific like "a certified public accountant with a Ph.D. in English Literature and 9.2 years experience filing income tax returns for circus performers." Employers don't need to pay for an ad in the paper to attract "an energetic recent graduate with a liberal arts major and a willingness to learn." Those, unfortunately, are a dime a dozen. It's more likely that you'll go knocking on their door than that they will come knocking on yours.

Sometimes, you *will* find jobs listed for entry-level candidates. Many newspapers even have a "College Grad" section within the Help Wanted ads. While some of these ads might describe jobs that are right up your alley, it's more likely that there's a catch to watch out for. Either the position is much more clerical than it sounds, with little opportunity for advancement beyond secretary, or the job might be with a fly-by-night company that folds a week after you sign on.

Many positions listed in the College Grad section are for sales jobs, some of which are with legitimate companies needing recent grads. Stockbroker trainee is also a typical position to see advertised. These and other sales positions are listed so frequently because there's often high turnover with these jobs. If you don't cut the mustard after a couple weeks of cold-calling for prospects, or if you find you can't survive on commission alone, then you're likely to bail out and the job will end up in the paper again. Administrative assistant jobs are also frequently found in this section of the paper. These postings are often the tuna surprise of entry-level jobs.

They can be springboards into higher positions with loads of cool responsibilities—or they can be the drudgery of life, leaving you with nightmarish dreams of evil file cabinets come to life.

If you do find a position in the paper that you're qualified for, brace yourself for some overwhelming competition. It's not that the quality of other applications is necessarily that much better than yours, it's a quantity issue. Job ads can attract hundreds or thousands of responses, so yours is just one of many that ends up on the recruiter's desk. Since we don't think sending a singing telegram or filling your resume envelope with confetti are particularly good ideas, there's not much you can do to stand out from the crowd except to write a top-notch letter and resume.

Despite all the negatives associated with classified ads, people do find jobs through the paper every day. We've witnessed success with our clients time and again. To up the odds of having this approach work for you, consider these tips:

1. Use More Than One Source for Ads.

Most everybody turns to the Sunday edition of their local big city paper for classified ad reading. Remember the Sunday ritual we described with our waffle-eating friend in chapter 1's virtual reality? There's nothing wrong with using the Sunday paper since it *is* where you'll find the most extensive array of listings; just keep in mind that positions are listed during the weekday editions, too, and may get fewer responses and therefore have less competition.

Check out the ads in other types of publications as well, including neighborhood and community papers, trade and professional association papers, journals, or newsletters, and also some magazines. Hone in on publications with content representative of the job you're looking for. A New York job seeker is more likely to find an ad for a tattoo artist in the *Village Voice* than in the *Wall Street Journal*.

2. Get Your Timing Right.

Generally speaking, you want to answer ads promptly. It's the old "early bird gets the worm" mentality. Sometimes jobs being advertised in the paper have already been announced on the company bulletin board, so interviews may be underway with current employees looking to advance within the company or with friends and relatives of those employees. By law, a position advertised in the paper cannot already be filled, but in reality, the legal lines get a little blurred. If you respond to an ad right away, you might pique the employer's interest before any final decisions are made.

There is also a school of thought that says to wait a few days or even a week before mailing a resume so that your entry stands out and doesn't get lost in the shuffle. This is pretty logical advice since most employers get a flurry of responses in the first two days and often don't even go through the resumes until a week or two have passed.

What if you find an ad that's a few weeks old? It's still okay to reply because interviews might not have started right away and a decision hasn't been made, so you can still get in the race. Sometimes you see ads listed repeatedly for a few weeks because there might be no rush in filling the job. If the ad is a few months old or more, the job is likely to have been filled, but it doesn't hurt to respond. The person originally hired might not have worked out and the position opened up again, or at the very least, you've tossed your name into the hat for any future openings.

3. Read Between the Lines.

Realizing that all that glitters is not gold, you should scrutinize ads with a critical eye. Remember a job ad is an *ad*. Just as the Coca-Cola Company wants you to drink Coke, and PepsiCo wants you to drink Pepsi, Company Y wants to get more responses from well qualified applicants than Company Z. The more responses they get, the better their chances of finding the right person for the job, thus justifying the expense and trouble of advertising.

Don't be swayed by the big display ads—the ones that appear in a box and take up more space than the little ads, maybe with some eye-catching graphics or bold type. Bigger does not always mean better jobs. The traditional small ads may come from smaller to medium-sized companies that are more secure employers anyway.

"Nothing in fine print is ever good news."

Andy Rooney

Watch out for jobs that sound overly glamorous:

> *"Get your start in the dynamic world of television! Interact with top media executives! Creative, energetic, self-starters with college degrees needed! No experience necessary."*

Sound too good to be true? Read the fine print: "Typing 60 w.p.m." "Call Ms. Jones (333) 555-5555." Ms. Jones works for an employment agency that is looking to place a receptionist who will pour coffee and type very fast for high-strung middle managers in a television assembly plant.

As we'll tell you later in this chapter, there's nothing wrong with most employment agencies. They can often be a good resource for entry-level jobs, and sometimes pouring coffee and answering the phones is the only way to get a foot in the door of a career. We're just saying here that you need to keep your eyes wide open and not be swayed by the commercial nature of some classified ads.

4. Take Extra Care with Your Resume and Letter.

Unlike with other job search methods, everything is riding on the resume and cover letter, and to a lesser extent, on your credentials and experience, when you answer ads. You're just an anonymous applicant reduced to words on paper and subject to the whims of the person interpreting your qualifications.

To avoid papering your walls with rejection letters, first realize that your letter and resume will probably be read by a screener, not by the person doing the actual hiring. If you don't directly meet the basic criteria outlined in the ad, your resume is likely to be tossed into the circular file. The screener is unlikely to have the time or ability to make a connection between your transferable skills and experience and those required for the job.

It obviously then becomes extremely important to present yourself effectively on paper. The advice we gave in chapter 4 on writing trashproof resumes and cover letters applies here, with a few special points to pay attention to. You must look extra closely at what the ad is *really* asking for, and highlight those qualifications in your cover letter. Listing those highlights as a bulleted list of statements is particularly effective when answering ads since the reader would rather scan a quick list of reasons why you should be interviewed than to have to plow through paragraph after paragraph hunting for your qualifications.

It's also important that the letter be extra concise and short (unless the ad asked for a "detailed" cover letter) since yours is just one of many to be read. If you don't know anything about the employer because it's a "blind ad" (See Tip #5 for an explanation of blind ads), take a fairly traditional approach to the style of the letter. Neutrality works better than humor or a slanted tone when you don't know with whom you're dealing.

Be sure to give all the information asked for in the ad. Requests for salary requirements or a salary history are the most often ignored parts of a classified ad. They wouldn't ask for it if they didn't want it, and your resume is likely to end up being tossed if you don't address the issue. Refer back to pages 110 to 122 of Composing Cover Letters in chapter 4 for guidelines on dealing with the salary issue.

Once you've put together a winning letter and resume, you might be responding to the ad by fax, if requested in the paper. Always follow up a fax with a hard copy by mail if an address was provided or if you can track down the address when a company name is given. If you're given the option of faxing or mailing, do both. If the ad says "No calls," then DO NOT CALL.

5. Understand Blind Ads.

You'll see that many jobs listed are through "blind ads." These are ads that don't tell you the name of the company or organization. They usually include just the company's address or maybe only a post office box or instructions for replying directly to the newspaper. Some companies use blind ads to keep competitors from knowing they're looking for people. It might imply that the company is short-staffed or restructuring and therefore volatile. Sometimes the ad is confidential because they're looking for candidates to fill the position of someone they're about to fire and don't want that person to know. In other cases, they just want to remain anonymous to avoid being barraged with calls or walk-in job seekers.

If only a contact person's name and phone number is given in the ad, or if a name is listed that doesn't tell you anything about the nature of the business like "O'Brien Associates," the ad may have been placed by an employment agency or executive recruiter. They don't give out the name of the company where the job is, because you could then apply directly to that employer, and the agency would miss out on collecting a commission if you're hired.

There's usually no harm in answering a blind ad if the job description sounds appropriate for you. Beware, though, that you are announcing yourself as a job seeker to unknown employers, and your resume could very well end up on your boss's desk. Not a smooth move.

6. Use Your Time Effectively.

Don't waste your time replying to ads for jobs you have only a snowball's chance in hell of getting. The screeners who read five hundred resumes after an ad is placed are not inclined to play mentor for you, saying to themselves, "Well, this guy doesn't have any of the qualifications we're looking for, but he seems to have potential." It's just not going to happen.

Take the case of Barbara, a client of ours who had worked for several years after college as a research and administrative assistant at a university. Barbara was looking to get into sales or marketing to change the nature of her responsibilities and make more money. She was therefore attracted to ads for jobs that she didn't necessarily have experience in but wanted to transition into. She spent several unsuccessful months applying for jobs in sales and marketing through the paper. We know she could have done well in the positions, but she just couldn't get interviews because she didn't have the direct experience and skills they were looking for.

Finding a job through the paper is a tough way to make a career change. We advised Barbara to consider applying for jobs that were closer to what she'd been doing (administration and research) but that were in the sales or marketing department of companies. She did just that and started getting plenty of interviews from her ad responses, eventually getting an administrative position that could lead to the sales and marketing job she wanted.

One exception to the "don't-bother-I-don't-have-what-they're-looking-for" rule is to wait a few weeks after an ad runs and write to express interest in positions that might not have been advertised. If a company advertises for a Director of Marketing to head up a new division, then it stands to reason that other positions might be available in that growing area of the company. They might need administrative assistants or associate directors, or any position you're likely to qualify for. Don't write immediately because your letter is likely to be tossed out as not right for the job advertised. Wait a couple of weeks or even more until their piles of mail have dwindled, and then send a carefully crafted letter explaining your interest and what you have to offer. This works best, of course, with ads that listed the company name so that you can first do a little research to tailor your letter even more to the organization's needs.

7. Start with Low Expectations and End Up Pleasantly Surprised.
Like we said in the opening section of this chapter, never put all your job search eggs in one basket. Answering ads can be an exhausting process, so it's easy to feel justified in resting on your laurels after scrutinizing a bunch of ads and sending out letters and resumes. All too often we hear job seekers regret having put their searches on hold while they waited to hear from the places they'd applied. You could grow really old waiting, so we don't recommend it.

It's not unheard of to get a response months or even a year after an ad was run. Some companies put ads in the paper just to collect resumes for future reference. Others *do* have a current opening available, which they fill soon after placing the ad but then find themselves needing to fill it again several months later. Rather than advertising again, they might simply go to the resumes on file from the last ad, and yours could be one of those. That was the case with a recent client of ours who responded to several ads in July and got two calls from that effort the following January. She was actually still looking for a job since she'd been working all that time and hadn't been in a hurry to leave, so she was surprised but pleased to have the better-late-than-never response.

The basic approach to answering ads is to start out with very low expectations and end up either no worse for the wear if nothing comes of it or pleasantly surprised.

JOB HOTLINES

Although they won't connect you to Wayne Manor or the White House, job hotlines are nevertheless a useful job hunting resource with which you should be familiar. They were created by organizations (generally large corporations) as a cost and time effective measure for coping with the hordes of job hunters that were besieging their human resources departments on a daily basis. Instead of having a staff member devote precious time to responding to each job seeker's inquiry, these companies created recordings listing up to the minute information on job availability and application procedures, which could be accessed simultaneously by multiple callers via a touch-tone phone. Job hotlines save the employer time and money while putting the most salient employment-related information in the hands of the job hunter in a fairly efficient manner. Better yet, job hotlines don't call in sick or go on vacation. They are generally accessible 24 hours a day, 7 days a week, and are typically updated once weekly.

THE COLD SIDE OF HOTLINES

While hotlines can be a useful addition to your job hunting bag of tricks, they also have their down side. For starters, you often must wade through several menus and submenus before you finally get to the information you really want. This can be extremely time-consuming, as well as expensive, particularly if your call is long distance. If the number you're accessing is not toll-free, we recommend calling at off-peak hours to keep your bill down.

Another frustration cited by many job hunters is that hotlines spew forth so much information at such a rapid rate that unless you're a speed writer or know shorthand, odds are you'll have to call back at least a couple of times to get everything down on paper. In our test runs with a variety of job hotlines we had a great deal of difficulty accurately recording, let alone spelling, the information we needed. Our recommendation is to use a speakerphone with a microcassette recorder so that you don't miss anything and then transcribe the tape later.

If you're still willing to give job hotlines a try, check the career section of your local bookstore or library for the *1997 National Job Hotline Directory*, by Marcia Williams and Sue Cubbage (McGraw-Hill). This handy book can help you access thousands of employment opportunities in the private, nonprofit, and public sectors.

DESIGNING DIRECT MAIL CAMPAIGNS

Although for many, the term direct mail conjures up images of frivolous retail catalogs, and annoying offers and solicitations, direct mail is actually a useful technique that on occasion has brought about promising results. A direct mail job search campaign involves three basic steps:

1. Compiling a list of employers that you most want to work for (see Compiling Your Hit List in chapter 3),

2. Developing and sending out customized cover letters and resumes to each employer, regardless of whether or not they have any openings on their staff, and

3. Following up with each employer by phone to try to arrange an interview.

While the success rate of direct mail generally is not high, a recent study conducted by the career center of a major northeastern university found that 15 percent of that institution's 1995 graduating class obtained their first job out of school by contacting the employer directly, typically by mail.

Even if you don't actually land a job or an interview via direct mail, you have at the very least gotten the word out to a group of highly select employers about who you are and what you can do for them. True, they may not have a position available for you right at the moment, but who's to say that two weeks from now something might not open up. Using the direct mail approach demonstrates to the employer that you know what you want, that you know how to do research, and that you have adopted a take-charge attitude with respect to your job search—three positives that just might help you get your foot in the door.

The down side of direct mail (you knew this was coming didn't you) is that, like cold calling, it can be a time-consuming, frustrating, and expensive venture. Let's face it, when you opt for the direct mail approach you're reaching out blindly to employers who in all likelihood have no need for additional staff—in fact, some of them may even be letting employees go. Secondly, tailoring cover letters and resumes to meet the needs of each employer is, to put it mildly, a highly labor intensive process. Finally, sending out dozens of resumes can be quite costly, as can follow-up phone calls, particularly if you're targeting organizations that are far away from home.

If you're going to use direct mail in your job hunt we suggest you go for quality as opposed to quantity, meaning don't do a mass mailing and blanket every firm in your industry with your resume. Instead, make a list of the 15 to 25 firms that you most want to work for, as well as a back-up list of another 25 to 50 should you have no luck with your top choices. Research each one of your target organizations to death. Leave no stone unturned. Make sure that every letter you write and every resume you send makes it painfully obvious to the reader that you understand their organization's needs, and most importantly, that you know how to help them accomplish their objectives.

To guarantee that the person on the receiving end views you as a viable candidate deserving of serious consideration, put your direct mail package together with the care and attention befitting a rare gem. Proofread all your materials carefully, and double check for spelling and grammatical errors. Address your letter to a specific person at the target organization, never just, "sir," "madam," or "to whom it may concern." It is generally best to send your direct mail package to your potential future boss. However, you may also want to send your materials to a human resources representative so that all bases are covered. If you don't have a contact name, call the company directly to get one, and don't forget to ask how the person's name is spelled—also make sure to get their official title. Even if you do already have a contact name it won't hurt to call and doublecheck that the individual is still with the company and is still working in the same capacity.

Feel free to enclose samples (e.g., articles, research, computer programs) of your work if you feel they might help the employer to gain a better sense of your skills.

Once your precious packages have been placed in the hands of the U.S. Postal Service, don't sit back and wait for the phone to ring—it probably won't, at least not for a while. About a week to ten days after each wave of letters (shoot for about 10 per week) goes out, you'll need to conduct a follow-up phone campaign to determine if your packages were received. More importantly, you'll need to try to convince each prospective employer to grant you an interview (review Phone Tactics—chapter 4). Consequently, you'll need to adopt that confident and upbeat phone manner we discussed earlier, in addition to rolling out your job search sound bite.

Even if the employer bluntly tells you that there are no jobs available at her company, try to arrange a personal meeting anyway, or at least a more in-depth phone conversation. Once you meet with someone face to face, there's no telling what could happen next. If nothing else, you've made another contact in your field who might be able to provide you with some useful information, or connect you with other employers.

WORKING WITH EMPLOYMENT AGENCIES

Whether you locate an agency through the classified section of a newspaper, through a friend, or through your networking efforts, you want to target agencies that find jobs for recent grads. Sometimes these agencies specialize by industry. For example, there are agencies that exclusively recruit for the legal, publishing, and human resources industries, among others.

There are also agencies that recruit only for temporary workers. They can place you in a short-term position such as for a day or a week or two. Or they can place you in a long-term temp position (three to six months) with an employer who needs temporary workers to replace employees who are on leave or to supplement their staffs during the busy times of the year. There are instances, however, when such temporary jobs can become permanent positions. For example, if you take a temp job to fill in for someone who's on maternity leave for three months, she may not return and you may be asked to become a permanent employee. Or if you work at an accounting firm during tax season, do a great job, and they have open positions at the end of the season, they may convert you from a temporary to permanent staff member.

Your challenge is to determine on a case-by-case basis whether or not an agency has jobs with growth potential, that are promotable, and that require a college education. This may be difficult, since some agency reps might hedge when describing their positions in order to get a better qualified candidate. They may not tell you the whole story or accurately represent the situation. Sometimes, the only way to find out is to pursue a position to the interview stage and learn from the employer directly what's going on.

One way to improve your chances of hooking up with a reputable agency is to get a recommendation from a friend who has used or who knows people who have successfully worked with a particular agency. Another way to find a good agency is to contact the National Association of Temporary and Staffing Services in Alexandria, Virginia.

Choosing a Reputable Agency

When you're trying to decide whether you should go ahead and give an employment agency a shot, or run for the door with your coat tails flying behind you, ask yourself questions like:

Are they treating me with respect?

Do they talk at me or with me?

Do they thank me for my time?

Do they reasonably accommodate my work hours when scheduling appointments with them or with a prospective employer?

Do they hook me up with the type of positions I'm really interested in or just random positions they want to fill?

Are they communicating with me all of the time?

Do they let me know up front how their agency works in terms of policies and procedures?

Do they brief me well about the organization and interviewer before an interview?

Do they follow-up thoroughly with me after an interview, getting feedback from me and giving feedback to me from the employer in a timely manner?

Do they negotiate effectively by communicating my terms to the employer and letting me know every step of the way what's going on?

Are they professional in other ways?

Is their office neat and clean, even if it's not glamorous?

Do they dress professionally?

Is their demeanor poised and businesslike?

Smooth Operators

You should prepare for your meeting with an employment agency recruiter the same way you would for a real job interview. Dress appropriately, act professionally, and bring a couple of clean copies of your resume. The agency recruiter will evaluate you as a prospective job candidate largely based on how you present yourself. If you go to an interview with an agency recruiter dressed in jeans, acting casual and unprepared to fill out an application or answer questions, it doesn't matter how qualified you are for a job. The recruiter will not consider you as a viable candidate and most likely will not take you seriously in the future. If they send you on an interview with one of their client organizations, you are a reflection of their judgment.

First Things First

When you arrive at an agency, expect the receptionist to give you an application to complete. This form generally asks for basic information about your educational and employment histories. You need to list the names of schools, dates attended, major areas of study, and degrees received from high school forward. It's also a good idea to bring with you the names, addresses, and phone numbers of your prior employers, your starting and ending salaries, job titles, dates of employment, and reasons for leaving. In addition, you sometimes need to list two or three personal references who are not related to you and their phone numbers. Specific information about computer skills, such as the types of computers and software packages you know, is typically another category.

As a recent grad, your work history may not fit easily into the designated categories. Just fill it out the best you can and attach your resume. Agencies understand that part-time work, summer employment, and internships make up most of your experience. The application will also indicate that you must complete the form even though you are attaching your resume. This is an employment agency policy because they need these forms completed for their records. Be prepared to take a few extra minutes to do this without questioning or resisting the process.

Never, ever write "see resume" on an application.

Sometimes agencies will ask you to take a computer skills test of your word processing ability and speed or spreadsheet knowledge. You may wonder why this is necessary, since you are not applying for a secretarial position. Again, this is just another standard procedure in some places. Since computer skills are critical to many entry-level positions across industries, the agency just wants to ensure that you have these skills before sending you out to meet with an employer.

Many aspects of the employment agency scene may not appeal or make sense to you. The sometimes impersonal, hustle and bustle of agency settings can turn you off and make you wonder if you're in the right place. Try to give it a chance and realize that it's just the way it is. You have to go through the motions to gain the potential benefit of being hooked up directly with an employer. Besides, this is just one job search resource of many that you can choose from.

Minding Your Own Business

Agency reps vary widely in how they do business. Some work exclusively with you. Others may have you meet with one or more of their colleagues who may also send you on interviews. You, however, should not initiate contact with multiple members of the same agency without letting them know about the others. This could potentially cause friction within the agency and work against you. The staff may choose not to represent you at all.

Whether or not you work with multiple members of the same agency, you are responsible for managing your job search. The quality and consistency of recruiters varies greatly. You need to keep in mind that agencies that handle jobs for recent grads are usually contingency, rather than retainer firms. Contingency firms do not have exclusive job listings and only get paid if they place a candidate with an employer, while retainer firms have exclusive listings and get paid on a regular basis by an employer to provide placements.

As a recent grad, you are one of many candidates vying for the same job that may be farmed out to many agencies. The agencies are focused on their profits, not on your career needs. They are recruiters, not career counselors who have your best interests at heart.

Since employment agency recruiters are focused on the bottom line, they attend mainly to the needs of the employer. As such, *you should never pay an agency any money for any reason*. Their fee, should they place you, will be paid by the hiring organization and will represent a certain percentage of your salary. Sometimes they don't receive this fee until you have been on the job for several months. But, either way, it has nothing to do with you. If an agency presses you for money, get out of there immediately.

What's in it for Me?

An agency recruiter's primary role in your job search is to serve as a liaison between you and an employer. Remember that even if an agency wants to send you on a job interview, it's still your ultimate choice whether or not you want to pursue the position.

Once you give an agency recruiter the okay, he will pitch you to an employer by sending your resume and talking to the organization contact. If the employer wants to interview you, the recruiter should prepare you for it by giving you an overview of the position, the people you'll meet, any key insights into what they're looking for, and the details about the date, time, and location of the interview. Again, some agency reps are more thorough than others and will give you varying amounts of information about an employer. It's always important to do your own research about the organization before you go on the interview.

After the interview, the recruiter will call you or expect you to call him with an update about your impressions of how things went. Then the recruiter will call the employer to get feedback about you. Finally, the recruiter will contact you and let you know the status of your candidacy and the next steps in the process.

Assuming the employer wants to hire you and you're interested in receiving an offer from them, the agency recruiter will help you negotiate the offer. This can be helpful at times, and sticky at others. It's helpful to have a third party to do the dirty work and rally for you. Since the recruiter's commission depends on your starting salary, he'll want your salary to be as high as possible. But it can also be tough to deal with a middle person, especially because he may want to get you in the job so much that he won't necessarily risk bargaining as hard as he could to get you what you want.

That's why it's important to think through what you want and strategize about what you're willing to give up before you communicate your needs to the recruiter. Treat the recruiter as an extension of the employer, not as your personal job coach or confidante. Be professional and positive. Be savvy enough to let the recruiter know enough to speak on your behalf but not too much to sabotage you by compromising too early in the negotiation process.

Once you get the offer you want, you can give the recruiter a verbal yes. But make sure that he understands that you won't resign from your current position or take the new one officially until you have the offer letter in hand stating the terms of your employment.

Somewhere Down the Road

There are many employment agencies out there. So you may think there's no harm in letting a not-so-great recruiter know what you really think of them after you've already accepted a job. But, since that recruiter has a relationship to some extent with your new employer, it isn't a good idea to vent your frustrations with them.

Also, as you build your career, you'll discover that within each industry word gets around about who's good on both the candidate and agency recruiter sides. Your work world can become very interconnected and you want to maintain a professional demeanor at all times.

If you have a positive experience working with a recruiter, they may contact you in the future about other positions, ask you to refer other prospective candidates to them, or want to place others with you at your workplace. It's therefore always in your best interest to maintain a good relationship with them.

CHAPTER **6**

Talking Your Way to a Job

PREPARING FOR INTERVIEWS

For most people, interviewing for jobs falls into that category of Life's Most Dreaded Activities, ranking right up there with having your teeth drilled. To allay any fears you might have about talking your way into a job, we have one thing to say:

> *A job interview is simply a conversation between two or more human beings.*

It's as simple as that. "But what about all those other things people say about interviews?" you're probably wondering. We don't mean to imply that an interview is no more important than a casual conversation with a stranger at a bus stop. Interviewing *is* a crucial part of your search. It's true that an interview is a chance to sell yourself and it *can* be a make-or-break opportunity to clinch the job, and if you don't prepare and practice you can really blow it. All we're saying when we call it "simply a conversation" is that getting panicked about interviewing will only work against you. It's better to start with the premise that an interview is just two or more people talking, then slowly work up to the realization that it happens to be a very important conversation.

Some people don't dread interviewing but actually look forward to it, seeing it as a chance to present themselves more impressively and persuasively than they can on paper. If you're that type, congratulations on your positive attitude, but watch out for the traps that overconfidence can lead to. Even those with calm nerves and dry palms must take great care in preparing for interviews and learning the best strategies. There's no room for complacency in a job search.

The steps you take before an interview are just as important as the interview itself. Your strategy actually begins when you schedule the appointment. Waiting until you get to the interview to employ savvy interviewing techniques is too late, so consider these seven steps that go into the preparation, and we'll tell you how to handle each one.

1. Schedule the appointment

2. Research the employer

3. Decide what to wear

4. Prepare your "repertoire"

5. Practice, practice, practice

6. Pack your "Bag of Tricks"

7. Relax and compose yourself

Got the Time?

Believe it or not, there is an art and science to scheduling interview appointments. A common mistake job seekers make is to be unrealistic about timing. Whether you have only one interview offer or ten, scheduling the appointments can be tricky. First, be sure to overestimate all timing. Don't try to squeeze too many interviews into one day, even if you're not working full time and have all day free. Three in one day is usually the maximum and two is more realistic. You need to be fresh for each one and allow pockets of time in between each in case any last longer than you had expected. Also be sure to consider travel time and allow for the unexpected, like traffic jams, bus or train delays, or difficulty hailing a cab.

If you have a choice about the time of day to schedule the appointment, try to make it at a time when you are at your peak energy level. Having a crack-of-dawn appointment isn't the best way to showcase your potential if you're a zombie until noon. Unfortunately, you can't always control when the appointment will be. You might have all the time in the world, but the interviewer is rarely as flexible. Be careful that you're not too demanding about when you want to come in. Ask what's convenient for the interviewer and try to accommodate his or her schedule.

If you're job searching while working full-time, then the scheduling might be even more difficult. When squeezing an appointment in over a lunch hour, or before or after work, be extra realistic about your ability to get there. Having to cancel an interview at the last minute because you have to work late or through lunch is not only an inconvenience for the prospective employer but also implies that the interview is not a priority for you or that you have difficulty managing your time.

Allow one hour for a first interview, but be aware that it could be as short as fifteen minutes or could last more than an hour. Sometimes you will first meet with someone in human resources for an initial screening, then you might be passed on to someone in the area where you would be working, and you might even talk to a third or fourth person if they're all available. If this is a second or third interview, it could last even longer, perhaps all day including lunch. You'll usually be told what to expect for a second or third interview, but not always.

Rarely do you know the length of time to expect for a first interview. It's kind of like a blind date. You know how you're never sure if a blind date is going to turn out to be a lifelong soul mate or a dud you can't wait to get away from? Well, employers feel the same way. Just as a blind date usually starts with plans for only a drink or coffee with the hopes it will turn into dinner and a movie if you click, a first interview also starts out with minimal commitment.

When scheduling an appointment you'll either be talking to the person who will do the actual interviewing or to a support person such as an administrative assistant or receptionist. Remember that this initial phone contact is your chance to make a good first impression, so don't forget about the Phone Tactics section of chapter 4: Be courteous, clear, and professional. (Note: Interviews through on-campus recruiting programs at colleges are usually arranged for you, so you don't have direct contact with the interviewer until the day of the appointment. We talk more about this method of interviewing later in this chapter.)

When you're on the phone making the appointment, be sure to get all the relevant details. It's easy to get caught up in the excitement of actually scheduling an interview and forget to find out the exact address, floor or office suite number, name of the person who'll be interviewing you, their phone number, and even a fax number. If you sense that the company is technologically progressive, you might want to get the interviewer's Email address too. Don't hesitate to ask for all this information, because you never know when you'll need it before or after the interview. It's embarrassing to call five minutes before the interview to find out where you're supposed to be or to let them know you're running late. It's even more embarrassing not to be able to call because you didn't get the direct line of the person you're meeting and no one's answering at the main phone number.

Also, be sure to ask for detailed directions so you know how to get there, but don't sound like someone who can't read a map. If going by train, subway, or bus, simply ask which stops they're closest to. Don't make the person take you through every step of the route. Figure it out yourself later or with the help of any friend who knows how to navigate the public transportation system. If you'll be driving, don't make the person describe every twist and turn from your driveway to the interview site, just pick a location you're familiar with and get accurate directions from there.

The exception is when you're interviewing out of town in an unfamiliar area, it's all right then to ask for more explicit instructions. Remember that the person giving instructions might be used to driving to work, while you'll be taking public transportation, or vice versa, so their directions might not be so accurate. To avoid any last-minute mishaps, verify the instructions with a hotel concierge or with the transit information phone service well before the time of the interview. You don't want to be rushing to your interview and hear "That #44 bus hasn't come by here in two years. The route changed and now you have to walk five blocks and catch the #39 then change to the #206. That trip'll take you at least an hour without a car." If you'd known all that the night before, you'd have that extra hour to travel.

Sometimes It's Not Who You Know, It's What You Know

If you can sound knowledgeable about the organization you are interviewing with and the specific type of job you are interviewing for, as well as the overall career field and industry, you will distinguish yourself from all other candidates. You'd be amazed how many students and recent graduates walk into an interview knowing almost nothing about the people they'll be talking to. Now is the time to go back to the information you gathered in the Compiling Your Hit List section of chapter 3.

Don't feel that you have to recite every statistic from a company's annual report. What really impresses an interviewer is simply knowing enough about that prospective employer to show that you know why you're there and you know what you're getting into. Remember in chapter 3 we gave you guidelines in the form of questions to ask as you did your research? Now is the time to go back to the copious, detailed notes we're sure you took and turn them into "Interview Cheat Sheets" for each interview. On the following pages, we've given you a blank form to photocopy and use for all your interviews, as well as an example of how it can be filled out.

BASIC DATA	
Organization name:	Verbatim Publishers, Inc.
Position available:	Editorial Assistant
Department:	Children's books
Address:	222 Sesame Street
	Candyland, New York 11111
	Human resources dept. is on 23rd floor
Contact person:	Mr. Rogers, Human Resources Manager, ext. 365
	(remember to get first name for thank you note).
	Also spoke briefly with Miss Piggy, Associate
	Editor of children's books, but will interview in
	personnel first.
Phone #	Main co. #-212/111-1111
	Children's dept. is 111-1112
Fax#	212/222-2222
E-mail:	Ask for at interview
Interview date:	Will be finalized 6/26

ABOUT THE ORGANIZATION	
Number of employees:	500
Year organization was founded:	1902
Locations of offices:	NY (headquarters), London and L.A.
Relevant financial stats:	Highest profits ever in 1995 after decline in late 80's
	and early 90's. Growth due to expansion of trade
	paperback division.
Key managers or principals:	CEO is Mr. Curious E. George (bluebood type; co. founded
	by his father; will be retiring at the end of this year.)
	Mr. George's thirtysomething grandson
	Curious E. George III just became Editor-in-Chief.
Products/services:	All major book publishing divisions except textbooks
New directions:	Children's dept. growing. Heavily involved in educational
	multimedia.
Organizational culture:	Changed from conservative to more progressive and
	risk-taking due to grandson's influence.

WAYS TO MAKE BROWNIE POINTS	
Media coverage:	Mention articles in *Time*, *The New York Times*, and *The Washington Post* last summer about change of leadership and new directions. Article last month in *Publishers Weekly* on new CD-ROM. Profile in *Forbes* on Curious George III last Jan.
Flattery:	Mention CD-ROM I tried out. Great graphics, innovative educational approach.
	My contact at Women in Communications said Verbatim has most respected children's books in the industry.
Inside info:	Jane (former Verbatim intern I met at conference) said they like strong computer skills—also like experience with children. Remember to mention the nanny job that's not on my resume.
Questions I can ask :	How will the new direction into educational multimedia affect day-to-day operations and staffing? Is the person who last filled this position still in the company?

BASIC DATA

Organization name:
Position available:
Department:
Address:

Contact person:

Phone #

Fax#
E-mail:
Interview date:

ABOUT THE ORGANIZATION

Number of employees:
Year organization was founded:
Locations of offices:
Relevant financial stats:

Key managers or principals:

Products/services:
New directions:

Organizational culture:

WHATEVER SHALL I WEAR TO THE BALL?

Every spring, college campuses are swarming with seniors in navy blue suits. Despite the prevalence of these azure seas, rigid standards for interview dress codes are not necessarily the reality. Companies that recruit on campuses tend to be predominantly (but not exclusively) large corporations or firms with conservative cultures, such as law firms or banks, so navy blue and charcoal gray are usually the way to go. For interviewing in the real world, you'll find a wider array of appropriate attire. It's important to tailor your appearance to the industry in which you're interviewing and to the nature of the specific organization. You don't want to interview for a management trainee position at the Gap looking like you're on your way to the law firm of Stuffy, Grumpy, and Tweed.

We're not going to get into all the nitty-gritty of what to wear. It's pointless when people say things to men like "Don't wear a brown suit" or to women, "Make sure your skirt comes one inch below the knee." You might look fabulous in that brown suit of yours or your best skirt length might be an inch *above* the knee. These and other rigid rules of interview dressing rarely work for everyone, so it's best not to put too much stock in them. This doesn't mean, however, that you should care less about your interview attire. You should care. The choices of what to wear are infinite and the decision is highly personal. Don't worry, though, we *will* give you some concrete advice to help with the inevitable dilemma of how to suit up. Before trying on everything in your closet and buying out the local department store, take a look at these basic rules of interview garb:

1. Find Out What People in That Industry or That Company Wear

Are they creative? Casual? Conservative? If it's Bloomingdale's training program you're after, then obviously you need to pay extra attention to style and can take more liberty with colors and cuts. For corporate jobs, you'll generally need to stick to the navies and grays and traditional styles, although there are some companies with a younger, more casual feel.

Considering the specific industry is particularly important. Sometimes you can go against conventional wisdom like: "Women should never wear pants to an interview." Meredith, a client we coached through a job search in the music industry, came up with two perfect pants outfits that got her through her search. She was able to look casual (important since many of her interviewers wore jeans) but also professional because the outfits were polished and neat. They were also trendy enough to make her look in touch with the market of oh-so-hip, young music-buyers she'd be responsible for keeping on the pulse of. Her wardrobe wouldn't have gone over well outside of the creative industries, but it was just right for her Hit List.

2. Err on the Side of Professionalism

Always aim for being just a little more dressed up and a little more conservative for the interview than you might actually be on the job. Just as Meredith didn't wear jeans, even though she knew her prospective employers often did, you shouldn't be tempted to underdress. As long as the overall style and effect of what you wear fits with the organizational culture, you won't miss the mark by being a little more dressed up. Doing so simply shows respect for the person you are meeting and conveys an air of professionalism.

By the way, be aware of the phenomenon "Casual Friday" that many companies have adopted. If your interview is on a Friday, don't be surprised to find most everyone at the company in casual clothes—sometimes even in companies that are usually conservative and formal. *You*, though, should still dress to impress.

3. Be Comfortable

No matter what you wear, make sure it fits well and is comfortable. Interviews can be nerve-wracking enough without the need to tug at something tight or hang onto something loose. Nothing should be held together with safety pins, masking tape, or staples (a popular hemming method for non-sewing types) unless it's due to a last minute emergency and there's no time to change. As for your shoes, you should be able to walk miles in them without a pinch, squeek, or rub.

One of the main goals of interviewing is to be relaxed so that the interviewer can have confidence in you. If you are uncomfortable or nervous about something you're wearing, then you'll be distracted from your "sales pitch." Remember that episode of *Seinfeld* where George fights his way past other customers in a men's clothing store to snatch up a drastically reduced designer suit, only to find out at a job interview that the suit made a loud swishing noise every time he took a step in it? Well, swishing generally isn't a quality employers seek in their prospective employees. Neither is somebody who can't sit still because he keeps sticking his finger in his too-tight collar, or who keeps tugging at her skirt that keeps shifting back to front. Be smart about what you choose to wear and have a dress rehearsal before it's showtime.

4. Be Neat and Clean

Along with fitting well, it is crucial that whatever you wear be impeccably presented. Whether you're wearing a forty dollar outfit or a four hundred dollar one, it has to be clean and pressed. Take along a little wardrobe emergency kit in your bag for last minute mishaps. An extra tie or pair of hose can be a real saving grace. If you're packing for an interview out of town, don't take a chance on just one suit or outfit. When that baby next to you on the plane throws up all over your one and only shirt, you'll be buying a new one in an unfamiliar city unless you packed a change of clothes.

Go for a simple look as well. Unless you're interviewing with a fashion designer, most interviewers care more about who you are and what you have to offer than what you wear. You don't want them to be distracted by a cloud of cologne or perfume, dangling, clanking jewelry, and asymetrical, two-toned, neon clothes.

The clean-and-tidy rule applies to you, too, not just your clothes. Okay, we probably don't have to tell you to shower, wash your hair, brush your teeth, and shave before an interview—but we will anyway. If your fingernails are dirty, the interviewer won't necessarily know it's because your favorite hobby is fingerpainting. She'll assume you just have poor hygiene. And if you can't pass up that garlic, anchovy, and onion pizza just before the interview, be sure to pack some powerful breath mints. In fact, pop in a breath mint anyway, even if your lunch was as innocuous as cottage cheese and jello. You may just be nervous and get the ever-dreaded dry mouth just before you go in. You'll be glad you brought those Tic Tacs along.

If you smoke, don't even *think* about doing it anywhere near the interview site. Smoking just before an interview, even outside, can make you smell like a walking ashtray when you go into an enclosed office. And one last rule, while we're playing dictator: Don't chew gum at the interview!

INTERVIEWING AS REPERTORY THEATER

Once you know where you're going, when you're going, and what you're going to wear, it's time to decide what you're going to say. After all, an interview is a conversation, not a fashion show, so looking good is only going to get you through the first impression stage, then you have to open your mouth and impress them with who you are.

Rather than anticipating all the possible questions that could be asked and all the possible answers you could give, we want you to develop a "repertoire" that will enable you to answer any question you could encounter. The reason you can get away with this is that most all potential questions can be boiled down into a handful of categories. There might be an infinite number of ways a question can be worded, but there's a finite number of issues that are typically raised.

For example, the following questions are really all asking the same thing:

- Tell me about yourself.

- What are three adjectives that describe you?

- What are your strengths and weaknesses?

- Why should we hire you?

- Why would you be right for this job?

They're all asking you to talk about your personal qualities and how those would be assets in the job. Sound familiar? It's what we had you do in chapter 1 when you put together your Skills Package. You can now use that package as a foundation for answering many typical interview questions. Being able to talk about yourself in terms of "I am, I can, I know" is all the ammunition you need to answer even the toughest questions.

The key to preparation, therefore, is not to prepare five different answers to the questions above, only to be thrown when the question ends up being asked in a sixth, unexpected way. Instead, it's better to have one general answer that is flexible enough to adapt to various specific questions.

To supplement your Skills Package, think of specific examples that back up what you say about yourself. Anyone can give a general answer. Only a strategic interviewer will use hard evidence. For example:

Typical question:
What one thing would your last boss say about you?

Lousy answer:
She would say I was a quick learner.

Mediocre answer:
She would say I was a quick learner because any project she gave me I figured out quickly and got done on time.

Winning answer:
She would say I was a quick learner because every project she gave me I figured out quickly and completed on time. For example, I had to redesign their database to track the success of various marketing strategies and print several types of reports—all in two weeks. I had never used a program like that before so I took the manual home with me for a few nights to study and then took the initiative to find someone in another department who used the program. I got them to spend a few minutes showing me parts I didn't get from the manual. That way, I learned how to do it without bothering my boss. I got the file set up and the reports printed out three days before my deadline and all the managers were very pleased.

Now that's an answer! Not only does it state the quality ("I'm a fast learner"), but it tells *why* with a concrete example of what you did and what you are capable of.

You want to prepare a mental archive of at least five examples like this one, which represent accomplishments and challenges and illustrate your best qualities. Voila! That's your repertoire.

The old fashioned way of approaching interviews is with a script, memorizing answers to hundreds of possible questions, which is much less effective. It's like the difference between a comedian who can improvise and the amateurish or less talented ones who have to stick to a script of jokes and one-liners. With thorough preparation, you too can be a successful improvisationalist. How's that for an paradox?

The script method is less effective because...

- preparing answers to all potential questions is futile. You can never anticipate the exact wording of all questions, and it's a waste of time to construct many different answers when you can prepare fewer responses that will apply to most questions.

- it perpetuates the imbalance between the almighty interviewer and you, the lowly interviewee. The Q and A format is an uneven playing field. Interviews should be more conversational, like two peers solving a problem together. The problem just happens to be whether or not you and the job are a good match.

- you're more likely to get nervous and blow it if you're worried about remembering rehearsed answers. It's easy to be caught off guard if a question isn't worded the way you expected it to be. With the repertoire method, you're ready for just about anything thrown your way.

Your repertoire should include:

1. Specific terms taken from your Skills Package that relate to you and are relevant for the job.

2. Several examples that illustrate those qualities from your package and that bring to life the experiences listed on your resume. (The more you can remember, the better, but have at least five good examples prepared.) The examples can be taken from work experiences (paid and unpaid), academic work (e.g., group projects, major written assignments, oral presentations, etc.), and activities or sports.

Try to have at least one or two examples that fit each of the following categories:

- an honor or accomplishment
- a challenge you overcame
- an ethical dilemma you resolved
- an innovative approach to something

- a team-oriented activity
- a solo activity that showed perseverance and autonomy

3. At least one or two facts about the organization that relate to your interests, skills, and potential, so that you can spell out for the interviewer how you would be a good fit for the job and the company.

4. Two or three "tidbits" of general knowledge about current events relevant to the job or simply relevant to being an informed adult. These may be recent happenings in local or world affairs or industry-specific developments. You don't have to be an expert on everything, but read (or at least watch) enough news to be able to carry on an intelligent conversation.

   With these four elements in your repertoire, you'll be able to answer any question effectively and also make that all-important small talk. To make you feel a little more comfortable with the repertoire approach, we have included lists of typical questions later in this chapter.

Practice Makes Perfect

Just because we say it's better to improvise from a repertoire than recite from a script doesn't mean you shouldn't practice. Even the best improvisationalists practice, so that in the midst of spontaneity they sound polished, professional, and experienced. Think back to the teenage years when you stood in front of your bedroom mirror and rehearsed the conversation you were going to have in study hall with what's-his/her-face. Come on, admit it, we know you did it. Well, now you get to do the more mature version of that embarrassing little ritual. Only the stakes are higher this time. It's one thing to look and sound like a jerk when you're trying to ask out that cute sophomore for a Friday night date; it's another to mess up when a job is at stake.

Now, let's go step-by-step through your interview prep:

1. Write out your repertoire. Writing down the stories that will serve as the evidence of your stellar qualities is an excellent way to get "fluent" in them. If writing is not your forte, at least jot down some keywords and phrases that describe the examples and then go immediately on to Step 2 if you're more of an auditory learner than a visual one.

2. Get used to talking about yourself. Be fluent in the language of you, i.e. the terms on your Skills Package. Also get comfortable with the stories you've written about your accomplishments. Learn to tell the stories in a concise, positive, persuasive, and coherent way.

3. Now look at the list of typical questions we've provided at the end of this chapter and practice pulling from your repertoire to answer them.

4. It's inevitable that you'll have difficulty expressing some things and answering some questions. Be patient with yourself as you fine-tune the rough parts. Call on your job search support team to give you input on how you're coming across.

5. Tape-record yourself talking about your strengths, goals, and accomplishments. Pay special attention to your voice. Is it energetic, animated, and clear? Are your statements littered with uhs and ums? Does your voice go up at the end of a statement as if you were asking a question, and making you sound unsure or immature? Look in the mirror as you make the recording so you can watch your nonverbal communication too.

6. Participate in a mock interview either at your college, at a career counseling center, or with friends or family. If the interview can be videotaped, even better.

Repeat these steps as often as you need to feel comfortable with the interview process. Beyond that, remember that real life interviewing will help you get used to this unusual type of conversation. We don't advocate wasting employers' time interviewing for jobs you don't even want just to get interview practice. You should, though, look at interviewing for jobs that do interest you as a way to practice until that much sought-after offer comes along. In fact, some entry-level job seekers with little or no interviewing experience make sure not to schedule appointments with their top choice of prospective employers until they've had a chance to practice elsewhere. This strategy works for more experienced interviewers, too, if you're feeling rusty.

Pack Your Bag of Tricks

One of the final steps in the preparation for an interview is to pack up what you will take to the interview. This may seem kind of silly since it's not like you're going to give a slide presentation or something, but you . You don't want to be rushing around for the crucial items you'll need them on your way out the door. Arm yourself by going over this checklist well in advance:

- several copies of your resume
- your reference list and/or copies of reference letters
- your portfolio, if applicable
- your Interview Cheat Sheet(s)
- tissues or a handkerchief
- a pad of paper and professional-looking pen
- an emergency kit containing safety pins, breath mints or spray (don't let anyone see you spraying—it's so cheezy), and a small mirror. Men might want to include an extra tie if you'll be eating lunch in between appointments and might spill something. Women should include an extra pair of hose and earring backs if you have pierced ears so you don't have to walk around looking like a pirate if one falls off.

The bag that all this goes in is important since it's a very visible part of the first impression you'll make. Everything on the checklist above should fit into a small briefcase, small to medium sized portfolio case, attache, or shoulder bag. Do not carry a large briefcase. You'll look like a kid playing grown up if all that's in it are a few sheets of paper and a pen. *Absolutely, positively avoid backpacks* (unless it's a stylish leather one suitable for the place you're going). Be sure any bag you choose is simple, professional, and of good quality.

CHILL OUT!

Now that you've spent all this time preparing for the perfect, flawless interview, there's still one very important thing left to do—relax. Just like when studying for a big test, you want to be fresh and composed for an interview. Try to get as much preparation done in advance so that you can do something relaxing the night before. Lay your clothes out (or at least know for sure what you're going to wear), review your Cheat Sheet, practice any tricky parts of your repertoire one last time, then forget about it all. Do something fun (but not too fun!) and relax.

If you'll be going to an interview straight from work, be sure to allow a little downtime to compose yourself rather than rushing to the appointment with no time to spare. That may be hard to do if your schedule is tight, but do the best you can. Even closing your eyes for a few minutes on the way (unless you're driving!) can be a mini-refresher, or just take some deep breaths in the elevator on the way to the appointment. Whatever works for you, do it.

KNOWING WHAT TO EXPECT

Even though interviews come in all shapes and sizes, the basic strategies for handling them are generally the same no matter what the setting, length, or purpose of the appointment. There are, however, certain tactics that are unique to particular types of interviews. In this section, we've listed the main types of interviews you'll encounter and what you should know about them.

On-Campus Interviews

As we discussed in the campus Resources section of chapter 5, you might have access to an on-campus recruiting program. Interviews on campus are quite different from those you encounter out in the world. First, they tend to be shorter. Since a recruiter is likely to be seeing many students in one day, they are rarely scheduled for more than thirty minutes and might end in less time. Interviewers usually spend anywhere from half a day to two or three days on campus interviewing one student after another, so you have to work extra hard to distinguish yourself and to make an impact in a short time. It's particularly important, therefore, to be focused and concise and to come across as motivated, professional, and basically a nice person.

Studies have shown that the questions asked in on-campus interviews are likely to center primarily on your college experiences, as would be expected. The typical questions about your major, specific classes, campus activities, why you chose this college, and how you like it are likely (but not guaranteed) to be asked. You might be asked about work experiences, career goals, and personal qualities as well.

We'll let you in on a little secret. If you find that the interview is focusing too much on college stuff, try to direct the conversation (subtly and tactfully) toward other topics. The interviewer will come away with new information about you that wasn't necessarily on your resume, and it's a surefire way to distinguish yourself from all the other history majors who play sports and like their college.

On-Site Interviews

Once you're out of college, most interviews take place at the site of the company or organization. While in college, you might be called to the company site for a second or third interview after you have passed the initial screening on campus. Strategies for handling second and third interviews are discussed a little later in this chapter. Here, our discussion of on-site interviews applies both to those that result from on-campus recruiting and those for graduates who arrange the interviews on their own.

The timing issues we discussed in the preparation section of this chapter are especially important here. You're not just strolling across campus, so how you get there is important. Some dedicated job seekers even make a trial run to the interview site so they can be sure to get there on time on the actual day.

Your on-site interview might start in the human resources department, especially if the organization is large and you didn't get in through a personal contact. Remember that the personnel interviewer's main function is to screen you for the people who would make the actual hiring decision.

While they do care if you are a congenial person, they're not so much interested in getting to know you as they are in getting to know your credentials and experience. They need to find out if you meet the basic qualifications for the job to determine if they should pass you along to the next phase in the interviewing process. The same is true for a screener in the actual department in which you'd be working. You might meet with a junior staff member who assesses your basic fit before sending you on to meet with a manager or two.

In a screening interview, the way you handle the closing of the appointment is particularly important. Because the person speaking with you might not have the authority to ask you back on the spot or to give you an idea of your chances, it's essential that you find out how to proceed from that point on. Don't be bashful about asking what happens next, who this person will be passing your resume along to, and when the position needs to be filled.

Another way to take control of this first interview is to see it as an opportunity to check out the organization. Being on-site lets you get a feel for the environment and the people who work there. Be sure to ask a lot of questions at this stage. Doing so can give you information about the company, the job, or career paths within the organization. That knowledge can then put you in a more powerful situation during future interviews.

INTERVIEWS BY PHONE

It's not uncommon for initial screenings to be conducted by phone to save the interviewer time or if there is geographic distance between you and the interviewer. The obvious difference with this method is the lack of nonverbal cues. The content of what you say, the way in which you say it, and the sound of your voice are much more important here.

Be sure to sound energetic and enthusiastic. So many times we have prospective clients call us who sound blah on the phone because their speaking style is flat or they mumble, only to find that in person they are dynamic and sharp. It's human nature to form a negative opinion of someone based on how they sound before you see them, so remember how crucial that first impression is over the phone. Of course, you can't change your voice overnight (although there are great voice coaches who can work wonders), but you can make an effort to speak more effectively.

Dealing with silences in an interview is always difficult, but in phone appointments they can be even more uncomfortable. You don't know if he is listening animatedly or has tuned you out and is reading his mail. Resist the temptation to keep babbling on if the interviewer is silent. Simply ask, "Would you like me to elaborate on that?"

As we discussed in the Phone Tactics section of chapter 4, phone etiquette demands that you project a professional image, which means no music or barking dogs in the background, no screaming kids, and no TV blaring. Disable call waiting if possible, too, to avoid interruptions.

GROUP INTERVIEWING

Sometimes interviewing is not a one-on-one interaction. There are basically two types of group interviews. It can be just you with a panel of interviewers or you and a few other candidates with one or more interviewers. Sometimes you'll know the situation before going in, but you might not. If someone says you will have a group interview, it doesn't hurt to ask which of the two types it will be.

If you find yourself in a room with multiple interviewers, eye contact and body language become key. Avoid focusing on just one person, even if that person is doing most of the talking. As you give a reply, direct your answer at the whole group by alternating eye contact. Also be sure you don't physically position yourself in such a way that you're facing only one person. Give them all the feeling that you're connecting with each of them.

When you're first introduced to all the interviewers, pay extremely careful attention to their names so that you can refer to them by name during the course of the interview. It gets awkward to have to refer to someone in the group as "he" or "her." If you don't get all the names at first, you can always politely ask one or two people again in the first few minutes of the meeting.

Finally, with panel interviews try to get business cards of each person you meet so that you can follow up with them. Don't be afraid to ask which person you should consider as the main contact for this job. Doing so will help streamline your follow-up efforts and keep you from pestering the ones who won't be directly involved in the final hiring decision.

If you find yourself in the other situation—one interviewer with a group of candidates, the main thing to know is that you might be judged heavily on how you get along with the others and what role you take in the group. The obvious disadvantage of this format is that you don't have as much opportunity to give your sales pitch, especially since these group interviews often double as information sessions about the company. You might also hesitate to speak out lest you look like a brownnoser to the other interviewees. Keep in mind that you have to get your point across or the interview is a waste of time, so try to strike a balance between blowing your own horn and showing interest in, and cooperation with, the other applicants.

UNUSUAL SITUATIONS

Sometimes interviews aren't conducted at school, at the office, or on the phone. Depending on the circumstances, they can take place just about anywhere, including conferences, career fairs, or even via computer.

Some national or regional professional association conferences have special times in the schedule when you can interview with employers attending the meeting. These interview sessions are usually set up like career fairs where you wander from table to table chatting briefly with the representative and dropping off your resume. Others might be more formal, with resumes circulated before the conference and interviews scheduled in advance.

If you will be attending a conference that does not have such a program, be on the lookout for ways to create your own on-the-spot interviewing opportunities. If you meet someone in the course of the conference who works for a place that's of interest to you, why not try to arrange a meeting while you're both at the same place, even if just for an exploratory interview? Find a quiet but public spot (no hotel rooms!) at the conference hotel or convention center to have a meeting.

One nice thing about interviewing at conferences, and sometimes career fairs, is that the environment tends to be more relaxed and casual. The semi-vacation atmosphere of a conference can put interviewers in a good mood, making the situation more conducive to that "conversation between two human beings" we talked about in the beginning of the chapter. Beware, though, of getting too casual. You still have to get your points across and maintain a modicum of professionalism. Getting drunk in the hotel lounge with a prospective employer does not make for an effective first impression.

Another atypical method of interviewing that is growing in popularity is video-conferencing via personal computers. A Wisconsin-based company called ViewNet established this system which lets interviewers, typically in large corporations, communicate with students, typically in large universities, over computers. With sound and image transmission, the process is almost like being face-to-face.

With the growth of computer networking, particularly through the Internet, we predict that more and more screening of job candidates will take place electronically, and not just through large corporations and universities that can invest in systems like ViewNet. In lieu of a telephone screening, all types of employers can communicate with you initially in a flash session over the Web before seeing if it's worth setting up an appointment. Better brush up on those writing skills and raise that typing speed!

Second, Third, and Even Fourth Interviews

After you've been screened in an initial interview on campus or on-site, you hope to be asked back for more meetings. At this point, the employer knows the basics about you and your background and believes you at least reasonably meet the criteria for the job, so now the interviewers' objectives are different. These follow-up interviews are more about getting to know you, not your qualifications. Their goal is to assess your fit with the job, the company, and your prospective colleagues. You're likely to meet a number of people involved in the hiring decision to see if they think they could get along with you.

These interviews can be time-consuming and tedious, often involving many hours and many people. Despite that, you must treat each encounter with the enthusiasm and assertiveness that you brought to the first interview. Don't assume each person knows what you've told the others. Give your sales pitch to each one and try to stay fresh. Also keep track of the names of everyone you meet for your follow-up.

The length and format of these interviews varies but often includes some activity other than straight interviewing. You might have to go to lunch with one person or a group so that they can get to know you better. It's essential that you be on your best behavior, chew with your mouth closed, know which fork to eat your salad with, and as always, generally err on the side of professionalism.

The Worst Things to Order When You're Being Interviewed over Lunch

- Onion soup
- Barbecued ribs
- Buffalo wings
- Mu Shu anything
- A whole lobster, crab (or any shellfish that requires careful manipulation and could possibly fly across the table and splat all over the interviewer)
- Spaghetti (or any long-noodle like food that can end up dangling from your teeth.
- Three martinis
- Salad (the leaves are always too big and then you have to contend with those little, slippery cherry tomatoes).
- Anything that arrives flaming.
- A banana split

One final note on these interviews. The questions *you* ask are especially important because they want to know that you're interviewing them as much as they are you when it gets to the final stages. You're looking to make the right match here as much as they are, so be sure to get all the information you'll need to evaluate any job offer that might be forthcoming.

ANTICIPATING TYPICAL QUESTIONS

Since there is an infinite number of questions that can be asked in an interview, no list of so-called typical questions can ever do justice to the range of possibilities. Below are just some of the ones you might encounter when applying for entry-level positions. To answer these questions, you'll use the repertoire you developed in the previous section as well the "guiding principles" we give you in the next section, Steering the Interview Your Way.

College Experience Questions

- Why did you choose your major?
- Which classes in college have you liked best/least? Why?
- Why did you select your college? How have you liked it?
- Has your college experience prepared you for a career?
- Describe your most rewarding college experience.

- If you could do it over, how would you plan your education differently?
- What teaching styles do you react best to?
- Do you plan to go to graduate school?
- Are your grades a good indicator of your potential?
- What have you learned from your extracurricular activities?
- Tell me about one of your papers or your thesis.

Questions About You

- Tell me about yourself.
- How did you choose this career direction?
- What are your strengths and weaknesses?
- How would you describe yourself?
- How would a friend or your last boss describe you?
- What motivates you to work hard?
- What does success mean to you?
- What are you most proud of?
- In which kind of environment do you work best?
- How do you handle pressure?
- What's important to you in a job?
- Do you have a geographical preference? Would you relocate? Travel?
- Describe a major obstacle you've encountered.
- What have you learned from mistakes you've made?
- What would you do if you won the lottery?
- What else should I know about you?

Questions About Your Experience

- Tell me about your jobs/internships.
- How did your liberal arts background prepare you for this job?

- What work-related skills do you have?

Questions About Your Goals

- What do you see yourself doing five years from now? ten? fifteen?
- What do you really want out of life?
- Why do you want to work for us?

Questions to See if You Know What You're Getting Into

- What do you know about this organization?
- What do you think it takes to be successful in this organization?
- Why do you want to work for us?
- What do you look for in a job?
- How can you make a contribution to our organization?
- Where do you think this industry is headed?

BRAIN TEASERS

Some organizations that demand cream-of-the-crop intellectual skills such as financial institutions and management consulting firms, among others, like to ask brain teaser kinds of questions to see how you think. Why are manhole covers round, and other "trick" questions might throw you for a loop, so be prepared for anything off the wall. Even though you can't study for these types of riddles, you can be alert, apply analytical thinking and logical reasoning, not to mention a sense of humor if you just don't get it. Whatever you do, don't get flustered.

QUESTIONS YOU ASK

At some point in the interview, you'll be given a chance to ask questions. This usually comes at the end, but you should take the initiative to ask questions throughout the interview. Doing so can give you the upper hand, because every bit of knowledge you get about the job or the organization will help you present yourself in a way that matches what they're looking for.

When the interviewer does come to the final stages of the meeting and asks if you have any questions, the worst thing you can do is say "No." It's often difficult to come up with any, especially if the interviewer has already told you a lot about the job or the company. Try to have one or two questions in mind before going to the appointment and add to the list once the interview gets underway. Just be sure to avoid asking anything too basic or that can be answered in the company literature. The following are some ideas that are a little more insightful.

About the Organization

- How does your organization differ from its competitors?
- What are the company's plans for future growth?
- What challenges are your department/organization facing?
- What do you like most about working here?
- How would you describe the corporate culture (or work environment) here?

About the Job Itself

- Where does this position fit into the structure of the department and the organization as a whole?
- What are the future plans for this department?
- How much contact is there between departments or areas (if a large organization)?
- To whom would I report?
- What percentage of my time would be spent in the various functions you described that this job involves?
- Is it organizational policy to promote from within?
- What is a typical career path for people in this position?
- Why is this position available?
- What personal qualities make someone successful in this job?
- May I talk to someone in the company who currently holds or recently held this position? (Only appropriate if an offer has been extended or seems imminent.)

ILLEGAL QUESTIONS

Inquiry Area	Illegal Questions	Legal Questions
National Origin/Citizenship	Are you a U.S. citizen? Where were you/your parents born What is your "native tongue"?	Are you authorized to work in the United States? What languages do you read, speak, or write fluently? *(This question is okay, as long as this ability is relevant to the performance of the job.)*
Age	How old are you? When did you graduate from State University? What's your birth date?	Are you over the age of 18?
Marital/Family Status	What's your marital status? Who do you live with? Do you plan to have a family? When? How many kids do you have? What are your child care arrangements?	Would you be willing to relocate if necessary? Travel is an important part of the job. Would you be able and willing to travel as needed by the job? *(This question is okay, as long as ALL applicants for the job are asked it.)* This job requires overtime occasionally. Would you be able and willing to work overtime as necessary? *(Again, this question is okay as long as ALL applicants for the job are asked it.)*
Affiliations	What clubs or social organizations do you belong to?	List any professional or trade groups or other organizations that you belong to that you consider relevant to your ability to perform this job.
Personal	How tall are you? How much do you weigh?	Are you able to lift a 50-pound weight and carry it 100 yards, as that is part of the job? *(Questions about height and weight are not acceptable unless minimum standards are essential to the safe performance of the job.)*
Disabilities	Do you have any disabilities? Please complete the following medical history. Have you had any recent or past illnesses or operations? If yes, list and give dates. What was the date of your last physical exam? How's your family's health? When did you lose your eyesight? How?	Are you able to perform the essential functions of this job with or without reasonable accommodation? *(This question is okay if the interviewer has thoroughly described the job.)* As part of the hiring process, after a job offer has been made, you will be required to undergo a medical exam. *(Exam results must be kept strictly confidential, except medical/safety personnel may be informed if emergency medical treatment is required, and supervisors may be informed about necessary job accommodations, based on the exam results.)* Can you demonstrate how you would perform the following job-related functions?
Arrest Record	Have you ever been arrested?	Have you ever been convicted of _____? *(The crime named should be reasonably related to the performance of the job in question.)*
Military	If you've been in the military, were you honorably discharged?	In what branch of the Armed Forces did you serve? What type of training or education did you receive in the military?

Most experienced interviewers, especially human resources department recruiters, will know better than to ask an illegal question, but some do either inadvertently or deliberately. It's more common to get them from people who have never been trained to interview or in small companies where the atmosphere is casual and it's kind of like you're joining a family.

Your responsibility is to be aware of what cannot be asked according to Equal Employment laws and then to decide what strategy you will use to respond. You can choose to answer if you don't object to the question, but you have a right not to. On the other hand, if you refuse to answer, you risk offending the interviewer and losing any chance at that job (which might not be a bad thing if they were concerned about something that's irrelevant to your ability to do the job).

An intermediate option is to look at what they're really asking and give the information they need without actually answering the question. For example, if a college senior is asked if she plans to have a family some day, she can say something like, "Whatever type of lifestyle I choose in the future, I plan to be committed to a career and to this first job." The chart on page 201 shows you what topics are off limits in an interview and what related questions can be asked.

Steering the Interview Your Way

So we've prepared you for the interview and warned you about what to expect, now let's look at what actually takes place during an interview, starting with the moment you set foot in the building.

If you haven't figured it out by now, we think that first impressions are pretty important. Don't wait until the interviewer calls you into the office to be on your best behavior. Consider everyone you come into contact with up to the point of the interviewer as being someone you need to impress with courtesy, congeniality, and your ability to have your act together (or at least look like you do). Whether it's the parking attendant, the security guard in the lobby of the high rise building, or the receptionist, consider everyone as a spy of the person you're on your way to meet. It's not that they actually are spies (except maybe the receptionist), it's just that you never know who might say something in passing about your behavior to the powers that be.

As you report to the office where the interview will take place, by all means stay relaxed. You can help yourself get that way and stay that way by arriving early so that you have enough time to compose yourself. Give yourself a chance to sit down, take a deep breath, and glance over your Cheat Sheet (but avoid last minute cramming). If you're wearing a coat or walking shoes that need to be traded for interview shoes, or if you're lugging a bunch of bags, take care of all these things before you go in so that you don't greet the interviewer with a coat dangling from one arm and a grimy running shoe on one foot while the other foot sports a leather pump or wing-tip.

For a final check of your appearance, grab that tiny mirror we told you to pack in your Bag of Tricks. If you discover spinach in your teeth or a hair standing straight up don't panic. Ask the receptionist to direct you to the restroom before he or she notifies your interviewer that you're there.

When the interviewer comes out to great you, smile, extend your hand, and introduce yourself (even though it's obvious who you are). Make sure the handshake is firm but not bone-crushing. It's especially bad when a limp handshake is given to a woman by a man, suggesting she'll break if you apply the slightest bit of pressure. Or if you're female, avoid giving an unfirm, dead-fish handshake. You're there to make an impression—and the first face-to-face one usually begins with that handshake.

Always make good eye contact with interviewers and listen carefully for their names in case you had any concerns about how to pronounce a name. Greet the interviewer with an air of confidence (but not cockiness), self-assurance, and friendliness, and you'll have won half the battle before you even get into the actual interview. People will like you or hate you in the first thirty seconds. You'll still have time to change their opinion later, but why not start out on a positive note?

Be prepared for a few minutes of small talk at the start of an interview. Did you have any trouble finding us? Crazy weather we're having, isn't it? They're not looking for you to spew forth rocket science here, and these usually aren't trick questions. Just answer politely to show that you are fellow homo sapiens who experiences the weather just like the next guy.

Don't mar the polite banter with anything that could make you look difficult to get along with or incompetent. Don't say you had a difficult time getting there or that the receptionist was rude or that the carpet in the office is an ugly color.

When the interview finally gets going, it can follow any number of formats depending on the interviewer's experience or mood and the nature of the job or organization. The categories are typically:

The Structured Interview
This is the classic human resources textbook type of interview in which you're asked typical questions, possibly even from a form

that the interviewer is filling out as you talk. The interview follows a fairly coherent line of questioning covering all the main topics like education, work, strengths and weaknesses, and career goals. Often this type of interview is conducted by people with little experience interviewing or in situations where interview procedures need to be standardized to elicit the same information from all candidates. This kind of interview is usually pretty easy to handle since it's likely to mirror your practice sessions and rarely conceals any hidden agendas. There's a danger, though, that the interviewer might not really get to know you as a person, so make sure not to come across as a robot just churning out answers with no conviction.

The Unstructured Interview

Some interviewers take a much looser approach to the process. They may ask many of the traditional questions but the questions seem to come in a random order not building on each other. This is often the case with inexperienced interviewers or busy people who have other things on their mind and haven't thought through what they want to ask you. The danger here is that the interviewer will end up not really knowing anything about your credentials or potential. If the conversation is all over the place, you may need to tie up loose ends for them to spell out what you have to offer and why you'd be a good fit for the job.

The Conversational Interview

Some interviewers go from the opening chitchat to a discussion of international politics or where to go for the best hiking trails or to get the best quesadilla in town. Somewhere in there, they skipped the whole part about why you majored in philosophy or what you did on your last job or why you should get the job. You might leave the interview on cloud nine, feeling like the two of you became fast friends, but remember they're hiring a worker not a friend. So, if a question about your art history major leads to a discussion of the image of the camel in seventeenth century Moroccan painting, be sure to get in a few plugs for that award-winning thesis you wrote or that challenging internship you had at a museum.

The Confrontational Interview

Also called the stress interview, these situations are likely to arise when interviewing for jobs that would be in high-pressured, fast-paced environments. Testing out how you react to stress in the interview gives the prospective employer an idea of how you'd handle the real thing. If you find that the interviewer is being confrontational, putting you on the spot, disagreeing with everything you say, and asking you to solve hypothetical problems in seconds, don't take the aggression personally. Also don't worry about exactly how you answer a particular question or whether your opinion on an issue is objectively right. The content of what's said here is not quite as important as how you handle yourself under pressure. Show that you can think on your feet, but also remain calm and composed, then breathe a sigh of relief when it's over.

The Sales Pitch Interview

In some cases, an interview is not really an interview at all but is more of a chance for the recruiter to sell you on the company. Rather than answering questions about yourself, you may find yourself listening to a lengthy description of the job and an enthusiastic endorsement of why XYZ Company is such a great place to work. Then, when time is almost up, they'll say, "So, do you have any questions?" How could you after they've told you more than you'd ever want to know? If you find yourself in this situation, look for opportunities to direct the discussion toward you *before* time is up. Take the information you're being given and relate it to what you have to offer and what you're looking for.

No matter what format the interview takes, there are several general categories of qualities that employers are looking for, particularly at entry-level. If you keep these in mind, you can direct the interview in such a way that these qualities will be revealed in you. What employers really look for in a candidate:

- An ability to communicate effectively
- Evidence of having thought through your career plans and identified a goal that fits with the position available
- Flexibility
- Initiative and drive
- Intelligence and critical thinking skills
- A confident, self-assured air
- Ability to handle responsibility
- Emotional maturity
- Leadership potential (if applicable)
- At least some organizational skills
- Self-awareness
- Ability to be self-directed and insightful

In addition to relying on your repertoire to answer any and all questions, you'll need to keep in mind certain guidelines for handling an interview. Think of these as guiding principles that, if followed, make every reply you give a winner.

- Direct the course of the interview wherever possible without monopolizing the conversation or avoiding questions.

- Be positive about everything and everyone. If you must discuss a negative experience, be as neutral as possible— never bitter—and talk about how you resolved it or what you learned.

- Read the interviewer's body language and mirror his or her demeanor without being an obvious mimic.

- Handle nervousness by remembering that the interviewer may be just as nervous or inexperienced as you are and by remembering that, all together now, "IT'S JUST A CONVERSATION!"

- Back up all statements you make with evidence taken from your repertoire. Never give a yes/no or one-word answer.

- Beware of cultural differences and the protocol that accompanies them, but don't assume that just because someone looks different they have a different standard of behavior from yours.

- Avoid taboo subjects like salary, vacation time, etc. You want to sound like you're interested in doing the job, not just picking up a paycheck and heading to the beach.

- Listen well. To answer a question effectively, you have to hear it. Focus on what the interviewer is saying. If you do drift away or don't understand something, it's okay to ask politely for clarification or a repeat of the question.

- Be comfortable with silences. If there's a lull in the conversation, don't fill it by rambling on and talking your way out of a job. If a silence seems to go on too long after you've answered a question, ask, "Would you like me to say more about that?"

- Always keep the employer's perspective in mind. Anything you say should be from the perspective of what the employer needs and wants to hear.

- Think before answering. If a question requires a complex response, it's all right to take a few seconds (which will seem like hours) to reflect instead of just blurting out a response.

Tests During Interviews

In addition to talking about yourself persuasively, keeping all the strategies in mind, and chewing lunch with your mouth closed, you might have to take a test or two.

Skills tests are not uncommon for some entry-level positions, especially if you're going through an employment agency. You might be asked to take tests for typing speed and accuracy, clerical skills and attention to detail, knowledge of specific computer programs, and possibly basic math skills. Even if you're not applying for a secretarial position, don't debate the agency's or organization's hiring practices. Just take the tests like a good sport even if you expect to be hired for your critical thinking skills and not your typing speed.

If you're applying for a job that requires specific content-based skills (like we talked about in the "I know" section of the Skills Package in chapter 1), you may have to take a test that relates to that job. Areas that can be tested include accounting, bookkeeping, editing or proofreading, computer programming, and language translation, just to name a few.

Occasionally psychological tests are administered, but this is rare for anything but senior level jobs because these tests cost the company several hundred or thousands of dollars per applicant to administer. They're usually reserved for management positions where personality fit with the job and the corporate culture is of utmost importance, and only after a candidate is being seriously considered.

There are also tests of sales skills, management potential, and organizational abilities that fit into that gray area between skills measures and personality assessments. You might have to "act out" a work-related task in a simulated exercise, but again, these are not common at entry-level.

One type of test that can be given for any level or type of position is a drug test. Many organizations have a policy of administering tests for illegal drug use to all new hires. You wouldn't be given a drug test until well after a first interview when you have been offered a position. Your actual hiring may be contingent upon having your references check out and passing the drug tests. The obvious strategy for this part of the job search process is don't do drugs and you'll pass the test. If you happen to be on prescription drugs, or have been lately, to treat an illness or injury, be sure to make the hiring people aware of the situation in case your results are affected.

PARTING IS SUCH SWEET SORROW

The final stages of an interview are the point at which many inexperienced (and experienced) interviewees fall short. The way you leave an interview is just about as important as the way you enter it. Here's the wrong way for an interview to end:

Interviewer:	Well, if you have no further questions...(stands up and extends her hand for the final handshake)
Job Seeker:	Thank you for taking the time to speak with me. I'm very interested in the position. (Shakes hands and starts toward the door.)
Interviewer:	Fine. We'll call you.
Job Seeker:	Good-bye.

What's wrong with this interchange? The job seeker has left with no idea of how to proceed from this point on. Being passive does you no good; expressing your thanks and interest in the position is only the half of it. The parting moments are your chance to do more—to take control of the situation and gain valuable information that can guide you through the follow-through procedures, which we'll talk about in chapter 9. How can you be more effective? Here's an example:

Interviewer:	Well, if you have no further questions...(begins to stand up and extends his hand for the final handshake.)
You:	Actually, I'd like to know how I should proceed from here. Should I contact you in a few days?
Interviewer:	(Sits back down.) Well, we have a few more people to interview this week then we'll be making a decision soon.

You:	When would I start if I were hired?
Interviewer:	We'll need the position filled by the first of the month.
You:	I'm available to start any time with just a few days' notice. [assuming you are not employed] I'm very interested in this position, above any others I'm currently a candidate for, and I know I could make a contribution to this company. Would it be all right if I called you next week to see how your decision is going?
Interviewer:	That would be fine. I can't guarantee I'll have much to report, but you can try.
You:	Great. Thanks for your time. I'll be in touch. (Stand up to shake hands and leave.)

Without being pushy, clingy, or desperate ("Pa-leeease give me this job!"), you've taken charge of the situation and opened the door for further communication. It's easier to be assertive now while you're still face to face with the interviewer than a week later when you're home alone staring at the phone wondering if you should call, wondering if you'll be a pest. You've also shown genuine interest in the position and have come across as more of a professional-in-demand than a powerless job seeker. You're now ready to tackle the follow-through in chapter 7.

CHAPTER 7

Getting to Your Destination

LANDING THE JOB

Now that you've survived the interview process, you may think your work is done. Well, not so fast. Unfortunately, you can't just kick back and decide that it's out of your hands now and you'll just wait and see what happens. If you stop actively pursuing a job at this point, you're making a risky choice. You may end up wasting all the time and energy you've already put into your search. And you probably don't stand a chance against your competition.

Imagine what would happen if Hootie and the Blowfish stopped singing three-quarters of the way through a song. Or if Maya Angelou decided not to write the last verses of her poems. Or if Pete Sampras finished only half a serve each time he played in a tennis game.

Would any of these people be successful if they didn't complete their work? Of course not. And just like them, you have a full-time job, which requires follow-up. Consider yourself to be a professional job searcher, whether or not you are employed at the time. In your job search, a good interview will get your foot in an organization's door. But, you're only partially there. Good follow-up will enable you to land a job, because it demonstrates to your prospective employer your interest, assertiveness, and potential capacity to see work through to the end.

Debriefing the Interview

One way to keep on top of where you are is to debrief yourself after each interview. Here are some sample questions you can use to start:

- What did I learn from this interview about the job? the organization? the supervisor? the culture? my prospective peers?
- What was my impression of the job opportunity as a whole?
- What key needs did the interviewer communicate that the organization has to meet with the position?
- How do my qualifications match these needs?
- Which aspects of my background did I emphasize and which did I neglect?
- Did the interviewer have any explicit or implicit concerns about my candidacy?
- How did I address or fail to address these concerns? Which questions did I have a hard time answering?
- Who has input into making the hiring decision? Who has the final say?
- Where do I think I stand as a candidate?
- What is the hiring time frame for the job and next steps I need to take?

The Thank-You Letter

Timing

Timing is everything when it comes to follow-up. Your initial follow-up, in the form of a thank-you letter, ideally should be sent within twenty-four to forty-eight hours of your interview. This is especially important in this high-tech age, when other candidates may send their letters by fax, e-mail, or overnight mail as well as by regular mail. We generally don't advocate sending a thank-you letter by fax or e-mail, as it won't look polished or personal. However, use your common sense. If you're applying for a job at a high-tech company, for example, then the hiring managers may not get to their regular mail for days, but will be sure to check e-mail.

Format

It's usually best to type your thank-your letters and envelopes on nice paper. Make sure the color and weight of the paper and envelopes match each other. In special cases, it's acceptable to handwrite a note on a folded card or plain paper if the place at which you interviewed was informal. Make sure your handwriting is legible if you choose this route.

Address the letter to your interviewer using their correct title and address from their business card. If you've misplaced the card or didn't get it, call the receptionist at the organization and confirm the spelling of the person's name, title, and mailing address.

Almost always begin your letter with the interviewer's proper name. Mr., Ms., or Dr. are all acceptable after the "Dear." On rare occasions, you might use the person's first name (for example, if during the interview, they asked you to call them by their first name, or if you knew them personally from another context before the interview). Use the standard business format we covered in chapter 4's section on "Composing Job Search Letters."

Make sure that you check your spelling and grammar before sending your letter. Spelling mistakes, in particular, stand out to a prospective employer and work against you. Many job candidates have been rejected simply because they neglected to proofread their letter.

Finally, if the employer has not yet been given your resume, this is the time to enclose it.

Tone

Picking a tone for each letter is like selecting what to wear to a party. Base your decision on the tone of your interview, just as you take your cue from a party invitation. If your interviewer was generally laid back, used casual language, and the workplace was relaxed, gear your tone accordingly. Toward the other extreme, a very formal interview requires an equally formal thank you note. No matter what, it's safer to err on the side of being too formal, rather than too casual.

Content

Your letter should be brief, not more than three or four paragraphs. Think of it as another opportunity to sell yourself. You need to write a targeted, persuasive letter that will convince your prospective employer that you are the candidate they should hire.

Paragraph 1: Review

In the first paragraph, review the purpose and events of your interview. Immediately acknowledge your interviewer for meeting with you. For example, "Thank you for taking the time out of your busy schedule to meet with me yesterday...," or "It was a pleasure to meet with you today...," or "I appreciated the opportunity to meet with you today..."

Cite by full name any other members of the organization you met through your primary interviewer:

> "Thank you for introducing me to _____ and _____,"
> or "It was a pleasure also meeting _____," or "I
> enjoyed having the opportunity to speak with _____
> about (name of organization or position)."

Mention one or two specific things you learned and/or were impressed by:

> "I enjoyed learning more about the _____ position,"
> or "It was a pleasure to learn more about the structure
> of your organization, its business philosophy, and current
> initiatives." "Specifically, I was impressed by ....," or "Our
> conversation helped me to gain a better understanding
> of ....". These specifics will give the reader a mini preview
> of what's coming in the rest of the letter.

Paragraph 2: Highlight

In the second paragraph, briefly highlight any key aspects of your academic background, work experience, or skill sets that are critical to the job. You can introduce these aspects in the context of your interview by saying things like, "Our conversation reinforced that my background and experience are an excellent fit with the position," or

> "As we discussed, my background in _____ and three
> years as a _____ with _____ have required
> strong _____, _____, and _____ skills."

Don't repeat your entire resume or interview responses in this paragraph. You'll make a solid impression if you include those examples that support these sources of information in a new, concise way. Your thank you letter then becomes another way for you to demonstrate your ability to exercise good judgment, to synthesize what the interviewer told you, and to communicate your understanding of how your assets match the interviewer's needs.

Whenever possible, link your attributes with the job qualifications and reinforce what you will contribute to the organization: "My experience doing _____ will enable me to promote your _____," and "These skills would enable me to add immediate value to (name of department and/or organization)," or "Based on my experience and academic preparation, I would hit the ground running with (name or organization), as a (name of position)."

Paragraph 3: Supplement

In the third paragraph, include any additional information about yourself. You may want to cover the attributes you didn't discuss, bring up points you didn't fully explain, or elaborate on responses you felt were incomplete during your interview.

If it was clear that the interviewer had reservations about your candidacy, this is your opportunity to say something to turn your situation around. You may feel that your GPA was of concern, or that the employer was troubled by your lack of direct experience. Acknowledge the hesitation and provide a strong, positive counter-argument.

Be careful, though, not to remind the interviewer that something didn't go well in the interview. Instead, state the thought in a strong positive tone: "In addition to the skills we discussed during our meeting, I also have _____years of experience doing _____ or have taken _____ courses in _____," or "I am proficient in _____ as well as in the _____, which we discussed." As in the second paragraph, make sure to get specific about and quantify your skills or accomplishments whenever possible.

Paragraph 4: Move Forward

In the fourth paragraph, summarize the rest of the letter. Make sure you thank your interviewer again: "Thank you again for the opportunity to discuss my candidacy for the _____ position." Keep it simple here. Don't go overboard and ingratiate yourself too much or you'll sound fake and like you're kissing up.

Also, this is the place to reinforce your level of interest in the position. For example, "I am very interested in the position." Only express your enthusiasm for the position if you sincerely feel this way. If an organization is your first choice, let them know. If you don't feel enthusiastic, either say nothing or let them know diplomatically that you are not interested in going further with them in the process. Include a sentence that leaves the door open for the interviewer to contact you before your next meeting: "If you have any additional questions, please contact me at (phone number or numbers)."

Finish the letter by referring to the next step in the process: "I look forward to hearing from you on Monday, as you mentioned, concerning the next step," or "I will call you next Wednesday, as you suggested, to discuss the possibility of meeting with your colleagues." As in the former three paragraphs, be specific. State the day and terms of the next step directly without being pushy. Make sure you refer back to your debriefing notes to determine the interviewer's cue about how to proceed.

No Russian Novels for Me, Thanks

So now that we've finished spending all of these pages giving you the basics of thank you letters and telling you how important it is to be thorough and detailed, we're going to put your mind at ease. You don't have to write a manifesto. As we said at the beginning of this description, the thank you should be brief. No more than four paragraphs long. So it should comfortably fit on one page with space left over.

Multiple Interviewers

If you were interviewed by more than one person on the same day, either in a group or in consecutive interviews, it is appropriate to acknowledge everyone you met with in one of two ways. One way is to write everyone a thank-you note. Be sure that each letter is slightly different, because interviewers from the same organization sometimes share notes with each other or even keep them together in a file.

Another way is to write one letter to the person responsible for organizing your day, or the most senior level person, and ask to thank the others. Mention the others by full names. This approach is okay if you only spoke briefly with the others.

Samples of Past Work

It may be helpful to include selected samples of your work in your thank you letter. (See chapter 4's section "Assembling Your Portfolio.") You should do this if it is requested, or if you believe it'll make a difference in helping you get the job. But it isn't a good idea to overload your prospective employer with too much paper, especially if they didn't request it.

Remember, again, that in many organizations, the work you produce while you are there remains the property of that organization after you leave. You must be very careful when you present samples of your work that belong to another company. And if your work includes any confidential information, black it out or do not use that particular work. Whatever you do, remember that a potential employer will evaluate your sense of discretion as part of their decision whether or not to hire you.

The Art of Persistence

Persistence, or the degree to which you contact your prospective employer, can be a tricky part of follow-up. There is a fine line between being persistent and blowing it by being annoying. There are no hard and fast rules. Depending on what the interviewer told you about the time frame for hiring and how they planned to communicate with you—call you, send you a letter, contact you through your headhunter—follow these cues and act accordingly. Don't, for example, call your interviewer every few days. This will be interpreted as poor judgment or desperation.

The Top 5 Ways to Be a Pest

1. *Call your prospective employer collect.*
2. *Send your thank you letters postage due.*
3. *Dump last year's file of your work into a UPS box and mail it to your employer marked "FYI—samples of my work."*
4. *Have your best friend call the hiring manager to give a recommendation, pretending to be your former manager.*
5. *Send e-mail messages to check in with smiley faces at the end.*

Also, if you're working through an employment agency rather than directly with your prospective employer, you'll need to direct your persistence toward the agency. As the liaison between you and the organization, the agency is responsible for keeping the communication channels open. Your agency representative will most likely contact you by phone after your interview or request that you call them to let them know how it went. They will then call your prospective employer, get feedback about your interview, and contact you to let you know what the interviewer said about your interview as well as the next step. (See pages 167–168 for more on how to deal with and select agents.)

PHONE CALLS

Be clear about why you will call an interviewer and make sure it's for a good reason. For example, you may have received another job offer and need to know where you stand. You may just be curious after a week or so about the status of your candidacy. Or, if your interview was not as effective as you'd hoped, you may want to try to make a better impression during a follow-up call and possibly keep yourself in the running. These all are acceptable reasons. It is important that you're clear in your own mind about the purpose of your call so that you can be direct with your prospective employer during the call.

THE MOMENT OF (TELEPHONE) TRUTH

How soon you call after your interview depends on the reason why you are calling. In general, don't call before your follow-up letter arrives, and give the employer at least a few days before checking in with them.

See chapter 4's section on Phone Tactics to determine the time of the day and week to call and what to do if you don't reach who you want to.

Also, be courteous and brief when you call. Focus the call on your interest in the job and your ability to do it better than anyone else. Sometimes the employer will indicate that they have not made a decision yet. In this case, consider your call an opportunity to keep yourself fresh in the mind of your prospective employer. You may even want to follow up the call by having one of your key references place a call to the employer to support your candidacy.

If the employer responds that they have decided to hire someone else, try to get feedback about why you were not selected. Some employers will be more comfortable with this request than others. If they resist, thank them for their time and don't probe further. If they are receptive, take advantage of this chance to learn something from the experience and to see how you can improve your job search skills for the next time.

8

Reeling in Job Offers

THE BIG PICTURE

Remember when you were a child riding in the car during a long trip and every few minutes you asked your parents, "Are we there yet?" Sometimes the job offer phase can feel like that car trip, because it's a lengthy process during which you're continually trying to figure out when it will end.

After following up your interviews, you play the waiting game until you learn whether you receive a job offer or a rejection. Since you're pursuing many jobs at once, rather than waiting around to hear about just one, you may be so busy that you are surprised when an offer does come. Being surprised is okay, but being unprepared to respond is not. As we have pointed out throughout this book, *every* phase of the job search process is important.

Within a week or so after your final interview, either someone from your prospective employer's office, such as a hiring manager, human resources representative, or your head hunter, will contact you to extend an offer. The basic components of the offer include the position title, brief job description, work location, base salary (and other moneys, if applicable), and start date.

STOP, LOOK, AND LISTEN

Now that you know there's more to an offer than just the thrill of getting one, there are some other things you need to think about. Receiving a job offer is what you aim for in a job search, but it is not always wise to take the first offer that comes along. It is sometimes tempting to do so, but you want to make sure it's the right one for you. It's worth the effort to evaluate any offer carefully before accepting it. Few employers expect you to give them an answer on the spot, so you usually have a least a few days, if not a week or two, to make up your mind. Asking yourself the following questions can help you evaluate an offer:

QUESTION 1: AM I READY?

This may seem like a weird question considering that the whole point of a job search is to get a job. But, you might get an offer very early in your search, and you may be worried that there will be a better offer yet to come. You should be at least 99 percent sure that an offer is right for you. Otherwise, don't be afraid to turn it down.

If you think the job might be right for you, but don't feel comfortable accepting the offer, see how long you can put off giving an answer. Always convey enthusiasm for the job and appreciation for the offer so that you won't close the door too soon. Explain that you've just begun your search, have other interviews lined up, and need a little time. An employer wants to know that you're making as informed a decision as they are, so they'll usually respect your position.

Another possible situation is that you might really need to take a job even if it's not the ideal one, because of financial need. Relieving financial burdens will free you to pursue the right job later. Be realistic. No job is perfect and meets all of your needs. Especially one of your first jobs out of college. So if a job will help you pay your rent, is not the bottom of the barrel, and will buy you some time to find your dream job, you may want to take it.

A fourth scenario is that you may have other offers in the works. Often, job searches don't progress sequentially. You'll probably be at different stages with different organizations during your job search. For example, you might get an offer from an organization that is your second or third choice, and not have heard from your first choice.

If this happens, reevaluate your priorities. If you still feel very strongly about working for a particular organization or getting a particular type of job, then it may be right for you to turn down offers until you get the job you want. It's not easy to turn down offers, but it's a good idea to aim for what will make you happiest in the long run.

Moreover, be aware that you have control over your situation. Remember, you're an active job seeker, not a passive one. Use the offer you have as leverage with places you haven't heard from. For example, suppose you really want to work for Organization A, but they haven't made their decision. Call them and tell them that you have an offer from Organization B but would rather work for Organization A. This shows Organization A that you're genuinely interested in them and may help speed up their decision. Whatever your situation, communicate with all parties involved rather than just sitting back and passively getting or not getting offers.

QUESTION 2: WHAT DO I REALLY KNOW?

There are three main sets of criteria you should consider when evaluating a job offer: the job, the organization, and the compensation package. Using the list below as a guide, write a few words about each of the criterion in terms of how they would be in your ideal job.

The Job

- What are my duties/responsibilities? What percentage of my time would be spent doing each of these?

- Is this job a good match for my skills, interests, values, and personality?

- Does this job fit with my short and long-term career goals?

- How do I feel about my prospective supervisor? Anyone I'd supervise? Those who would be my peers?

- How would I be trained? Is the training sufficient? Does this method of training work with my preferred learning style?

- What would my hours be? How many hours per week would I work?

- Where would this job lead? Is it promotable? Could I transfer easily to another area of the organization? How much time must elapse and what other conditions must I meet (such as a certain performance review rating) before I can apply for another position within the organization?

- Is the job location convenient? Is there any chance of being transferred/relocated? How much travel is required for this position?

The Organization

- How financially stable is the organization?

- Is the organization growing? What has its past growth rate been? What are its long-term plans for growth? Have certain areas of the organization been targeted for growth? Is your prospective job in one of these growth areas?

- Have there been any recent or rumored layoffs of employees in the newspapers?

- Who are the organization's competitors and how are they doing?

- What is the organization's management style or "culture," including teamwork emphasis, dress code, work/family friendliness, and flexible work arrangements (telecommuting, job sharing, flex-time).

The Compensation

- Is the salary offered in line with typical salaries for this type of job?

- When and how would my job performance and salary be reviewed? What are typical increases?

- Is this position exempt (primarily professional positions) or non-exempt (primarily support staff positions)? If it's non-exempt, what are the rules about overtime and what's the hourly overtime rate?

- How are the medical, dental, vision, life, and disability insurance benefits?

- Are there retirement or profit-sharing plans? After how many years of service and at what professional level are you eligible to participate in these plans?

- How much time off would I get in terms of holidays and sick, personal, and vacation days?

- Is there a tuition assistance or reimbursement program? When would I be eligible to participate in this program? Would I have to take courses that are directly relevant to my current job? What are the guidelines in terms of: whether I would get the money up front or at the end of the semester with my grade report; what grades I must achieve to receive the money; and whether or not I would have to pay the organization back if I receive money and leave shortly thereafter? What are the tax implications of this program?

- Are there other subsidized support service programs such as an employee assistance program that provide free, 24 hour confidential personal crisis counseling; a child care program on site or nearby; an elder care referral program; a health club; or reduced fee commuting options?

QUESTION 3: HOW DOES MY PROSPECTIVE JOB RATE AGAINST MY IDEAL JOB?

Fill in your rankings of the criteria under the "Rank Real Job" column below. It's okay if you don't have enough information about all of the criteria to rate them. Do the best you can, ranking them from 1 (for a great fit) to 3 (for a poor fit).

Criteria	Put Check Marks In This Column	Rank Real Job In This Column
The Job		
Duties/Responsibilities	❏	___
Percentage of Time on Each Duty	❏	___
Skills Match		
Interests Match	❏	___
Values Match	❏	___
Personality Match	❏	___
Career Goals Fit	❏	___
Prospective Supervisor	❏	___
Prospective Subordinates	❏	___
Prospective Peers	❏	___
Training Method	❏	___
Training Sufficient	❏	___
Work Hours of the Day	❏	___
Work Hours Per Week	❏	___
Upward Mobility	❏	___

Criteria	Put Check Marks In This Column	Rank Real Job In This Column
Transfer Potential	❏	____
Conditions for Transfer	❏	____
Location Convenience	❏	____
Likelihood of Relocation	❏	____
Travel Requirements	❏	____
The Organization		
Financial Stability	❏	____
Current Growth	❏	____
Past Growth Rate	❏	____
Future Growth Projections	❏	____
Areas Targeted for Growth	❏	____
Recent or Rumored Layoffs	❏	____
Management Style/"Culture"	❏	____
The Compensation Package		
Salary	❏	____
Salary/Job Performance Review Method/Timing	❏	____
Typical Increases	❏	____
Exempt or Non-Exempt	❏	____
Insurance Benefits	❏	____
Retirement/Profit-Sharing Plans	❏	____
Eligibility for R/P-S Plans	❏	____
Time Off	❏	____
Tuition Assistance Program	❏	____
Eligibility for Tuition Program	❏	____
Other Subsidized Programs	❏	____

QUESTION 4: WHICH CRITERIA ARE A "POOR FIT"?

Place a check mark to the left of the name of each criteria that you rated a 3 in your Real Job column. Do not put check marks next to any other criteria.

Question 5: Are My "Poor Fit" Criteria Deal-Breakers?

Carefully review the criteria with check marks next to them and decide one by one whether you can live with having a poor fit with the criterion in your prospective job or whether it is unacceptable and therefore a potential reason for you not to take the job as is. Circle the check marks that represent criteria that you cannot tolerate having a poor fit with.

Question 6: Can I Remedy the Situation?

How many circled check marks do you have? If you've really thought it through before circling your marks and still have many, then ask yourself what's in the job for you. If you have only a few marks, review them each again and decide where you stand and what, if anything, could be done to remedy the situation and make the fit between you and that part of the job better. You can always refer back to your ideal job description notes about each criterion.

Question 7: Where Do I Stand Now?

Once you see how your final ratings stack up against your prospective job, you can use these factors as guidelines for a potential job negotiation. You can also get a handle on how much you really want or don't want this job. And in the big scheme of things, you have a working description of your ideal job criteria to use as a kind of reality check during your job search process as you evaluate potential jobs.

BURNING BRIDGES

While you are mulling over whether to accept, decline, or negotiate a job offer, keep in mind that it's never a good idea to burn your bridges. It can happen in any of the three instances all too easily. For example, when declining an offer never criticize any aspect of it or the organization. During the negotiating process, don't be arrogant or demanding about what you think you deserve; prove it by sticking to what you can contribute to the organization. When accepting the an offer, you may request a few days to finalize your decision. Never argue about the amount of time with your prospective employer or fail to respond within the appropriate time frame. Most importantly, don't ever renege on a job offer. Don't just take it, figuring that you can back out at the last minute.

Doing the right thing, or maintaining a professional demeanor at all times, is more than common courtesy. It's a strategic approach to your job search. Due to the mercurial nature of the job market, it's likely that you'll encounter the same individuals repeatedly during your career. They'll remember your behavior, for better or worse.

Burning Bridges 101

If you want to make a memorable exit from an organization, make sure you...

Call in sick your last two weeks.

Take lots of office supplies before your leave.

Finally tell your manager what a bad dresser he is.

Walk around the office loudly singing "I gotta get out of this place if it's the last thing I ever do..." over and over again.

DECLINING THE OFFER

If you decline an offer, you need to call your prospective employer and send a follow-up letter as well. Make sure when you do this that you do it graciously. It's always good practice to phone the hiring manager (or the recruiter, when applicable) and thank her for the offer, as well as explain why you have decided to decline it. You don't have to go into major detail; just cover the basics: "I've decided to pursue another opportunity," or "This job isn't the best fit for me because...."

In some instances, the employer may probe you for more specifics, so be prepared to politely say enough but not more than you feel comfortable or think is smart to reveal. Of course, never bad mouth any organization. Then thank them for their time and say that you enjoyed learning about the position and their organization.

It's okay to decline a position that's not right for you. Trust your gut as well as your evaluation of the job's criteria. If something just doesn't seem right for you, then don't go there. Even if your friends or parents are telling you what a great opportunity or how desirable a job is, you're the one who has to live with it on a day-to-day basis. It's also perfectly acceptable to decline an offer if you just want to wait to see what else is out there in your job search.

NEGOTIATING THE OFFER

Negotiating the offer, in particular, is a complex process. You must prepare for a negotiation by researching salaries appropriate for the position and coming up with a wish list of other items. To know what salaries are typical for the position you're considering, you can consult various sources of information on salaries. These include people who know the field or industry, surveys that professional associations frequently conduct, and other resources found in public library reference sections, job listings in newspapers, *The American Almanac of Jobs and Salaries 1994-1995 Edition* by John W. Wright (Avon Books), the *CPC Salary Survey* (College Placement Council, annual publication), and career guides for various fields. Most importantly, you must come up with a walk-away position. A walkaway position is your bottom line. It's the minimum offer you would accept and still feel good about.

The Preparation

The topics open for negotiation vary by level and industry, but salary is generally the main negotiation point. Sometimes, you can also negotiate benefits, title, and start date. For example, you may want tuition reimbursement to begin when you enter the company. However, the company policy is that new employees must wait six months to receive it. You may be able to negotiate this benefit so that you get what you want. If you do successfully negotiate such a benefit, get it in writing as part of an offer letter from the company, or as a second choice, in your acceptance letter to them.

Be sure to consider your whole compensation package—benefits, vacation time, profit-sharing, etc.—when deciding if you want to negotiate for a higher salary. It's important to count all elements of the compensation package that you would have to pay for yourself, such as health insurance, as if they were monetary. Add the dollar value of these elements to your salary as you consider the worth of your job offer.

The Approach

A major part of your approach concerns your timing. *When* you ask for what you want is as important as *what* you ask for. The time to negotiate your job offer is after you receive the offer and before you accept or decline it. If you eventually accept an offer, you can't go back later and say, "Oops, I forgot about that; let's add that in..." Likewise, if you decline an offer without trying to modify it, you may regret it and wonder if you could have made it work out.

Your attitude in the negotiation also matters. Your demeanor should be cooperative and open, rather than demanding and closed. In addition, flexibility is necessary in order to establish a rapport with the employer. By remaining open to a give-and-take discussion about your job offer, you'll most likely end up with a mutually acceptable outcome.

The Dialogue

We'll focus here on salary, since this is the main and most complex topic you'll negotiate. Having done your research, you're in a position of strength to get what you want. When you begin, try to let the prospective employer make the first offer. If they ask you what you want, ask them what they had in mind for the position. If they insist that you begin the bidding, aim 10-20 percent above what you really want. You can't negotiate up, only down from your initial bid. So start high enough that you ultimately can meet the employer in the middle. For example, if you want $40,000, then ask for $44,000. The employer may then come back with $36,000 and you can ask for $40,000.

In case they come back with an offer that is too low, such as $32,000, don't get upset, angry or shut down. Just focus objectively on getting where you want to be. Be direct and restate your interest in the job and the organization. Then tell the employer that the only thing holding you back is that you are not satisfied with the salary offered. Wait for them to respond without jumping in on the silence. This part is especially hard, since some employers are good negotiators and can keep you waiting for several minutes, which may seem like an eternity. It's like playing poker: sometimes you just have to wait it out with a straight face. If you receive another offer, continue the negotiation until you get to a reasonable point.

If the employer makes the first offer, they'll probably give you the lowest or a number on the low side of what they're really willing to end up with. This practice is referred to as low-balling. Many positions, even entry-level ones, have a salary range that varies anywhere from a few hundred to a few thousand dollars. Every range has a low, mid, and high point to accommodate your level of experience and future growth.

Your prospective employer will try to hire you for as low a salary as possible in this range to keep their department budget low. When you respond to a given range, make your counteroffer range overlap at the top of it. For example, if an employer tells you that the salary for a position is $29,000–$33,000, tell them that your salary research and skills make you worth $32,000–$35,000. This way you'll have a better chance at negotiating on the high end of a legitimate range.

The key to effective negotiating is demonstrating your value to your prospective employer. They won't give you more money just because you need it. But they might pay you more if they believe you're worth it. You need to prove how you can solve their problems or meet their needs. Tell the employer about your past accomplishments and relate them to the employer's needs. An easy, powerful way to present this information is by developing CBO statements. This technique is useful at many times during your job search, such as writing your resume, developing a phone pitch, and during salary negotiations. Here's how to create an CBO statement:

C: Think of a relevant professional *challenge* you have encountered.

B: Think of a corresponding *behavior* that you used to address this challenge.

O: Think of a strong, preferably quantifiable *outcome* that resulted from your behavior.

Use these CBO statements to convey to the employer how you have successfully met challenges in the past and can use these experiences to do the prospective job better than anyone else. In this way, you concretely show the employer how you would be an immediate asset to their organization.

Another way to get a negotiator to budge is to propose alternative situations to increasing your salary. For example, ask for a guaranteed six-month salary review based on your performance or suggest that the employer hire you for a slightly more responsible position in you desired salary range or pitch a position that you create for yourself in the organization with an appropriate salary.

Suggesting creative ways to supplement your salary is another option. You can ask to participate in a tuition assistance program, for instance, if you want to go to graduate school or take a few seminars as a way to get more bang for your buck. Or, in a for-profit organization, you can ask for a profit-share arrangement or stock options if it is public. These ideas don't immediately require your manager to get approval for a higher salary and so, may help you get what you want more readily.

Ending the Negotiation

There will be a point in the negotiation where you and your prospective employer have either reached an agreement about the terms of your job offer or are at a stalemate. If you're stuck in your negotiation process, you'll need to make a decision about whether or not to accept the offer as it stands.

If you're really undecided about where you stand, tell the hiring manager that you'd like to take a day or two to consider the offer. Remember your walkaway position, the offer you won't go below. If you are financially stable and really unhappy with the offer and think you can do better, then don't settle for a raw deal or one that is far out of your appropriate range. Or, if you really can't afford to make ends meet with this offer, then don't torture yourself. Find a way to supplement your income, or look for another job. Either way, starting a new job while stressed out about money will adversely affect your performance. It's not the end of the world if you have to leave the offer on the table.

At the same time, be realistic and remember to consider the dollar value of the compensation package as a whole when you mull over the value of your offer. Especially when you're just starting out in your career, you don't have much negotiating experience or leverage. Realize that you have to start somewhere and pay your dues. If you really want the job and are willing to forgo salary for experience, then reconsider your position.

This trade-off can be difficult not only financially, but in terms of your self-worth. For the first time in your life, your friends and peers are not moving at the same pace. Until now, you all progressed through your school years together from one grade to the next. Now you're entering different fields, and some of you are moving into entry-level jobs which pay differently and others are entering graduate school programs. This can be frustrating, since your pay rates will vary greatly, as will your titles and working conditions.

It's important to compare yourself to others in your field at your level, not to your friends in other fields. And realize that you may choose to gain solid experience for less money than you'd expected to earn which will pay off later.

Another approach to getting unstuck in a negotiation is to propose alternative solutions to increasing your salary. One possibility is to ask for a guaranteed six month salary review based on your performance. Or you could suggest that the employer hire you for a slightly more responsible position which comes with a salary in your desired range. Another creative response, for the bold and imaginative among you, is to pitch a position which you create for yourself at the organization. This position would, of course, come with an appropriate salary.

After you negotiate an offer, you again need to decide whether to decline or accept it.

ACCEPTING THE OFFER

If you're happy with the offer and you know from your research that it's a fair one given your experience, the occupation, and the industry, then go for it. In most cases, human resources will send you a written offer for your signature, indicating that you agree to the terms of the offer. If not, you should send your new employer a letter summarizing the terms of your mutually agreed offer.

Although receiving an acceptable offer is the desired end to your much-labored-over job search, there are a couple of possible scenarios that you might encounter and should be prepared for:

Scenario #1: Accept, But Wait a Few Days

You may want to take some time to make sure it's the right move. In this case, you should immediately tell the employer that you are very interested in the position and want to think it over for a day or two. Make sure you indicate when you will get back to them with your decision, for example, by 5:00 p.m. on Wednesday, and phone them promptly within the time frame you agreed upon.

Scenario #2: Accept, But First Consider Other Pending Offers

If you have been interviewing for more than one position, you may be anticipating other offers in the near future. In this case, let the prospective employer who has made you an offer know where you stand. Tell them that you are very interested in the job, but that you need a few more days or a week to see through other possibilities. They'll then let you know if they're willing to wait or if they need a response sooner. As we discussed earlier in this chapter, use this offer as leverage with your other prospective employers. Then follow the last step of the process in Scenario #1 above and accept the job.

GIVING NOTICE

Don't give notice until you have an offer letter or an acknowledgment of your letter to the employer firmly in your hands. This is a key point, since you don't want to get caught between an old job and a suddenly withdrawn new one.

When you give notice, remember not to burn your bridges. You may really want to let your former employer know what you really thought of the organization, salary, your supervisor's personality, and other assorted things. But, resist the temptation and don't do it! Any momentary satisfaction you feel will be quickly replaced by the reality of the word getting around that you are a bitter ex-employee or by having your former supervisor suddenly show up at your new company in a position of power. You just never know what can happen, and it's better not to find out the hard way.

You can tell your supervisor that you are giving notice. Written notice, however, is typically required so that the organization can have a record of your resignation on file.

Dealing with Counteroffers

After you give notice, your organization may make you a counter-offer, or an offer to stay. This counteroffer may include a salary increase and other benefits. Beware of accepting counteroffers, though, because then your employer knows you may leave at any time and it might affect your future growth within the organization. Also, remember there was a reason or two why you pursued other opportunities.

Updating Your Network

Let the people in your job search network know when you begin a new job. Call or write them, informing them of your new place of employment and how to reach you. Thank them again for their help along the way and indicate your interest in keeping in touch with them in the future.

Updating your network will enable you to maintain your professional contacts for future reference. It'll also be a great way to grow professionally, since these individuals will become your colleagues in the field over time. You will undoubtedly contact each other again about professional activities and job opportunities.

From Learning to Earning

INTERNSHIPS, APPRENTICESHIPS, AND OTHER WAYS TO BRIDGE THE GAP

So far we have discussed specific ways to prepare you for the job search. Most of these chapters have focused on short-term strategies for acquiring job leads, whether it be tactics for creating an award winning resume or how to "surf the net" for that perfect job. In this chapter, we're going to dig a little deeper. We'll take a look at opportunities that allow you to gain more in-depth exposure about particular career fields while conducting a job search. These methods include:

- Internships
- Externships or Cooperative Education
- Apprenticeships
- Fellowships
- Volunteer Opportunities
- Continuing Education

These experiences can help you gain more knowledge about a career field while equipping you with additional skills to make you a competitive job candidate for a particular job. Even better, they can be used while in college to help you gain focus for your first job *as well as* later in your career, to provide the missing link for a different job search. Which method(s) you use will largely be determined by financial needs, time constraints, and required training for a particular job.

You may look at these options and think, "Nah, that's not for me." But let's say you decide you are interested in public relations and marketing. These fields are somewhat interrelated, but the jobs within each are *very* different. Rather than jump into one or the other, it may be wise to get a clearer idea of what each job entails. The methods we'll discuss will give you a clearer idea about what those jobs actually involve, help you gain marketable skills, and allow you to develop networking contacts in those fields. Not bad, eh?

EXPERIENTIAL EDUCATION

Internships, Fellowships, Externships/Cooperative Education Programs, Apprenticeships, and Community Service/Volunteer Opportunities are all considered "experiential education." These terms can be a complicated matter because some people use the words interchangeably. For instance, an internship working with the veterinarian at a zoo may also be considered a volunteer experience *or* an apprenticeship. Similarly, an externship at an architecture firm could also be labeled an internship. So, how do you know what you should apply for and why you should apply for it?

Let's try to simplify the confusion by differentiating between the terms. Keep in mind, though, that they all have two things in common:

1. They all have specific start and end times, and

2. They are not viewed as an actual job, but rather as the training ground or path to a job.

Internships

Internships are usually viewed as opportunities to gain experience in a given field, and in this case, to assist with the job search. They are usually longer in duration than an informational interview or shadowing experience. They can last for several weeks, to a month, to a semester, to a full one- or two-year period. Both full- and part-time opportunities are also available. Internships can be paid or unpaid, or can include some variation of the two (such as stipends, which may include a small hourly rate, or may refer only to transportation and meals). This is where it is important for you to determine your time/financial limitations with regard to undertaking such an experience.

Internships usually require some formal application process. This can mean a resume, cover letter, personal interview, and even an essay, transcript, and letter(s) of recommendation. For these reasons, it's important to do your research and be aware of application procedures and deadlines. Be aware that some deadlines can be a full year before the internship actually starts. For instance, the deadline for the United States Department of State is usually November 1 for the following summer!

Internships allow you to become immersed in a job, giving you the most comprehensive exposure to a particular career field. This method of the job search is most appropriate for those who can take an extended leave from a job, or for college students and recent graduates.

Information about specific internship programs can be found by checking with your college career center, by asking professors, or by reading specific books about internships (like The Princeton Review's *Top Internships* or *Internship Bible*). Many internship sites focus on certain populations, such as women, students of color, high school students, college sophomores, juniors, seniors, or graduates, while others are more flexible and may consider all populations. In addition, many companies list their own internship programs through their personnel or human resources departments. If you're interested in a particular organization, call them and inquire about opportunities.

Fellowships

Fellowships are typically postgraduate programs and are offered for training or volunteer opportunities, as well as graduate study. They can be merit-based, need-based, or some combination of the two, so they can be extremely competitive. There is usually a formal application process that, in some cases, can be quite extensive. Many require academic transcripts, resumes, and letters of recommendation, so plan ahead! Keep in mind that, like internships, they have formal deadlines that can be up to one full year before the fellowship actually begins. The duration of these programs can be one to two years, and they usually have stipends. One example of a fellowship program is The Peace Corps, a worldwide volunteer organization, which fights poverty, hunger, and disease. They require a two-year commitment, providing living expenses, medical and dental insurance, and a stipend upon completion. Fellowships can also be used for graduate study, as is the case with the Jacob Javits Fellowship. This grant program is for students studying in the arts, humanities or social sciences. Fellows receive a stipend based on financial need and available funding, which can be used for educational and living expenses.

If you're still in school, information regarding fellowships can be found at your college career center or dean of studies office. If you're out in the real world, The Foundation Center in New York City (79 Fifth Avenue, New York, New York tel: 212-620-4230) also has extensive resources for information on fellowships for certain projects and for certain populations.

Externships or Cooperative Education Programs

Externships or cooperative education (co-op) programs differ from internships in that they are more structured and are typically part of a degree program at an academic institution or trade school. In other words, you may receive a certain number of credit hours (and a grade!) toward your degree for participation in an externship. These programs are usually a semester or year in duration, depending on the requirements of your school. What's more, you are usually paid for these experiences. Your school will usually have an office (such as a career development or cooperative education center) that will assist you with finding an externship or co-op site.

Apprenticeships

The term "apprenticeship" is most often found in specific craft or trade careers and refers to working under an experienced person or master tradesperson in that field or trade union. Apprenticeships are usually paid, and a certain number of hours must be accrued before entering the field as an actual professional. People often assume that these types of programs would not be appropriate for college students or postgraduates, but if you are interested in trades as varied as carpentry or hat making, an apprenticeship might be just up your alley!

Take Paul, a young man who was finishing his degree in political science at a well-known university. He'd always enjoyed building things, making bookshelves and chests for family and friends during summer months and vacations. Even though he had done an internship while in college at a law firm, upon graduation he felt unfocused, having no real interest in pursuing the "law thing." After careful consideration he decided to apprentice with a carpenter in town. He is now a successful (and content) carpenter with his own business.

If interested in such programs, you should contact a career center, career counselor, or inquire with associations related to the field. Information about these trade organizations can also be found at your local library.

Volunteer Positions/Community Service

Volunteering at a homeless shelter or a community health organization often allows the flexibility of working beyond the regular 9-to-5 job constraints. These types of positions can also be a great way to do some insider networking. Sue, one of our clients, was working in financial services and was interested in making a career change. She thought she wanted to pursue a job with a focus on women's issues. It seemed interesting, a place where she could make a difference, but she had little experience in that area. Sue did not have the economic flexibility to leave her current job, nor did she have the time during the week to conduct an internship. We suggested that she volunteer at a local women's health clinic on weekends to see if women's issues was in fact a solid career interest and to gain experience in the field. The volunteer experience solidified Sue's interest and allowed her to acquire relevant skills that made her more marketable in her job search. She ultimately left her job in financial services and now runs a battered women's shelter in Chicago.

Information about such opportunities can be found at libraries, colleges, community organizations, or hospitals. This type of career exploration is beneficial for people with full-time job commitments and for students who may have some flexibility in their schedule.

I'M HERE, NOW WHAT?

Now that we have defined the different types of experiential education/job search opportunities, what do you do once you get there? It's not enough to get in on these opportunities—you have to make sure you make good use of them while you're there. What does this mean? Not only are you there to do a great job, you are there to make contacts for the job search. Here are a few tips to make that a little easier:

1. Act professionally while there. Dress in appropriate, job-related attire. Be punctual and adhere to your schedule. Don't use company time for personal concerns. If you find yourself with free time, ask if there are other projects to get involved in. Or, initiate a project of your own! Nothing is more impressive than an intern/fellow/apprentice/volunteer who has obviously found an area that needs attention and takes it upon herself to tackle the issue. Of course, it is proper to ask for permission first before taking on any new project.

2. Make contacts while at your internship site. Talk to people! It is hoped that these are the networking contacts that will ultimately assist you with your job search. Be professional, but don't be shy. Whether it be the president of the company or other office workers, introduce yourself.

3. Gather information about the entire industry. Don't just assume you can only learn about the company you work with, branch out and ask questions about other organizations in that particular industry. Make contact with people from related organizations, when appropriate.

In an environment where the economy is tight and the job search competitive, you want to give yourself as much of an edge as possible. Close your eyes and imagine this: You are in the running for a paralegal job with someone else who comes from a school comparable to the one you attended and with an academic background similar to yours. The only difference in you resumes is that you completed two summer internships with local law firms where you conducted legal research, in addition to other general office duties. Now put yourself in the shoes of the hiring manager. Who is the most competitive candidate for the job? Take a bow—you take the paralegal prize!

Similarly, when looking for jobs you may have a bunch of possible contacts right at your fingertips through the externship or fellowship you just completed. Sara, one of our clients, was finishing up an externship with an architectural firm in April of her senior year. Because she was looking for full-time work in the field, she put her "feelers out, talking with people both at her firm and others in the area. Within weeks she had interviews at two firms, and eventually ended up working for one of them. Who you know can make a difference.

Now, we can't promise that these types of experiences will win you a trip around the world, help you lose twenty pounds, or even make you one of *People* magazine's Most Fascinating People of the Year, but we can attest to what they can do: increase your chances of picking the career field that is right for you while gaining skills and making networking contacts. In all, not a bad return on your time.

CONTINUING YOUR EDUCATION

"The job market is tight. I have nothing else to do, so I might as well go to graduate school." Does this sound like something you've said to yourself before? It's not such a crazy idea; sometimes, graduate school is a good move in this situation—but sometimes it's not.

It's easy to get caught up in the familiar frenzy of the school application process and wrap yourself in the warm blanket of campus life. To save yourself wasted time, energy, and application fees, it's a good idea to step back before immersing yourself. Once you're in it, the process takes on a life of its own and it's very difficult to have the perspective and guts to ask yourself if you're doing the right thing.

Among all of the reasons grad school applicants have for wanting to go, there are really only a few that will get you in and enable you to benefit from your experience. Something to pass the time is not one of these reasons.

So What Are Good Reasons?

Pursuing graduate work for Jennifer, Stan, and Hallie was a logical, appropriate step. Jennifer applied to law school to become an environmental lawyer. She obviously needed the training before she could get a job in the field. Stan wanted to go to business school to move forward in his career, from being a research associate to an analyst at an investment banking firm. An MBA brought him advanced status, increased responsibility, and growth. Hallie had always experienced an insatiable thirst for learning. She loved school and wanted to go as far as she could, by getting a Ph.D. in comparative literature and teaching at the college level.

Another thing to keep in mind is that graduate school is only one of many continuing education opportunities that can help you get the necessary training and credibility to get a job.

In our experience advising students and college grads about continuing their education, we've found that it's helpful to present the options in terms of their respective purposes. We'll discuss the many offerings called continuing education by grouping them into four categories: Avocational, Life Skills, Job Preparation, and Professional Enhancement.

Avocational means classes that you would take for fun to dabble in a hobby or casual interest not directly related to your paid work. Maybe you'll take a painting, music appreciation, sailing, or gourmet cooking class.

If you're looking for a course to teach you how to enhance your overall sense of wellness, check out a *life skills* course. You could take a class in CPR, self-defense, public speaking, financial planning, or stress management.

Since you're reading a book about job search, you know how important it is to get prepared to make successful transitions into a first or new job. Graduate school, or other programs that serve as either stepping stones to graduate school or substitutes for graduate school, can all be considered *job preparation*.

This category is broad, because it includes preparation for a wide variety of fields. You can take classes and complete programs in such diverse areas as broadcasting, career counseling, environmental science, fitness instruction, healthcare management, human resources management, marketing, multimedia technology, publishing, and vocational education in the skilled trades.

A fourth kind of continuing education, *professional enhancement*, covers ways in which your can improve professional careers that you're already involved in. If you're a health care professional, counselor, attorney, actuary, or outdoor education instructor, for example, you've probably taken courses to receive additional levels of training and certification.

SIGN ME UP!

As a job searcher, Job Preparation is the category that most applies to you. When you're exploring Job Preparation options, you'll find them in different formats. Individual courses (credit and non-credit), certificate programs, graduate school, and vocational education programs are the main ones. These programs are often flexible ways for you to pursue further training on either a part-time or full-time basis.

Individual courses are offered through many institutions on a noncredit basis. This means that you can take courses to explore a field of interest or to get comfortable with school again after you've been out for a little while. Even universities' regular as well as continuing education departments often let you enroll in courses as a non-matriculated student without filling out an application. You just need to get permission from the department in the case of a regular one, or register by phone, fax or mail in the case of a continuing education one.

Also, you can take individual courses through many other types of educational organizations as well as universities. Refer to the list of places in the next section of this chapter for ideas. Certificate programs are offered on a noncredit basis typically through continuing education divisions of higher-education institutions. They can be used as a stepping stone or alternative to graduate programs. These programs have open enrollment, meaning there are no specific qualifications required to enroll. Participants include recent grads and more experienced professionals in all careers who want to learn the basics as well as current developments in a field. Certificates can be short-term, intensive ways to move ahead in a career or to make a career transition.

Graduate school programs are probably the most familiar type to you. They include academic master's degrees and doctoral degrees in the arts and humanities, social sciences, and natural sciences, as well as professional degrees in areas such as business, law, and medicine. There are also many programs that offer combined or dual degrees in different fields, such as law and business.

These programs require an extensive application, which often includes letters of recommendation, official transcripts, essays, and standardized test scores. The requirements vary widely depending on the type of program and the level. For example, a master's in social work program does not usually require that you take a standardized test to gain admittance. Business school applications tend to have multiple essay questions, while law school applications usually have one. Grad programs in the arts require a portfolio or audition to gain admittance, while programs in other fields do not usually require a sample of your previous work.

Vocational education programs are often overlooked by college grads as not for them. But they are actually viable means to get solid career training in technical fields. If you have the interest and ability, consider training to become an electrician, medical technician, or computer programmer among other professions. Such training often leads to a lucrative and stable job because of the increasing demand for these services. Technical training institutes nationwide have specialized programs in trade as well as professional areas and offer financial aid as well as placement assistance to candidates who have demonstrated potential in their fields.

RESCUE ME

As we've mentioned, you can find these programs in many different places. Consider all of your options when you're thinking about continuing education as a means to a job. They include graduate schools at universities and colleges, continuing education departments or schools at universities and colleges, technical training schools, distance learning programs through accredited institutions, professional associations, community colleges, YM/YWCAs, Jewish Community Centers, and privately-run alternative learning centers. You can learn more about possible programs in several easy ways:

Conduct Library Research

Your local public library and undergraduate college's career services office library both have resources concerning continuing education. You can work with a reference librarian or information specialist at these places to investigate what programs might meet your needs and to get the information you need to contact the programs directly.

Ask Others

Ask professors, friends, parents' friends, colleagues, and contacts in your field of interest for their recommendation about specific courses of study. People in the field often are the most connected to such programs as both students and adjunct faculty members. They have informed opinions about what kinds of programs and places are the best fit with your background and interests.

Contact Local Schools and Organizations

Use the telephone book as well as the *Encyclopedia of Associations* to compile a working list of local schools and other organizations that might offer courses in your area of interest. Contact the institutions directly and ask them to send you their course catalog and any specific information available on your program of interest.

It's always a good idea to gather as much information as possible, since you may discover that your needs are best met in a course or program related to the one you considered initially. Just like with informational interviews, be sure to ask your contact at one organization for ideas about relevant courses of study at other places, especially if they do not offer continuing education that works for you. Also, be aware that it is worthwhile to request information from your programs of interest before assuming that they are either too demanding or not rigorous enough.

You can find a program that meets your needs for cost, time, rigor, credibility, and value and, in turn, strengthen your job search. All you need to do is to investigate thoroughly how these criteria can impact your ability to get your desired job.

RECYCLING

Given the changing nature of the job market, many recent grads find that they need to train or retrain either immediately out of college or shortly thereafter.

Nearly one-third of all U.S. adults are enrolled in a formal education program, according to the U.S. Center for Education Statistics (CES), and at least one-quarter of them are participating primarily for job-related reasons—to 'advance,' to 'improve skills,' or to get 'new training'."
(New York University School of Continuing Education "Changing Scene" Winter 1995, p. 1.)

Increasing numbers of recent graduates as well as mid-career transition professionals are enrolling in continuing ed programs, making the classroom an excellent networking *and* learning environment.

In some cases, networking and free placement services are offered by these programs, aiding your ability to obtain a job. When you investigate a program, read and ask questions about the placement services the institution provides students and alumni as well as their placement statistics. Make sure you take advantage of these services early on so that can use them to get employment while you're in school instead of when you're close to finishing your program.

You have so many ways to get ready for a job in your current or a new field. Continuing education, with its practical, real world approach, can give you the edge as a candidate in the job market now and for years to come.

10

Smoothing the Rocky Road

COPING WITH REJECTION

"Don't worry about it!" you hear your support team say as you embark on the job search track. It's easier said than done. Especially when it comes to the fear of rejection. Some of you have been burned before and are concerned about a repeat performance. Others just can't seem to get over the nightmares about the imaginary hiring manager from hell. Both of these scenarios can negatively affect your job search.

Because you fear rejection, you may be reluctant to actively pursue your job search. This fear is understandable, but you can't let it stop you. Acknowledge it and realize that it's a normal reaction to going after something you really want. Then get on with it and try not to take rejection as a personal rebuff.

There are many reasons why you may lose out on a job that are out of your control. The person who gets hired may be an internal candidate, have more targeted qualifications, and being connected through a network. Even if you don't get the job this time, though, it doesn't mean that you wouldn't be an asset to an organization or that you couldn't do a job. It just means that it didn't work out. Get back out there and give it your best shot. Somewhere along the line it'll be you who gets the job.

Another way that you may let the fear of rejection undermine your job search is by focusing exclusively on getting the employer to like you. Any recruiter or hiring manager will tell you that when you have this attitude inside, it comes across as phony and overeager outside. Instead, try to remember that an interview is a two-way discovery process to determine if you and the employer are a mutually good fit. Approach your interview and other interactions with the employer this way and you'll project confidence, interest, and a mature professionalism.

WHEN THE GOING GETS TOUGH

As you know, it's not just the fear of rejection that can get you stuck. It's also the reality of it. Rejection can feel devastating. You may want to go off on a vacation, hide in your home, or escape into a movie marathon surrounded by as much junk food as you can stomach.

There are many other, more productive alternatives for dealing with the emotional aspects of rejection. It's important to cope with your lows during the job search process as they happen, so that you can move on as quickly as possible toward ultimate success. The exercises below will help you to:

- identify and address your feelings
- draw upon supportive others
- review your past successes
- review your job search strategies

SEND YOURSELF A DIFFERENT MESSAGE

Often, we are unaware of the things we tell ourselves after we're rejected. When we take the time to hear these responses, we discover that many of them are destructive and blown out of proportion.

Make sure that you aren't sending yourself any self-destructive messages, such as:

"There's no point in following up on that interview. I'm sure they have better candidates."

"I hear there are very few jobs in my field for recent college grads. I'm not going to find a job."

"This wait and see thing after final interviews is torture. Maybe I'll just stop dealing with organizations after the interview so I can put them out of my mind."

These kinds of messages are powerful because you can sabotage your best efforts with them. It's only natural to have fears and feel down about your progress. But, the only way you're going to move forward successfully with your job search is to tell yourself more good stuff than bad stuff about how it's going. It's really a matter of not getting in your own way. Be real, but tell yourself a more optimistic story than the day before.

By changing the way we talk to ourselves about rejection, we can recover more quickly and with renewed strength and perspective. Here are some common messages we send ourselves and some new messages to deal with rejection more effectively:

When I feel...	I tell myself...	Instead, I'll try to think...
Anger	That organization is stupid!	Sometimes things don't work out.
Rejection	XYZ company jilted me!	It's not personal, but professional rejection; therefore, it's not a good fit for me either.
Worthlessness	I blew it and failed!	It's only one moment in time; I've been perceived as competent and valuable in the past and will be again.
Disappointment	I feel so deflated that I didn't get that job!	It's normal to be disappointed, especially when I wanted something to work out. The feeling will pass.
Denial	I didn't get rejected; they must have made a mistake when they addressed the letter!	Rejection happens. It's part of life. Nobody's perfect and we all experience it sometimes.
Confusion	What do I do now? I thought I did everything right and I don't have any idea what to do next!	It's okay to be unsure what to do next and feel overwhelmed. I can focus on approaching things in small steps until I regroup and re energize. I can also get help to gain clarity.
Embarrassment	I just want to crawl into a hole and hide! Maybe I'll just stay at home for a while and not socialize until I straighten my work life out!	It's not shameful to be rejected. I will surround myself with those I trust who are supportive of my endeavors.
Depression	All I can think of is how bad things are in my life! It's all doom and gloom!	I will focus as much as possible on the positives in my search and in my life every day, especially on the small triumphs.
Hopelessness	There's no way I'm ever gonna get a job. I can't seem to break this cycle of rejection!	This experience is part of my natural learning process. I have much to gain. I can survive rejection and more—on to success!

Develop a Support System

Having a support system of people who you can turn to when you're feeling down about your job search, can be an invaluable resource for you. Your support system can be as big or as small as you wish. Remember to refer to chapter 3's section on "Building and Maintaining a Support Team" for details on how to do this when you begin your job search.

It is, however, a good idea to have more than one supporter in order both to benefit from others' varied experiences and to avoid putting too much pressure on any one relationship. Remembering to select others whom you can also support at some point in their job searches will enable you to build a strong support system more comfortably.

Create a Success Lifeline

Another way to deal with rejection is to create a success lifeline. Take a blank 8 1/2" by 11" piece of paper and turn it horizontally. Draw a long, horizontal line from the left side of the page to the right side of the page. Place short vertical lines along this horizontal line at different chronological stages from left to right (earliest to latest). Then label the space underneath the horizontal line between each two vertical lines. These blocks of time might be broad, descriptive categories like your preschool years, elementary school years, junior high school years, high school years, etc., or they can be age-based categories, like 1-5 years old, 5-10 years old, etc. It doesn't matter how you label your blocks of time, as long as you understand that these blocks will potentially contain success events in your life.

Within each block of time indicate in any way you choose, a marker of one or more success events. These markers can be pictures, words, or a combination of these things. These success events can reflect accomplishments that you have been proud of in any aspect of your life—family, hobbies, personal growth issues, relationships, education, professional, or anything else.

Try not to think too long about your choices before putting them down on paper. When you've placed at least five success events on your lifeline, review them to see if you can discern any patterns or themes concerning your definition of success. The connections may be transformations or continuous threads of your definition over time.

Have you selected events in only one or two areas of your life, such as education and work? Are you surprised by your choices? Did they reinforce something you already knew about yourself and your values? Did your memories of success bring back any situations where your success was bouncing back from a rejection or other such difficult situation? What can you apply from these past experiences to your present one?

Review Your Job Search Log

Check your job search log (see chapter 3's section, "Getting Organized") to ensure that you're going after jobs that fit with your true career goals. If you're going after jobs that aren't what you really want or aren't going to be a step toward what you want, stop. Conserve your energy and redirect your search.

If you're headed in the right direction, see if there is another way you can approach your search to make the lows easier on yourself, using techniques such as those we've just described.

Take Care of Yourself

When you're caught up in being a professional job searcher, it's easy to forget about your other needs besides a job. Good food, exercise, sleep, hobbies, friends, and other fun activities improve your overall well-being and help you cope with stress. The less stressed you are, the more inclined you'll be to succeed at your job search. Besides, you deserve it. So give yourself a break and conserve your energy.

Some fun, inexpensive ways to cope with rejection are little things that just make you happy. When you're feeling blue, get a massage, get back to nature, practice aromatherapy, eat lots of healthy "comfort food" (your childhood favorites), watch classic comedy videos like The Three Stooges — whatever. Just make sure you do something that makes you not only relax, but brings you back to feeling like your old, great self.

KICK STARTING A STALLED JOB SEARCH

You know your job search is going down the tubes when the phone has stopped ringing, the mail brings nothing but rejection letters, and you've memorized the daytime TV talk show lineup. Even your friends and family have given up asking, "Do you have a job yet?"—the question you thought they'd never tire of. When the situation gets this grim, the best thing to do for your search may be to *stop* searching—at least long enough to regroup and figure out where the problem lies. Like a computer that malfunctions, a stalled job hunt requires troubleshooting tactics to get it back on track. Taking the five steps described on the following pages can help you zero in on the source of the problem and generate some much needed activity.

STEP ONE—CHECK YOUR JOB SEARCH "TOOLS"

Though it may seem unfair, something as simple as a typo in your resume could be the thing standing between you and a job. Before embarking on a complete overhaul of your job search strategy, take a careful look at the tools of your search. Just as a computer can come from the manufacturer with a bug or can catch a virus, so too can your job search "equipment." Look over the following list of your "tool kit" contents for places that might be sources of trouble. Then refer to the appropriate chapters for troubleshooting strategies:

- Resume(s) (chapter 4)
- Cover letters (chapter 4)
- Letters of recommendation and portfolio (chapter 4)
- References (chapter 4)
- Interviewing technique (chapter 6)
- Phone technique (chapter 4)

Even a minor flaw in any of these tools can stand between you and a job. You have to double-check and triple-check every component of your search even if you think there's no need to do so.

One woman we worked with got off to a great start with her job hunt, getting to third and fourth interviews but not getting any offers. She seemed to be doing everything right, and she had terrific experience and skills, having worked for several years since college for a large company where she'd moved up two notches from an entry-level clerical position. We couldn't imagine what the problem was until we had her check her own references. It turned out that through a data-entry glitch in her former employer's human resources department, prospective employers calling for a reference were being told that she had held only the entry-level position for all six years. They then assumed that she had fabricated two promotions on her resume. Even if they suspected there might be a mix-up, most weren't going to take the time to give her the benefit of the doubt and investigate. Fortunately, the job seeker did look into the matter and got the problem cleared up. She then landed a job two weeks later.

STEP TWO—CHECK YOUR STRATEGY

If you didn't find any problems in Step One, or if you found problems and fixed them but your search remains at a standstill, then it may be time to evaluate your overall job search strategy. When you run out of places to apply and people to talk to, it's essential that you stretch the limits of your creativity to come up with more effective tactics. There is almost always a way to generate new leads and expand your network. Contrary to what you might think, a job search is not born to self-destruct like those stars you learned about in astronomy class that eventually collapse in on themselves and disappear. You may feel like your search is sinking into a black hole in outer space, but the situation is rarely as dismal as it seems. There are solutions!

If you've turned straight to this section and skipped the rest of the book, then the answer is easy: Read chapters 1 through 9 and follow our advice!! On the other hand, if you've already read the rest of the book and have followed our suggestions but are still having problems finding a job, then your strategy may need more extensive first-aid. Try asking yourself the following troubleshooting questions, making sure to take your time in doing so. The whole point of the exercise is to take a step back from your search, reflect on what you've been doing, and identify glitches in the system.

WHAT AM I DOING WRONG?

1. Am I using the full range of job lead sources? (chapter 5)

2. Am I using the best job lead sources for the field/industry in which I'm looking? (chapters 4 and 5)

3. Am I presenting myself as a focused job candidate with something to offer? (chapters 1 and 4)

4. Are there people and places I've forgotten about that
   I could follow-up with now? (chapters 3 and 5)

If your answer to any of these was "I don't know" or "No," then review the chapter indicated after each question and look for strategies you might have overlooked.

Step Three—Get Feedback

So you've taken Steps One and Two but *still* don't see where the problem lies. If that's the case, then it's time to involve other people in your troubleshooting process. Sometimes no matter how hard you try to think of new approaches to finding a job you just can't come up with anything. The difficulty may be that you're too close to the search to see it with an objective eye, or you might simply be more of a details person by nature and less of a strategist, so new ideas just aren't pouring in. Or, maybe you're the type who can come up with all sorts of great ideas but you're not good with the details and still haven't spotted that typo. Whatever the case, it never hurts to call in someone with an outside perspective for a fresh approach.

Now is the time to review the list of people you came up with in chapter 3 as your inner circle of job hunting allies. You'll need to enlist the help of any people on that list who haven't driven you crazy by now (or who haven't run screaming from you, the "Friendly Neighborhood Disgruntled Job Seeker"). For the troubleshooting we're advocating here, the friends and family who comprise part of this support team need not have any special knowledge of job search techniques or of the field in which you're searching. Just having another pair of eyes and objective perspective is all the expertise needed to detect problems in your written materials or to assess how effective you are on the phone or in a mock interview. As we mentioned in Chapter 6 on interviewing, much of job-seeking involves simply communicating with other human beings—not unfamiliar life forms from another planet. Assuming your friends and family are fellow members of the human race, then it stands to reason that they can be good judges of your job search style. Pay attention to their feedback!

Once they've all helped look for typos, interviewing faux pas, and any other problems described in Step One, you should turn to the more creative and visionary members of your inner circle. Even without being professional job search coaches, they can probably come up with some effective ideas for generating activity. They'll say, for example, "What do you mean there's no one left to talk to about entry-level jobs in public relations, why don't you write to that new firm that was featured in the business section of yesterday's paper?" (You missed that article because you used yesterday's paper to wrap those genuine acrylic knickknacks you shipped back to the home shopping channel.)

When the people around you run out of ideas, remember that another important source of advice can come from the *outer* circle that has formed since you began your search. It consists of all the people you have come into contact with through phone calls, interviews, informational interviews, and other sources. These professional contacts can often give feedback on your interviewing style, phone manner, written materials, etc. Review some of the principles of networking in chapter 5 and follow-through in chapter 7 if you need help renewing or maintaining contact with this outer circle.

Also, don't forget to turn to a college career advisor or an independent career counselor for expert advice to balance the amateur (but valuable!) input of family members and friends. This decision worked for Morgan, a recent graduate with a major in business, excellent grades, and solid summer work experience who had been looking for positions in marketing with major corporations. After a fruitless five-month search in New York and Boston, he was beginning to despair. His parents were both successful corporate executives who had tried to help him by arranging informational interviews and circulating his resume among their colleagues. In addition, he had sent out over one-hundred resumes to companies on his Hit List and had received only a couple of responses.

Morgan couldn't understand what was blocking him from jobs. With a thirty-second glance over the cover letter he had been using, we saw the solution to one of the problems. In three brief paragraphs, he unwittingly made five negative references to his qualifications, including the famous "though I have very little experience..." phrase. The letter was also filled with claims of several admirable personal qualities that weren't backed up with any examples. He was clearly an excellent writer—the letter was coherent and eloquent, so to most readers, i.e., his parents and himself, it was a good letter. But to a prospective employer, it gave only vague notions of why he should be hired (or even interviewed), and immediately raised doubts in the minds of the readers with all its negative statements. With some minor reworking, the letter became much more effective and started to bring him positive responses.

The cover letter was clearly one problem, but that doesn't explain why he wasn't getting jobs from the interviews with his parents' contacts where a cover letter wasn't necessary. To solve *that* mystery, we suggested he call one or two people he had met with whom he would feel comfortable asking for feedback. He chose two older men who had been sort of surrogate uncles to him, yet weren't so close to him that they couldn't give objective criticism. He also knew that their no-nonsense manner would make them inclined to "lay it on the line." Morgan asked them for some candid observations on his interviewing style and interpersonal approach in general and did he ever get them. He found out he has a habit of interrupting and a tendency to come across as cocky. Though the criticism wasn't easy to hear, it *was* constructive and gave him something concrete to work on. With some practice interviewing, he managed to develop a much more effective style and got a good job.

STEP FOUR—CONSIDER RE-DIRECTING

Sometimes Steps One through Three just aren't enough. No matter how perfectly you polish your tools or how creatively you strategize, you just keep reaching dead ends and rejections. Or maybe you're not even getting far enough into the process to have rejections because you can't get interviews or find anyone who'll talk to you. If that's the case, it may be time to redirect.

What we mean by redirecting is making a slight shift in your short-term goals without jeopardizing the chances of reaching your long-term goals. For example, you might have your heart set on obtaining an entry-level position in the promotions department of a major record label in Los Angeles. You knew when you started that the music industry is one of the most competitive fields and that it was a long shot, but you were determined to give it a try. Plus, you had some relevant experience with your college radio station, had interned with a small music distributor one summer, and had worked part-time as a sales clerk at Tower Records during school. Despite all that, you've been searching for eight months without even a nibble.

If you don't have an urgent financial need for a job, you do have the option of continuing to look for another few months. But even so, keep in mind that the gap on your resume won't look too good. If you *are* going to let your search go on ad infinitum, at least be sure you have some kind of part-time job or volunteer work to put on paper so you can show that you are doing something productive with your time besides reading rejection letters.

Most of you probably don't have the luxury of letting your job search drag on for several months or a year or more. If that's the case, consider widening your search and slightly shifting gears. Your options for doing so are:

Broaden the Range of Job Titles You've Been Targeting

For example, if you're finding that a job in music promotions is too hard to come by, consider applying for positions in less competitive areas of a music company. People working in that field can advise you on the prospects for future mobility between departments so you don't get stuck. Just getting a foot in the door at a record company in any department may be a good first step. This strategy can apply to most any industry, not just music.

Consider Finding a Comparable Job Title in Other Fields or Industries

That same job seeker who wants music promotions could do just as well getting a start in a promotions capacity in another industry. Working in public relations, marketing, publicity, or sales in a different field would provide valuable experience and skills to bring to the music industry a year or two later. If the experience is in a related area of media or entertainment, then it's even better. What you're doing here is getting a foot in the door to a functional area (promotions) by targeting a different industry.

Target Smaller Organizations

Another option is staying in the same industry but targeting different sized organizations. With music, for example, you wouldn't concentrate on just the major record labels. There are many small, independent production companies that may be less competitive. This advice applies to most any field. Smaller doesn't always mean less competitive, but it can. As described in chapter 2, the growth areas of many industries are in small to medium-sized companies.

Consider Another Sector of the Work World

If you've been looking only in the private sector, consider the public sector/nonprofit world or vice versa. That music promotions experience, for example, may be available with a trade union or not-for-profit organization representing musicians. If you've already been looking in the nonprofit sector for, let's say, fund-raising, recognize that you can acquire valuable sales and interpersonal skills in a private sector business organization. You can then take those skills to the public sector where your experience will be in demand.

Think About Relocating Geographically

Sometimes economic factors beyond your control can have an adverse effect on your job search. If moving is an option, you should consider applying where the *jobs* are rather than where *you* are. If, for example, you are determined to be in advertising but can't get onto Madison Avenue or even into smaller, less well-known ad agencies in New York, then you may need to consider moving to a smaller city to get advertising experience. You can then come back to the Big Apple equipped with great hands-on skills, a solid portfolio, and maybe a better shot at a job. Regardless of the type of job you're seeking, the economic and job market conditions of a given geographic region may be standing in your way. Obviously, moving is a personal decision, not just a career issue, so it may or may not be an option.

STEP FIVE—CONSIDER A "TIME OUT"

If you seem to be doing everything right and you've taken Steps One through Four and still aren't making any progress, then it may be time for some fairly drastic redirecting. Sometimes the reality of competition, economic factors, or lack of experience and skills make the job of your dreams just about impossible to get. You may need to take an objective look at your qualifications and job market conditions and significantly alter your immediate goals by taking time out from your search.

By taking time out, we don't mean time *off* to hang around the house. What we mean is that you might need to defer your search for a while and pursue some other activity that can bolster your qualifications, not to mention rejuvenate you personally. Depending on your financial situation, time-out activities can include internships, volunteer work/community service, part-time jobs, travel, and continuing education classes. We basically mean a structured program of your own or someone else's design that combines one or more of those activities.

Not all time-out options require taking a vow of poverty. Depending on the cost of living where you are and your own expenses (i.e., living with parents versus supporting yourself), you may be able to combine an unpaid internship and a class with a paid, part-time job or temporary work. Or, consider a paid, full-time job that's not in your area of interest or that doesn't even require a college degree but pays the bills while allowing time in the evening or weekends to take a course or do volunteer work. The key here is to piece together a career that provides for your financial needs and prepares you for your long-term career goals.

There are so many interesting things to do on this planet, that finding something to match your interests, talents, values and wallet is only hard because there are so many choices. You can build houses in Africa, teach English in Japan, learn stained-glass-making in Italy, work on a kibbutz in Israel, or "Teach for America." The list is endless and the growth opportunities immeasurable. College career centers and public libraries are good places to find out about these types of experiences.

A valuable resource for productive gateways is TIME OUT, a highly personalized service that finds time-out opportunities in the U. S. and abroad for students and working adults. Contact David Denman at (415) 332-1831.

By the way, the time-out option is not limited to recent grads. Even if you've been working full-time for a while, you do have the option of taking time out. Doing so is especially helpful if you want to make a career change or feel burned out from your career path so far. "Voluntary downshifting" is the term that's been coined by demographers for the 1990's trend of getting off the fast track to do anything from starting your own business, to being a full-time parent, to sitting around contemplating a blade of grass. What you do with this time out is up to you, so long as it's rewarding to you in the present and building on your future.

CHAPTER 11

Sample Resumes

Carla Delacroix

28 Ratchett Street
Denver, CO 11111
(888) 555-0000

Profile
- Ability to impartially analyze disputes and conflicts, and resolve them diplomatically; knowledgeable about arbitration, contracts, and labor law.
- Completing M.S. degree in Human Resource Management & Labor Relations.
- Elected as the youngest Chairperson of the Executive Board in the history of the Transport Workers Union - Local 553.

Labor Relations Experience
- Solely responsible for the expeditious processing of complaints and grievances for 800 union members; served as official union spokesperson.
- Promoted the interests of flight attendants locally and nationally; safeguarded individual and collective rights of all members; successfully lobbied Governor Cuomo to obtain unemployment benefits for flight attendants.
- Conducted legal research regarding labor disputes; interpreted contracts and prepared contract amendments; clarified rules and regulations for the union membership.

Management Experience
- Organized and chaired numerous committees; oversaw publication of newsletter.
- Supervised up to six flight attendants; trained new personnel.
- Responsible for budget management and allocation.

Education
- **M.S., Human Resource Management and Labor Relations**, May 1996
  University of Denver, Denver, CO
  Center for Labor and Industrial Relations Scholarship
- **Leadership Certification in Management and Labor Relations**, 1993
  Florida State University, Tallahassee, FL
- **B.A., English Literature and Marketing**, 1986
  McGill University, Montreal, Canada

Work Experience
- **Flight Attendant, United Airlines**, 1986 - present

LIBERAL ARTS MAJOR

Lianna Maria White

15 River Street, Apt. #3
Pittsburgh, PA 10000
(412) 555-5555

EDUCATION

Carnegie Mellon University, Pittsburgh, PA
Bachelor of Arts, Politics/History, May 1996

Minor: Spanish
Major GPA: 3.2
Honors: College of Arts and Science Scholarship

• Financed 50% of college costs through various part-time jobs.

Relevant Courses

Power and Politics in America	American Constitutional Law
International Politics	Women in Law
Comparative Politics	United States History

EXPERIENCE

1994 - Present

Carnegie Mellon University, Pittsburgh, PA
Admissions Ambassador

Conduct campus tours for up to 25 prospective students and their parents. Respond to phone inquiries regarding admissions and specific academic programs. Represent Carnegie Mellon at open houses and other special events. Provide administrative support within the Admissions Office.

Fall 1993

Investors Associates, Pittsburgh, PA
Sales Assistant

Supported sales efforts of brokers by maintaining up to date client records and daily logs of stock purchases and sales. Coordinatedfollow-up mailings to clients.

Summer 1993

Edward Isaacs & Company (CPA's), Pittsburgh, PA
Telemarketer

Laid the groundwork for the sale of financial software by convincing potential clients to register for a free evaluation of their computer systems. Heavy phone contact with high level executives. Maintained client leads via computer.

ACTIVITIES

Democratic Club—Organized and promoted club activities and events; assisted with voter registration drive.

Pre-Law Society, Member

ESL Tutor

SKILLS

Languages: Fluent in Spanish
Computers: Macintosh: Microsoft Word, IBM: WordPerfect 5.1

INTERESTS

International travel (have visited several countries in Central America and Europe), flute, art museums, ethnic fairs and festivals, Spanish literature, foreign films, African history

Rose Berger

14 West 2nd Street, Apt. F
New York, NY 10000
(212) 444-0000

Education	Phillips Beth Israel School of Nursing, New York, NY
Associate in Applied Science Degree, December 1996

GPA: 3.9
Dean's List: 1993 - 1995
Hillman Scholarship: 1993 - 1995 |

Health Care Experience

Fall 1995 - Present	**Beth Israel Medical Center**, New York, NY
Student Nurse Extern, P.A.C.U.

Perform various tests and procedures under the supervision of a Registered Nurse including the following: |

- Admit patients to ambulatory and in-patient units.
- Remove IVs and catheters; monitor vital signs; administer glucose tests, urine tests, and enemas; perform suctioning; teach crutch walking.
- Conduct discharge teaching.
- Attend in-service training sessions.

Fall 1994	**Lenox Hill Hospital**, New York, NY
Volunteer, Aids Unit

Provided companionship to patients, their families, and significant others. |
| Summer 1994 | **Children's Hospital Medical Center**, Washington D.C.
Volunteer, Adolescent Unit

Played with and comforted children, most of whom were suffering from leukemia, cystic fibrosis, or anorexia nervosa.

Coordinated and led group excursions. Provided general assistance to nurses. |

Professional Affiliations

1992 - Present	National Student Nurses Association

ENVIRONMENTAL FOCUS

Lorraine J. Talisman

✉ 222 Seventh Avenue , Marietta, Ohio 45750 ☎ (614) 333-3333

Profile

Seven years of experience providing for the needs of companion animals, farm livestock, and native and exotic wildlife in a variety of animal care facilities.

Highlights of Experience

Animal Care and Wildlife Rehabilitation

- Developed expertise in all areas of the care and treatment of injured, sick, and orphaned wildlife, including animal rescue, physical examinations, daily management of wounds and fractures, coordinating release of recovered wildlife, and hand-rearing baby mammals and birds.

- Completed International Wildlife Rehabilitation Council's Basic Skills Seminar.

- Expanded behavior training regimen for imprinted bald eagle at The Conservancy's Wildlife Center in Naples, Florida.

Environmental Education

- Conducted tours of The Conservancy's Wildlife Center for visitors of all ages. Provided information about wildlife rehabilitation and the wildlife of South Florida. Presented complex scientific concepts in an accessible, easy to grasp manner.

- Led interpretive and experiential outdoor education classes for children in the Summer Adventures program at Aullwood Audubon Center and Farm, Dayton, Ohio.

Training and Organizational Skills

- Trained and supervised numerous interns and volunteers. Taught basic medical skills, animal handling techniques, and facility maintenance. Contributed to the development of The Conservancy's volunteer training program.

- Assisted with organizing the International Wildlife Rehabilitation Council's 15th Annual Conference.

Education

Marietta College, Marietta, OH • Bachelor of Science, Biology, May 1994

Internships & Employment

The Conservancy, Naples, FL • Intern	1994 - Present
Osprey Reintroduction Program, Blennerhasset, WV • Volunteer	Summer 1994
The Cincinnati Zoo, Cincinnati, OH • Intern, Animal Care Department	1993 - 1994
Chesapeake Wildlife Sanctuary, Bowie, MD • Intern, Wildlife Center	Spring 1992
Aullwood Audubon Center & Farm, Dayton, OH • Intern	Spring 1991
Animal Medical Center, New York, NY • Volunteer	Summer 1990

PERFORMING ARTIST

TARA ANNE DIONNE
Contact: (213) 999-0000

Height	5'3"	*Eyes*	Brown
Weight	106	*Voice*	Soprano
Hair	Brown	*Age Range*	20 - 35

THEATRE

The Mystery Of Edwin Drood	Rosa Bud	Duncan Theatre
Hair	Chrissy	Utah Rep
Rags	Rebecca	Duncan Theatre
Pirates Of Penzance	Mabel	Duncan Theatre
She Loves Me	Amalia	Village Players
Loose Ends	Susan	Duncan Theatre
Elizabeth & Essex	Lady Anne	Utah Rep
Fiorello!	Nina/Florence	Utah Rep
Red Noses	Camille	Duncan Theatre
You Can't Take It With You	Alice	Village Players
No Sex Please, We're British	Barbara	Village Players

TRAINING

acting: **Bachelor of Arts**, Drama, Utah State University, May 1995
Gately-Poole Acting Studio - Kathryn Gately
Gillian Moore Commercial Workshop
FPTA Advanced Acting Workshop

voice: Winston Clark
Patricia Adams-Johnson

dance: Scott Shettleroe
Salt Lake Ballet Center (ballet, jazz, tap)

musical theatre: Musical Theatre Works Conservatory
Donald Oliver

SPECIAL TALENTS

Dialects (English, Brooklyn, Southern, French), Hair & Make-Up

ARTS FOCUS

Larry Fitzpatrick

West 12th Street • #10 • Washington, D.C. • 10000 (202) 222-2222

photography experience

Associated Press, *1994 - Present*
Print black and white photos to accompany news releases in
publications such as the *New York Times,* the *Washington Post,* and
the *Herald Tribune.* Handled trafficking and proofreading of all AP
third-party graphics over various networks.

Smithsonian Institute, *1993*
Produced black and white prints for journalists and delegations.

Laumont Color Lab, *1992 - 1993*
Reproduced color correct slides from originals; mounted and packaged
slides for promotional purposes; clients included PBS and HBO.

film / video experience

MTV Networks, *1994 - Present*
Production Assistant for rockumentaries on Aerosmith, Janet Jackson,
and Whitney Houston; viewed and logged tapes.

Collective for Living Cinema, *1993 - 1994*
Teacher's Assistant for beginning filmmaking workshops; taught
students use of Super 8mm equipment; facilitated discussion groups.
Coordinated screenings, projected films, oversaw box office.

gallery experience

Aperture Foundation Gallery, *Summer 1992*
Matted, framed, and hung works for exhibits by artists such as
Mapplethorpe, Eggleston, and Strand. Coordinated gallery openings;
liaison between clients and artists.

education

Georgetown University, Bachelor of Fine Arts, Photography, 1993

American University, Coursework in Video Production, 1994

Carrie Richards
6 East Arrow St., #1
Durham, NC 10000
(919) 111 - 0000

Design/Fashion Experience

1994 - Present **Freelance Designer**, Durham. NC
- Design curtains, pillows and other home furnishings; use expertise to guide clients in the selection of fabric, style, color, and texture.
- Designed and constructed backpacks and evening bags.
- Implemented bi-coastal marketing and promotional campaigns; coordinated promotional/sales events.
- Major clients include Fred Seigal, Santa Monica, CA, and Wrights, Manhattan Beach, CA.

Summer 1993 **Keeble Cavaco & Duka**, Raleigh, NC
Freelance Coordinator
- Organize invitations and RSVP follow-up for fashion shows for various designers including Richard Tyler and Anna Sui.
- Coordinate seating arrangements for media and retailers.
- Plan and facilitate a variety of special events including, receptions, openings, and book signings.

1992 **The Surrogate Chef**, Durham, NC
Events Coordinator
- Catered events for up to 3,000 people; clients included major corporations as well as celebrities.
- In charge of event styling; planned and selected color schemes, flower arrangements, tablecloths, place settings, and props.

Additional Experience

1988 - 1991 **American Airlines**, New York, NY
International Flight Attendant
- Responsible for the comfort and safety of up to 350 passengers per flight.
- Provide efficient and courteous service to a diverse, multicultural clientele.

Education **Duke University**, Durham, NC
Bachelor of Arts, Visual Arts, May 1995
Honors: Art Scholarship granted by the Neptunian Women's Club

Study Abroad **L'Ecole du Louvre, Le Sorbonne**, Paris, France
Studies included Interior Design, Art history, and French

AFS International Exchange Program, Minas Gerais, Brazil

Languages Conversational French

SCIENCE FOCUS

Andrew Viosta

15 Maple Place #5
Hackensack, NJ 06600
(201) 999-8888

Education

B.S., Mechanical Engineering, 1994
Rutgers University, New Brunswick, NJ

Special Projects: *Machine Design*
Created rubber band powered cars capable of performing figure 8s and other complicated movements.

Turbo Pascal
Designed a program to calculate the optimal air conditioning requirements for a college classroom. Created a program to assist bowlers with accurately scoring their matches.

Design Experience

1994 - Present **ACME Laboratories**, Camden, NJ
Design Engineer

Designed a hammering machine for indenting steel bars, an electric dryer for silk-screen printed garments, and a complete manufacturing line for quick acting automotive battery terminal clamps. Fabricated all molds and tools. Trained and supervised technical staff.

Computer Skills

Languages: C, Turbo Pascal

Software: DOS 5.0, Mac/OS, LOTUS 123, Quattro Pro, Excel, Pagemaker, Harvard Graphics 2.0, Flowcharting, Windows 3.1, WordPerfect 5.1

Hardware: IBM PC/XT/AT 386, Macintosh

Sales Experience

1993 - 1994 **Sears, Roebuck and Co.**, Hackensack , NJ
Sales Associate

Top ranked salesperson in the Lawn & Garden and Sporting Goods Departments. Scored 100% on the Shop and Check Service evaluation survey.

Activities

Gears and Pinions - Association of Engineering Students

Organized a university-wide contest to promote the preservation of library resources on campus. Solicited alumni to raise $5,000 in prize money.

BUSINESS MAJOR

Yanni Metaxis

Local Address (until 5/12/96)
11 Third Street
South Bend, IN 10003
(317) 999 - 2222

Permanent Address
91 Berry Avenue
Wilmington, DE 00000
(302) 444 - 3333

OBJECTIVE

Position as a Tax Accountant

EDUCATION

Notre Dame University, South Bend, IN
Bachelor of Science, Accounting, May 1996

- Overall Grade Point Average: 3.5

Related Courses

Principles of Financial Accounting
Micro- and Macroeconomics
Computer Based Systems for Management Support
Introduction to Computers and Programming

Study Abroad

BMT, Jerusalem, Israel, 1992 - 1993

Gained a deep appreciation for Israeli culture and history through a balance of formal education and extensive travel.

EXPERIENCE

Summers '93 & '94

United Video & Electronics, Inc., *Sales Manager*

- Supervised a staff of 5 sales representatives.
- Oversaw entire business operation during owner's absence.
- Contacted wholesalers via phone to place orders.
- Matched incoming shipments against invoices and resolved any discrepancies.
- Researched media options for advertising campaign.
- One of two employees entrusted to handle the cash register.

Summers '91 & '92

Camp Maya, *Waiter/Cook*

- Efficiently served up to four tables simultaneously during breakfast, lunch, and dinner.
- Prepared meals for 500 diners at a time.

ACTIVITIES

Investment Society, *Member*

- Discuss market trends, attend lectures, write for club newsletter.

SKILLS

Computers

Quattro Pro 5.0, DBase III+, WordPerfect 6.0 & 5.1, DOS, Pascal, Basic

Languages

Fluent in Greek

SOCIAL SERVICE

Ann Perkins   111 Elm Street • Rochester, NY 11111 • (716) 555-5555

Education

BACHELOR OF SCIENCE, May 1994
Syracuse University, College for Human Development

Major: Child and Family Studies
Coursework included education, psychology, and family dynamics.

Counseling and Teaching Experience

COMMUNITY MEDICAL CENTER   Syracuse, NY
Child and Family Counselor   Spring 1994

• Interacted with children and parents while children received medical treatment.
• Modelled effective childcare techniques and provided feedback to parents.
• Established on-going relationships with families.

SYRACUSE UNIVERSITY EARLY EDUCATION CENTER   Syracuse, NY
Student Teacher   Spring 1993

• Designed and implemented instructional activities for children ages 3 to 6.
• Researched learning styles and cognitive development of children.
• Organized and supervised educational field trips.

ELIZABETH M. WALL NURSERY SCHOOL   Syracuse, NY
Student Teacher   Fall 1992

• Coordinated and led educational activities for groups of four-year olds.
• Planned new activities daily to teach group interaction skills.

Additional Experience

Clinique   New York, NY
Assistant to Director, Creative Services   10/94 to present

• Assist art director in coordinating photo shoots.
• Created and organized filing system for Directors.
• Identify new products and displays by speaking with vendors.

Receptionist   8/94 to 10/94

• Greeted and directed executive clients and guests and routed phone calls.

LEIGH BARRETT BOUTIQUE   Rochester, NY
Sales Clerk   Summers 1988-89

• Created window displays and performed in-store merchandising.
• Assisted customers in selection of merchandise; maintained inventory.

Skills

Type 55 wpm; Familiar with IBM PCs (WordPerfect, Multimate 4.0 and Lotus)

Additional Information

Volunteer, United Jewish Appeal and American Red Cross.

Haved lived in Australia and London; travelled extensively in Europe.

BUSINESS FOCUS

Martin Thomas

32 East Barnacle Street • Las Vegas, NV 10000 • (702) 888-8888

PROFILE

- Professional experience in Marketing, Operations, and Applied Computer Technology plus a solid academic background in Information Systems and International Business.
- Ability to conceptualize the big picture, as well as pay careful attention to every last detail. Excel at organizing, coordinating, and managing projects.

EXPERIENCE

Avon Products, Inc., *Marketing Intern*   **1994 - Present**

Provide administrative and technical support to the Planning, Analysis, and Research team. Assist with the coordination and moderation of focus groups conducted nationwide; collect qualitative data to be used in forecasting.

Contributed to the development of a database designed to store information collected during quantitative and qualitative clinics.

Digital Equipment Corporation, *Project Specialist*   **1992 - 1993**

Oversaw course enrollment for a 10 room training facility serving up to 100 students per week. Identified and resolved issues concerning payment and invoicing.

Troubleshooting required extensive contact with key personnel in Administration, Sales, Education, and Finance.

Recipient of the Digital Equipment Corporation Excellence Award for Service.

Free-Room UK, England, *Account Executive - Key Accounts*   **1991**

Sold over 500K in consumer incentives and sales promotional items to Marketing Directors of companies throughout the United Kingdom.

Arranged board meetings and presentations in conjunction with Sales Director.

Served as key contact for resales and troubleshooting for major clients.

EDUCATION

University of Nevada, Las Vegas
Bachelor of Science, Information Systems/International Business, Summer 1995

Honors: Summa cum laude

Worked an average of 30 hours weekly while attending classes full-time.

SKILLS

C programming, Access, Excel, Lotus Organizer, Microsoft Word

---

About the Authors

L. Michelle Tullier

Michelle Tullier has been a career counselor in universities and private practice since 1985 advising adults of all ages on career choice and job search issues. Through her New York City-based practice, which attracts clients from across and the country and abroad, she specialties in the career development needs of high school and college students, recent graduates, and young professionals in their twenties and thirties. Michelle holds a Ph.D. in counseling psychology from UCLA and a BA from Wellesley College. She is on the faculty of New York University's School of Continuing Education where she teaches beginning and experienced career counselors and has held positions in the career centers at Barnard College of Columbia University and UCLA. Michelle is the author of Job Notes: Cover Letters (The Princeton Review/Random House, March 1997) and was a contributor to the Seagram's Chivas Regal CD-ROM Career Toolbox. Michelle serves as a Career Committee Chair for the Independent Educational Consultant's Association (IECA) and is a frequent public speaker, seminar leader, and consultant. Her e-mail address is CareerDr@aol.com.

Timothy D. Haft

Since 1988, Tim Haft has helped thousands of job seekers from all walks of life and all corners of the globe to find meaningful and satisfying work, and in some cases just a plain old job. Mr. Haft is the author of Trashproof Resumes (The Princeton Review/Random House, 1995) and Crane's Guide to Writing an Effective Resume (Crane & Company, 1995) and is coauthor of Job Smart (The Princeton Review/Random House, 1997). He is also a contributor to The Career Toolbox, an interactive CD for job hunters. Mr. Haft has served as a career counselor at New York University and the Fashion Institute of Technology, and has held roughly thirty-five other positions over the past fifteen years. He is currently Senior Editor at a national, nonprofit association that assists high school students with the transition to college. Tim holds a B.A. in history from the University of Virginia and an M.A. in Sociology from New York University.

ABOUT THE AUTHORS

Margaret M. Heenehan

During a six year tenure with the Office of Career Development at Barnard College, Columbia University, Meg Heenehan has advised students and alumnae regarding internships, jobs, and career decisions. She also leads job search and career development seminars for graduate students at Columbia University's School of International and Public Affairs and is an adjunct faculty member at NYU's School of Continuing Education. Her prior experience includes several years as a high school guidance counselor. Meg holds a Master of Education degree in counselor education from Penn State University and a bachelor's degree from the University of Delaware. She is a member of the Association for Multicultural Counseling and Development.

Marci I. Taub

Marci I. Taub, M.A., is a career counselor in private practice. She specializes in on-site and long-distance career counseling and testing, job search coaching, and educational advising services for clients from teens through early thirties. As an adjunct faculty member of New York University's School of Continuing Education, she develops and teaches courses through the Center for Career, Education, and Life Planning. She is also the coauthor of *Job Smart* (The Princeton Review, 1997). Her professional affiliations include memberships in the American Counseling Association and the National Career Development Association.

Prior to entering private practice, she consulted and was employed in human resources with major financial institutions, including Chase Manhattan Bank and Smith Barney. She has also held positions in colleges in New York and New Jersey, advising students on career planning and job search issues. Marci has an M.A. in Counseling from Montclair State University, a Certificate in Adult Career Planning and Development from New York University, and a bachelor's degree from Oberlin College. Her e-mail address is marcitaub@aol.com.

NOTES